The

POWER OF MANTRA

• WISDOM CULTURE SERIES •

The
POWER OF MANTRA

VITAL PRACTICES
for
TRANSFORMATION

Lama Zopa Rinpoche

Compiled and edited by Gordon McDougall

Paintings by Peter Iseli

Wisdom

Wisdom Publications
199 Elm Street
Somerville, MA 02144 USA
wisdomexperience.org

Library of Congress Cataloging-in-Publication Data
Names: Thubten Zopa, Rinpoche, 1945– author. | McDougall, Gordon, 1948– editor. |
    Iseli, Peter, illustrator.
Title: The power of mantra: vital practices for transformation / Lama Zopa Rinpoche;
    compiled and edited by Gordon McDougall; paintings by Peter Iseli.
Description: First. | Somerville: Wisdom Publications, 2022. |
    Includes bibliographical references.
Identifiers: LCCN 2021032862 (print) | LCCN 2021032863 (ebook) |
    ISBN 9781614297277 (paperback) | ISBN 9781614297437 (ebook)
Subjects: LCSH: Buddhist mantras. | Mantras. | Buddhism—Tibet Region—
    Prayers and devotions.
Classification: LCC BQ5050 .T48 2022 (print) | LCC BQ5050 (ebook) |
    DDC 294.3/437—dc23
LC record available at https://lccn.loc.gov/2021032862
LC ebook record available at https://lccn.loc.gov/2021032863

ISBN 978-1-61429-727-7 ebook ISBN 978-1-61429-743-7

25 24 23 22   5 4 3 2

Cover image by Peter Iseli. Cover design by Gopa & Ted 2 and Tony Lulek. Interior
design by Tony Lulek. Photographs of *Four-Arm Chenrezig, Tara, Solitary Vajrasattva,* and *White Tara* are by Daniel Allemann. Photographs of *Shakyamuni Buddha,
Manjushri, Medicine Buddha,* and the *Thirty-Five Buddhas* are by Peter Iseli. The
photograph of *Thousand-Armed Chenrezig* is by Dominique Uldry. The photograph of
Vajrasattva with Consort is by Elisabeth Zahnd Legnazzi. The photograph of *The Seven
Medicine Buddhas* is by John Bigelow Taylor.

Printed on acid-free paper that meets the guidelines for permanence and durability of
the Production Guidelines for Book Longevity of the Council on Library Resources.

Printed in Malaysia.

CONTENTS

EDITOR'S PREFACE

··

Two and a half thousand years ago, a man became enlightened. Prince Gautama, Siddhartha, the son of the king the
Shakyas, became Shakyamuni, the "conqueror of the Shakyas," usually
just known as the Buddha, the Awakened One.

Read one way, the story of the Buddha is of a person like us and
his search for the truth, which culminated in his enlightenment under
the bodhi tree. Read another way, the Mahayana way, he was already
enlightened, and his life was a teaching, showing us exactly what we
must do to become like him. Both readings are the truth. How that is so
is a quest we ourselves must undertake to discover what it means for us.

And that is the same with the countless buddhas there are in Tibetan
Buddhism. Why not just one Buddha, Shakyamuni? What does the
plethora of buddhas mean? What exactly are they and how do they
relate to our spiritual journey? I remember, in France in the 1990s, a student asked one of the great lamas, "Are the buddhas real or imaginary?"
In a wonderfully enigmatic answer, the lama replied, "Yes." Which I
took to mean that it's up to us to work it out.

Buddha, deity, meditational deity, *yidam*—the terms are synonymous, all referring to the enlightened mind manifesting in a particular
way to best benefit sentient beings. Thus, Chenrezig is the manifestation
of the buddhas' compassion, Tara is the manifestation of the buddhas'
enlightened activities, and so forth.

The many buddhas manifest according to the different propensities
of different people. They are there to help us in whatever way we need, if
we are able to open to them. Sometimes we need more compassion than
wisdom; sometimes we need a more wrathful approach, other times a
more peaceful one. We have a natural affinity for one or many buddhas.

That does not mean that one buddha is better than the others, but that one will resonate with us more.

Each buddha has a mantra. A mantra is a series of Sanskrit syllables that evoke the energy of that particular buddha. All sound has energy. It is said that every Sanskrit syllable creates a sacred vibration in the mind, and so each syllable of each mantra has the power to alter our psychic nervous system in subtly different ways. Some mantras run smoothly through the mind and invoke peace and contentment, some seem difficult to pronounce and have a markedly different effect. A mantra works in two ways: externally as a sacred sound that carries a blessing, and internally as a tool to transform our mind into one that is more compassionate and wise.

When we take an initiation into a particular deity, we are generally given a mantra commitment, such as saying a certain number of mantras of that deity every day. Although to our Westernized, individualistic mind, this might seem like an imposition at first, in fact it is the gift of liberation. If we get into the habit of saying mantras whenever the mind slips into a dull neutrality or into emotive overdrive—not only when we are doing a daily meditation practice but whenever we are going about our business—we can bring ourselves back to a peace and spaciousness that guards our mind from negativity. It is probably the most valuable mental tool we can have.

Generally, to practice a deity and say their mantra, we need an initiation given by a qualified teacher who is part of an unbroken lineage. There are some deities, however, who are so popular that their mantras are widely said by people whether they have had an initiation or not. Furthermore, even without an initiation, it is often permissible (and very beneficial) to do a simple version of that deity's practice. In such cases, it is generally said that rather than imagining yourself becoming the deity, as is often taught after initiation—you simply imagine them in front of you, and you receive the blessings of the deity.

By far the most popular mantra is that of Chenrezig (Avalokiteshvara in Sanskrit). There seems to be hardly a Tibetan person who doesn't constantly have OM MANI PADME HUM on their lips, and with non-

Tibetans too, this is very popular. Chenrezig is compassion, which we all desperately need, so chanting his mantra is incredibly worthwhile.

Over the decades, Lama Zopa Rinpoche has given countless initiations and instructed his students to say many different mantras. For specific situations, he gives very specific instructions, telling us which mantra will best protect or help us. For instance, for the recent coronavirus pandemic, to protect themselves and others from the virus, he requested his students to chant the Vajra Armor mantra, a powerful healing practice.

This book is a distillation of what Rinpoche has said of the most accessible deities and their mantras. These are the ones students of Tibetan Buddhism usually encounter first and practice longest, starting with Shakyamuni Buddha, the historical Buddha, the one who gave us the whole of Buddhism. Then, there is Chenrezig, the embodiment of compassion, Tibet's most beloved deity and closely associated with his Holiness the Dalai Lama, and Manjushri, the embodiment of wisdom. The entire path to enlightenment is encapsulated in compassion and wisdom, and so these two buddhas are extremely important. So too is Tara, embodying the buddhas' compassionate action. Then, after Medicine Buddha, the healing buddha, there are the mantras of the most effective purification practices, Vajrasattva and the Thirty-Five Confession Buddhas, and finally, the five powerful mantras Rinpoche often advises us to recite. Hopefully, this book will give you a feeling for the different deities and an appreciation of the power of the mantras—as well as the wish to use those mantras to transform your mind.

You might notice that there is not complete consistency in the way Tibetan terms are dealt with. Generally, Wisdom uses a simplified phonetic transcription that corresponds to the way the word sounds. However, because we have often used prayers from practices from Rinpoche's Foundation for the Preservation of the Mahayana Tradition, such as the prayers to the Twenty-One Taras, in those instances we have kept with the FPMT's system. Similarly, we write the Sanskrit terms without diacritics, except in one appendix, where Lama Zopa explains the differences in the sounds of the mantras in detail. When Sanskrit and/or Tibetan terms appear in brackets, we have not specified which is which, because the two languages look quite different, but generally if both languages are together, the Sanskrit comes first.

To compile this book I have used teachings stored in the Lama Yeshe Wisdom Archive that have been lovingly recorded, transcribed, and checked by a vast number of people, as well as the incredible books, booklets, and practices that have been created over the decades by the FPMT's Education Services, carefully following Lama Zopa's wishes so his students can practice the authentic Dharma. I would like to thank Tom Truty of Education Services for his invaluable help in checking the mantras and practices within the book, offering more recent alternatives, and giving permission for us to adapt and use the appropriate practices that we have taken from the FPMT's vast treasure house. I would also like to thank everybody who contributed to this book, those at the LYWA, the FPMT, and the many at Wisdom Publications, all of whom are an inspiration to work with. One person I especially want to thank is Peter Iseli. When we decided this book deserved the most beautiful buddha images to enhance it, we turned to Peter, who has been creating beautiful images for Rinpoche and other Tibetan masters for decades, and Peter not only freely offered his superb paintings but even created two new ones for the book. I think you will agree, the result is wonderful.

I apologize for any errors found in this book; they are 100 percent mine. May this book be a tool to allow people to develop their positive qualities to the maximum degree in order to help others. May whatever merits gained from the creation of this book be dedicated to peace in this troubled world; to the long life, well-being, and fulfillment of the wishes of all our holy teachers, especially His Holiness the Dalai Lama and Lama Zopa Rinpoche; and to the flourishing of the Foundation for the Preservation of the Mahayana Tradition and of the Dharma throughout the world.

Gordon McDougall
Bath, UK

INTRODUCTION: THE POWER TO TRANSFORM THE MIND

THE POWER OF MANTRAS

The Sanskrit word *mantra* (which is *ngag* in Tibetan) has two syllables: *man*, which means "mind," and *tra*, which means "protect," so a mantra is something that protects our mind.

The benefits of mantra recitation are vast. There are many stories about terrible diseases such as cancer being cured by mantras, or people or animals being helped to have a peaceful death and a positive rebirth through mantras being recited to them. But the supreme benefit of a mantra is its ability to transform our mind. When we recite a mantra such as Shakyamuni's mantra, we are recalling the Buddha's name over and over, helping us increase our closeness and devotion to the Buddha, and devotion is our real protection from suffering. By transforming our mind, it has the power to break negative habits and develop positive ones. As our mind changes, our ability to help others increases, so we are reciting mantras for others as well.

By linking us to the omniscient mind—the wisdom and compassion of the Buddha and all the enlightened beings—reciting a mantra invokes that great power, leading us from nonvirtue to virtue. The Buddha said,

> Do not commit any nonvirtuous actions,
> perform only perfect virtuous actions,
> subdue your mind thoroughly—
> this is the teaching of the Buddha.[1]

The whole Buddhist path comes down to these two pieces of advice—to not harm others and to benefit them. In order to do that, we must subdue the mind, which means both collecting merit through doing only virtuous actions and purifying any negative imprints on our mindstream from negative actions we have done in the past.

Reciting a mantra such as OM MANI PADME HUM, the mantra of Chenrezig,[2] is not only the most unbelievable purification—purifying defilements and negative karmas collected from not just this life but from beginningless rebirths—it also collects extensive merits.

In the West, when soccer players win, they throw their arms up in the air and run around. It's very intense. When I first saw this, I thought they were very angry because of the strong emotion. If they feel that strongly about winning a match, we should feel a billion times more strongly about being able to purify all that negative karma and accumulate all that merit, simply by reciting a mantra.

Westerners have asked me many times to explain how mantras work. This is a question that comes from the Western mind; it's not asked in Asia, certainly not among the Tibetans, because they have faith. When there is water, what does water do? It makes things wet; that is its nature. Fire has its own nature; its nature is to burn. Everything has its own nature. Mantras too have their own nature; their nature is to transform the mind. Any word we say affects another person's mind, making them happy or sad or angry or whatever. The power of the mantra comes from the sound, and that sound has the power to transform the mind into one of virtue.[3]

Thinking of mantras as just some Sanskrit sounds to be chanted is an extremely limited view of what they are; they are much more than that. The sound of a mantra has the power to protect us, holding our mind from nonvirtuous thoughts and fostering virtuous ones, thus allowing us to develop toward enlightenment. In the same way that the Dharma in general holds us, protecting us from suffering—*Dharma* literally means "that which holds"—mantras are mind protection. In *A Guide to the Bodhisattva's Way of Life,* the great being Shantideva said,

Therefore, I should focus my mind correctly,
and keep a careful watch over it.
What good will it do to keep many vows,
if one neglects the vow of watching over the mind?[4]

It is vital to remember Shantideva's advice. If we forget to protect our mind, what is the use of any traditional form of discipline? Even though we may do hundreds of other things, if we leave out this most important practice and leave the mind unprotected, we cannot stop our problems and achieve happiness, especially ultimate happiness. Everything comes from the mind; it is the source of all our suffering and all our happiness, so if we neglect to protect our mind, we cannot close the door to suffering or open it to happiness.

In the West, there are so many external rules: you can't do this, you can't do that. Sometimes I think there are too many rules. When we rely on external discipline, we can never solve our problems. The discipline has to come from our own mind. As a Buddhist, we might take certain vows to protect ourselves from committing any of the ten nonvirtuous actions,[5] but unless we protect our mind, those vows will be impossible to keep. As Shantideva said, what good will having vows be if we can't watch over our mind?

Modern Western life is full of distractions. Everywhere are objects of the senses to keep our mind busy, enticing us away from the Dharma. If you check you will see this is true. Being preoccupied with working for this worldly life, as so many people are, makes it extremely difficult to remember the necessity of Dharma practice and to find the time to practice it. Buddhism has many methods to overcome a distracted mind, such as meditating on impermanence and death[6] or on the disadvantages of the self-cherishing mind. When we are not meditating, however, what is the best method? Reciting mantras will keep our mind in virtue and protect it from nonvirtue.

THE WAY MANTRAS SAVE US

We *must* at least recite mantras when we have the chance. I often say, If you have a mouth, you must use it for that. (Of course, if you don't have a mouth, that's okay.) That is the minimum practice. We must *at least* recite OM MANI PADME HUM to develop compassion toward all living beings. Even if we have little understanding of karma and can't see how the mind is affected by mantras, we should have faith in the benefits of reciting them, benefits like the limitless sky. Reciting mantras really does protect our mind.

Mantras are there to protect us in everything we do. If we have a daily meditation practice, there are mantras to be said with the preliminary practices before the main meditation. Specifically, when we set up the altar, in order to dispel obstacles that can cloud our mind, we must recite OM AH HUM as we fill the offering bowls with water and offer flowers.

There are mantras we should say at the beginning of the day, such as mantras for blessing our speech, our mala, and our feet to protect any beings we might step on. There are also multiplying mantras that increase the power of our recitation when we recite them.[7]

Mantras That Heal

All mantras are mind protection; they heal our mind. By purifying the mind, by making the mind healthy, we can enjoy whatever success and happiness we want, now and in the future. There are some mantras, however, that are especially effective in healing sickness.

Probably the most common mantra is Chenrezig's OM MANI PADME HUM. We will later look at the Chenrezig mantra and how we can generate all-important compassion through it, but it is also extremely powerful for healing ourselves and others by transforming our minds into compassion toward all others, without distinction of race, nationality, gender, and so forth. We develop compassion without any barrier. Whether somebody likes us or not, whatever their beliefs, we only want them to have happiness and its causes and to be free from suffering and its causes. When we can take the full responsibility to ensure all others' happiness in this way, that is called great compassion and is the prerequisite to bodhichitta. Because our mind is free from the agitation of disturbing thoughts, we are naturally healthier in body and mind.

Another healing mantra is the mantra of Medicine Buddha: TADY-ATHA OM BHAISHAJYE BHAISHAJYE MAHA BHAISHAJYE BHAISHAJYE RAJA SAMUDGATE SVAHA. When we recite this mantra, we imagine that Medicine Buddha, the buddha of healing, is absorbed into us and into all living beings, and we receive all the blessings and power of Medicine Buddha's holy body, holy speech, and holy mind, all the qualities that enable us to help others. It heals our mind from all the disturbing emotional thoughts and makes it healthy—free, peaceful, contented, and fulfilled. Medicine Buddha's mantra does much more than heal us of our sicknesses; it enables us to serve all others in all our future lives, bringing them perfect happiness, and, as a side effect, bringing ourselves perfect happiness.

The texts explain that a being we might have inadvertently killed, like an ant we stepped on, can be saved from the lower realms and can obtain a good rebirth if we simply recite Medicine Buddha's mantra over the body. It seems hard to believe. So, how does it work?

Since things are dependent arisings, everything depends on causes and conditions. If we think about it, we can see that the power of mantra comes from the inconceivable qualities and power of the Buddha, from his holy mind that is completely trained in compassion and embraces all sentient beings without exception. The Buddha has infinite times more compassion and love for us than we have for ourselves, and the power of the mantra comes through the power of Buddha's omniscient mind.

The power of the mantra also comes from the power of the mind of the person who recites it. Of course, if we have some realization, there is much more power in whatever activity we do for other sentient beings; it is much more meaningful. However, even if we are still very far from attaining any realization, reciting the mantra can still be effective depending on how much compassion and love we have toward that sentient being, as well as how much devotion we have in the mantra, the guru, and the Three Rare Sublime Ones: the Buddha, Dharma, and Sangha.

Finally, there have to be conditions to do with the being itself: the dead or dying insect or animal. Not every sentient being has the karma to have somebody recite a mantra and blow over their body as they are dying so they can receive a good rebirth. When you think of the number of animals, worms, insects, and countless other forms of sentient beings who die all the time, the number who have the good karma to have somebody recite a mantra over them is incredibly rare, like stars in the daytime. Therefore, at that moment some very special positive karma is ripening, and it can definitely help them have a good rebirth.

Tara's mantra, OM TARE TUTTARE TURE SVAHA, is another very powerful mantra relied on by many people, including many healers and great meditators. Her mantra is effective to help us gain success very quickly in whatever we want to do, allowing us to overcome our problems and heal ourselves and others.

There are many other mantras that have the power to heal sicknesses, such as the mantra of Vajrapani: OM VAJRAPANI HAYAGRIVA GARUDA HUM PHAT. This was the first mantra I gave to a cancer patient, and they completely recovered, showing how powerful that mantra is.

When we do practices to help heal others, we should use the practice of a deity[8] we have a strong karmic connection with, because our close relationship with the deity will bring success more quickly. We should feel that the deity has *omniscience*, infinite *compassion* for us and all other living beings, and perfect *power* to guide us. The healing power comes more from our faith than from visualizing the deity clearly or reciting the mantra correctly. This is the essence of the practice. Wisdom and compassion are important in all practices, but in healing practices involving deity meditation and mantra recitation, generating strong faith is paramount. This mind is the actual healer.

The Importance of Mantras at the Time of Death

Because people in the West are usually very competitive, maybe we should make a competition between science and Buddhism. Which can help the most? The West has developed such incredible technologies. Now we can fly to the moon or send messages instantly all over the world, and we have limitless gadgets to make our lives more comfortable. There are huge advances in medicine, and many diseases that were fatal a few decades ago can now be cured. We can have a new heart if we want one, or even a new face.

None of these wonderful scientific advancements is at all capable, however, of helping us at the time of death. Nothing in science can save us from what awaits us after death. There has never been a machine made or a drug developed that has even slightly helped one person escape the terrible suffering of the lower realms. On the other hand, through putting into practice what we have studied of Buddhist philosophy, we can be ensured a rebirth in one of the fortunate realms, as a human or a god.

Similarly, when we are dying, if we just hear or remember the name of the Buddha—or of Vajrasattva, Chenrezig, Tara, or any of the other buddhas—let alone recite their mantras, we will be saved from the lower realms. Therefore there is no question that if we remember the various subjects of the graduated path to enlightenment, the *lamrim*,⁹ such as renunciation of samsara, the ultimate good heart of bodhichitta, and the right view of emptiness—if we can transform our mind into the Dharma—then a fortunate rebirth is assured.

Of course, if we have lived with a good heart, benefiting others with tolerance, patience, compassion, and loving-kindness, at the time of death—at *that* very important time, that important day, that important hour—the virtuous thoughts that we had during our life will help a great deal.

Unfortunately, because of fear and loss of capability, it is often very difficult to remember the Buddha or a mantra at the very moment of death. We are therefore very fortunate if we have a friend who can help us, someone to recite the mantra of whatever buddha we have an affinity with very loudly in our ear. For instance, say we have devotion to Tara. When our friend recites Tara's mantra, OM TARE TUTTARE TURE SVAHA, loudly in our ear, although our hearing faculty might almost be gone, something is absorbed, something goes inside. Our devotion to Tara fills our mind, making it very positive. In this way we are saved from the lower realms.

Even when the person who is dying has no knowledge of Buddhism, reciting a mantra and blowing in their ear is a great help. This is due to the power of the mantra. Besides reciting mantras, we should also pray with a bodhichitta motivation that they are never reborn in the lower realms but attain a perfect human rebirth[10] where they are able to meet the Dharma and progress along the path to enlightenment.

We can do this not just for dying human beings, but for animals as well: dogs, birds, flies—any being. Reciting a mantra such as Chenrezig's mantra and blowing in their ear has incredible power. It can even benefit a being already born in the lower realms, causing it to experience that state for the briefest period before being reborn in the upper realms.

The Importance of the Motivation

Each deity has a mantra, and which deity practice is best for us is determined by our individual karma and should be checked with a qualified lama. We should then receive the initiation into that deity practice or permission to practice that deity,[11] which also includes an oral transmission[12] of the deity's mantra.

Because the transmission of the mantra comes down in an unbroken lineage, it carries the blessings of the deity and of all the highly qualified lineage lamas through to the guru we received the lineage from. The purpose of receiving the lineage of the blessing is to give more power to the meditation on the deity and the recitation of the deity's mantra.

Whatever the purpose of reciting the mantra—to heal another person or help them gain a good rebirth, to stop (or start) rain, to have success in our life, or any other reason—its success depends on our motivation. Of course, the additional factors of visualizing holy objects and reciting the mantras correctly increase the power of the practice, but they are secondary to the motivation we have.

When we say a mantra for just some mundane happiness, such as saying a White Tara mantra to ensure our health, the mantra can be effective, but because that action is only for the happiness of this life it is not a virtuous action. Because the motivation is nonvirtuous, the mantra recitation is nonvirtuous, whether it helps in the short term or not.

In *Precious Garland,* the great Indian scholar Nagarjuna said,

> Desire, hatred, and ignorance, and the actions they generate are nonvirtues. Non-desire, non-hatred, and non-ignorance, and the actions they generate are virtues.[13]

Furthermore, Lama Atisha said:

> If the root is poisonous, the branches and leaves will also be poisonous. If the root is medicinal, the branches and leaves are also medicinal. Similarly, if the root is attachment, hostility, or benighted ignorance, whatever one does will be nonvirtuous.[14]

While there are still benefits from reciting a mantra with a nonvirtuous motivation, there is a great difference when we do it with a positive motivation. When we dedicate each mantra recitation or each prostration to others, we collect merit like the limitless sky.

Therefore our motivation should be as vast as possible. Perhaps we say the mantra with the motivation to be saved from rebirth in the lower realms. Even though it is a Dharma motivation, because we are only working for the happiness of our next life, that attitude is very limited.

The motivation we should strive for is bodhichitta: we should recite the mantra to become enlightened in order to lead all other beings to enlightenment. To recite it with bodhichitta combined with a realization of emptiness is even better. In fact, when we have attained each of the three principal aspects of the path—concentration, wisdom, and bodhichitta—then we can effortlessly benefit sentient beings. But even without these realizations,[15] if we can live in pure morality as much as we are able to, when we attempt to benefit other beings, we will be successful.

Therefore, when we recite one Vajrasattva mantra or one *mala*[16] of OM MANI PADME HUM, we should feel in our heart that this is all for the benefit of other sentient beings. When we can do this with bodhichitta as our motivation—with the mind that wishes to attain enlightenment in order to lead all sentient beings to that state—each mantra we do has the same benefit as reciting one hundred thousand mantras. The purpose of emphasizing the bodhichitta motivation at the beginning of every meditation session, and repeating it again and again, is to remind ourselves to generate bodhichitta and therefore make the most of every mantra we recite.

Besides a positive motivation, having devotion is an important factor in the effectiveness of mantra recitation. Different Tibetan texts can spell mantras slightly differently. Some versions have a few extra syllables, some less. The great translator Lotsawa Paltsig wrote a short book about how to read Sanskrit, which many Tibetan lamas follow in order to pronounce mantras correctly. This book says that you create much negative karma if you recite Sanskrit mantras incorrectly. However, the benefits of reciting mantras are not entirely dependent on correct pronunciation. Although it is good to try to say the mantra as accurately as possible, the power of mantra comes more from faith than from how we recite it. When there is strong faith in the mantra, it will be effective, whether we say it correctly or not.

There is a story about a woman in a time of great famine who used to recite OM BALE BULE BUNDE SOHA to cook and eat stones. One day her son, a novice monk, overheard his mother reciting the mantra and told her that the correct way to pronounce it was OM TSALE TSULE TSUNDE SVAHA. However, when his mother recited the mantra correctly, she could no longer cook the stones. Only when she reverted to her original recitation was she able to cook them again.

His Holiness Zong Rinpoche's previous incarnation told a story about someone with a big nose who came to ask for teachings from a lama in Kham. Busy, the lama brushed him off with "Your nose is like *rudraksha*." The monk must have had a big, rough nose like the big, rough beads of the malas that *sadhus*, Indian ascetic meditators, wear, which are made from rudraksha seeds. The monk, who didn't understand what the lama said, thought that he had received a mantra and faithfully recited every day, "Your nose is like rudraksha. Your nose is like rudraksha." Eventually he became able to heal many people by reciting this "mantra." Some years later when the lama had an infection in his throat, his attendant told him that there was a famous healer in the area, one who had helped many people, and the lama agreed to see him. When the monk came to see the lama, he recited, "Your nose is like rudraksha." Remembering what he had said in the past, the lama laughed so much that the infection burst and the pus came out, due to which he got better. That the monk became a famous healer by reciting "Your nose is like rudraksha" shows that his power to heal people mainly depended on his faith. It came from believing he had received a mantra from the lama, even though the lama had just said that to him as a joke.

THE DIFFERENT DEITIES IN TIBETAN BUDDHISM

Some people may wonder why there are so many buddhas in Tibetan Buddhism, besides the historical Buddha. Shakyamuni Buddha is just one manifestation of the primordial enlightened energy, or *dharmakaya*—just another name, in the same way that one person can have many names or designations during a lifetime. Perhaps you had a name given to you by your parents, another by your friends—your nickname—another if you got married, and maybe another when your guru gave you an ordination name. These different identities are all you, but different aspects of you.

Similarly, there are many different aspects of the Buddha, wrathful and peaceful, male and female. When we achieve the holy omniscient mind, we achieve all the buddhas, all the enlightened holy beings. "Shakyamuni" is just a different name, given to distinguish one particular aspect of the enlightened mind from another.

At first it might seem confusing to have many different buddhas rather than just the historical Buddha. Why can't there just be one buddha, the Buddha? If we look at how our society works, we can easily see that we need different people with different abilities and qualifications to ensure its smooth running. If we want to help others by healing their bodies, we need to train as a doctor; if we want to heal their minds, we need to train as a psychiatrist or psychologist. When we have that qualification, people will trust us and come to us for help.

In sort of the same way, the different buddhas, which are all different aspects of the enlightened mind, are there to perform different functions and fulfill the manifold needs of sentient beings—one aspect alone is not enough. There are numberless sentient beings, and even to fulfill the wish of one of them requires more than one particular aspect.

Chenrezig is the embodiment of the Buddha's compassion, and to take refuge in Chenrezig is to take refuge in the Buddha. In the same way, Tara is the embodiment of the Buddha's enlightened compassionate activities, and there is no contradiction in taking refuge in Tara and taking refuge in the Buddha. Tara is incredibly beloved by the Tibetan people and there are many stories of people being saved from death by taking refuge in her, by calling her name when they were in great danger. One aspect of Tara, White Tara, is evoked for long life.

With all these particular aspects of the buddhas, the main purpose is to bring sentient beings to the highest state, the sublime happiness of enlightenment. Of course, from our side, we must do everything we can to develop wisdom and compassion and progress along the path by extensively listening, reflecting, and meditating on the path.

1. SHAKYAMUNI BUDDHA

A S A YOUNG PRINCE, Siddhartha's life was as perfect as a life in samsara could be. His father, the king, received a prophecy that his son would either be a great king or a great sage, and because he was determined that Siddhartha would become king, he hid all suffering from him and totally immersed him in sense pleasures.

Despite his father trying to shield him from all suffering, there came a time as a young man when he saw four things in quick succession, one at each of the gates of the palace. First he saw an old person and he realized that we all have to age. Next he saw a sick person, something he had never seen before. Then he saw a dead body, and he understood that death comes to us all. This was a terrible revelation for a young man who had never seen the slightest suffering. At the fourth gate he saw a poor monk, a person who had none of the luxuries that Siddhartha had but nonetheless seemed incredibly happy. This was a like a light going on in a dark place for the prince. He saw all his palace life for the empty thing it was, and he knew that samsaric happiness was meaningless, something that only ever led to old age, sickness, and death. But he also knew there was a way out of this trap, if it could be found, and that it had something to do with the monk. This was the start of his spiritual quest.

Siddhartha chose the life of the ascetic, practicing with hardly any food in the most trying circumstances. He practiced concentration without moving, his whole body becoming like a tree, as if carved from wood, so much so that ants and insects made nests in his ears. After doing this for six years, he realized that austerity was as harmful as indulgence. When he was given milk and rice by a young girl, Sujata, his energy returned, and he went to the bodhi tree nearby to meditate. This led to that amazing night when he attained full enlightenment. Then he sought the companions from his ascetic days, finding them in

Sarnath, near Varanasi in north India, where he gave his first teaching, the first turning of the Dharma wheel, on the four noble truths.[17] Then, for over forty years he gave over 84,000 teachings and formed a great sangha around him, before passing away at Kushinagar.

The death of the Buddha was his last teaching to us, a lesson on impermanence. When it was time to die, he took off his robes, lay down, and said,

> All causative phenomena are impermanent.
> Work out your salvation with diligence.
> This is the last teaching of the tathagata.[18]

Everything is transient, subject to change, not just on a gross level but moment by moment. And every impermanent phenomenon is unsatisfactory; it is suffering by nature. Therefore why should we be attached to something that by its very nature will only bring us dissatisfaction and suffering? This is the most important lesson the Buddha could leave us. Then he passed away, entering parinirvana.

After that, all the arhats assembled and wrote down what they had learned by heart of his teachings and this became the core of the Buddhadharma we have today. From India, Buddhism spread to the other Asian countries and to Tibet, where it brought light to a dark country, and great teachers such as Padmasambhava, Lama Atisha, and Lama Tsongkhapa[19] helped make Buddhism an essential part of the Tibetan people's lives. In the West, before the middle of the last century, the teachings of the Buddha were almost unheard of, and so the causes of happiness and suffering were virtually unknown. Now the Buddha's teachings are widely available, from the basic lamrim teachings to the most advanced tantric practices with which we can attain enlightenment in one brief lifetime. None of this would have been possible without the achievements of the founder, Guru Shakyamuni Buddha.[20]

For followers of the individual liberation vehicle,[21] such as those in the Theravada countries like Sri Lanka and Thailand, the Buddha was like us and, by enacting the twelve deeds,[22] he attained enlightenment. From the Mahayana perspective, he had already become enlightened eons ago and the life he led as Siddhartha was an enactment in order to perfectly teach us what we must do if we want to likewise attain enlightenment. Furthermore, in this form, in the *nirmanakaya*, or emanation body, he was able to form the sangha around him and teach the holy Dharma to his followers for more than forty years.

We owe everything to the Dharma and the holy beings who came after the Buddha, who kept the teachings completely pure, and that means we owe everything to the holy being called Shakyamuni Buddha. The enlightened being he became arose from the bodhisattva who practiced for three countless great eons in myriad bodies, and that bodhisattva came from bodhichitta, which in turn grew from the compassion he felt for sentient beings. If, since we have met the Buddhadharma, our wisdom has grown enough to discriminate what is right and to be practiced from what is wrong and to be abandoned, all this comes from Buddha's compassion.

VISUALIZING SHAKYAMUNI BUDDHA

It is very good to visualize Guru Shakyamuni Buddha as clearly as possible, whether you are reciting the Shakyamuni mantra, doing a short meditation practice, or even an extended Shakyamuni *puja*.[23] Even though you might find the visualization too complex at first, don't worry. With time and practice it will come. Gradually, as the mind becomes more purified, the visualization becomes clearer. Even if you just have some sense that Guru Shakyamuni Buddha is there in front of you, that is an excellent start.

Straight in front of you, at about the height of the forehead and about a body's length away, visualize Guru Shakyamuni Buddha sitting on a throne. Everything is in the nature of light.

First visualize the beautiful throne, very large and square and adorned with many jewels. The throne is raised up by eight white snow lions, two at each corner. The snow lions look a little like Chinese lions, but with

white fur and a green mane and tail. These are not statues but living, breathing animals. They are in reality manifestations of bodhisattvas, the holy beings who have attained bodhichitta. They also signify the wisdom of the Buddha, because of all animals, snow lions are the only ones that have absolutely no fear at all. This is shown by the droopy ears. All other animals must keep their ears pricked for danger, but the snow lion has no such need.

On the throne is a large, beautiful, open lotus, upon which is a sun and moon seat. These are very radiant, very bright, with the colors of the sun and moon respectively, but flat, like disks or cushions. These three objects, the lotus, sun, and moon, represent the attainment of the three principal aspects of the path, renunciation (the lotus), emptiness (the sun), and bodhichitta (the moon).

Seated on this is the omniscient mind of all the buddhas, manifested as Guru Shakyamuni Buddha, who has attained these realizations. You can see the Buddha as the absolute guru. The Buddha is in the aspect of a monk. You should not see his body as something solid, like a bronze or plaster statue, but made of radiant golden light, representing his holy mind. Light rays radiate out from it. He wears the saffron robes of a monk. The robes don't actually touch his body. Our clothes cling to our body and always feel sort of uncomfortable, even if just a little, whereas the Buddha's robes float just free from his holy body. This is the power of his wisdom.

He is seated in a vajra or full-lotus position with the feet resting on the opposite thighs, soles upward. The palm of his right hand rests on his right knee, the fingers extended down and touching the moon cushion. This is called the earth-controlling *mudra*,[24] signifying that he has great control and that he is in touch with reality.

His left hand is in his lap in the meditation mudra, holding a bowl filled with nectar. The nectar is medicine capable of curing all the disturbing emotions, traditionally called the *maras*. It has the power to control death as well as purify the mind and body aggregates, caused by karma and delusion, from which all suffering arises. This bowl of nectar is not there to purify Guru Shakyamuni Buddha's delusions—he is already entirely free from them—but to purify ours. It is medicine for us.

His face is very beautiful, with smiling, compassionate, elongated eyes and a gentle look, just like a loving father, gazing at you and at the same time at all sentient beings. It is a face you can never tire of looking at, no matter how much you look, you can always look more, it is just so beautiful and so magnificent. Just seeing it brings incredible bliss. His look seems to tell you, "My child, if you want to be free from suffering, I will guide you."

He has long ears and reddish lips, and his hair is blue-black, with each hair individually curled to the right. At his forehead, between his eyebrows, there is a curl. It is unique in that it can be stretched out and it naturally curls again, like rubber. Every feature has significance, each part of the thirty-two major signs and eighty minor exemplifications of an enlightened being.[25]

Rays of light emanate out from every pore of the Buddha's holy body, touching every part of the universe. These rays are actually countless tiny emanations of the Buddha, going out to help all sentient beings and then dissolving back into his body.

THE MANTRA

The Meaning of the Mantra

Shakyamuni Buddha's mantra is this:

TADYATHA OM MUNE MUNE MAHA MUNEYE SVAHA

ཏདྱཐཱ༔ ༀ་མུ་ནེ་མུ་ནེ་མ་ཧཱ་མུ་ནེ་ཡེ་སྭཱ་ཧཱ༔

The first word of the mantra is TADYATHA (pronounced *tie-yata*). This is the introduction to many mantras; it means "this contains," and thus it tells us that what comes after contains the infinite knowledge of the Buddha's holy body, holy speech, and holy mind.

The second word, OM, contains the essence of all the Buddha's knowledge. By actualizing the paths of method and wisdom, all gross and subtle defilements cease, and our body, speech, and mind are purified, becoming the vajra holy body, vajra holy speech, and vajra holy mind of a buddha. This is signified by *a*, *o*, and *ma* respectively, the three syllables integrated into the one sound OM.

Next comes MUNE. Shakyamuni Buddha's name means "the subduer" (*muni*) of the Shakya clan and the word *muni* forms an important part of the Buddha's mantra. It used to be written in the mantra as "muni" but Kyabje Khunu Lama Rinpoche Tenzin Gyaltsen, the great bodhisattva His Holiness received many teachings from, clearly corrected this in a public teaching, saying it should be written and pronounced "mune." He also said that the last MUNE, MUNEYE, should be pronounced "mun-i-ye."[26]

MUNE is repeated three times, which relates to the graduated paths of the three capable beings—those of lower, middle, and higher capacity, who have the respective aims of a higher rebirth, nirvana, and enlightenment. This shows the route that the Buddha took over the three countless great eons until he became enlightened. It is the route we all must take.

The first MUNE, relating to the path of the lower capable being, signifies that the Buddha completely subdued attachment to this life's happiness. Through understanding subjects such as impermanence and karma, he was able to avoid rebirth in the lower realms and continue his spiritual journey.

The second MUNE relates to the path of the middle capable being; this is when the Buddha saw the shortcomings of the whole of samsara, even the highest attainment of the god realms, and having completely destroyed the false conception of the I, the principal ignorance that traps us in samsara, he attained liberation.

An arhat is free from samsara but not free from the dualistic mind and the subtle self-cherishing thought. MAHA MUNEYE, great control, the third MUNE, signifies the Buddha completely destroyed these and so overcame all duality between self and others and was able to fully see every single phenomenon. Like all the other bodhisattvas, when Guru

Shakyamuni Buddha entered the Mahayana path by attaining bodhi-chitta, he worked ceaselessly for the happiness of others, overcoming even the most subtle of obscurations and becoming enlightened. This is the graduated path of the higher capable being.

Guru Shakyamuni Buddha's mantra contains the whole path, both the path of the individual liberation practitioner, which encompasses the paths of the lower and middle capable being, and the path of the bodhisattva (the Mahayana), which encompasses the path of the higher capable being. It also contains the result of the path, the two *kayas* or bodies of a buddha: the *dharmakaya*, or truth body—the result of the wisdom side of the path—and the *rupakaya*, or form body[27]—the result of the method side of the path.

Finally, SVAHA (pronounced *soha*) means "so it is," the standard way to complete a mantra. It means basically, "May the blessings of Shakyamuni Buddha be rooted in my mind." I'm not sure what the connotation of the word "blessing" is in the West, but be careful not to think of it as something bestowed on us from outside. It's a beautiful word, but to receive blessings means to attain the wisdom and compassion of the Buddha, something we must do for ourselves. SVAHA means establishing the root. That can be guru devotion or faith in refuge and in karma. From that root, everything else flows.

This mantra contains the entire Dharma, from guru devotion, the first teaching of the lamrim, to the most subtle explanations on emptiness. It is just a few syllables, but the meaning is as vast as space. Reciting this mantra has the power to purify thousands of eons of negative karma. It is that powerful. Therefore it is extremely good to recite it as much as possible, not only during a meditation session, but whenever possible. It can be done standing up, lying down, while walking, while waiting at a bus stop—anywhere, any time.

To be able to attain enlightenment quickly for the sake of all sentient beings, to free them from suffering as quickly as possible, depends on how quickly we can develop on the path, and that depends on the strength of our bodhichitta. To attain not just wishing bodhichitta but actual engaging bodhichitta—the mind that spontaneously, completely, and continuously works for the maximum benefit of all sentient beings—we need the most powerful and skillful means possible, and this mantra is a vital tool to obtaining this.

Don't think that reciting a mantra is something to do when there is nothing better to do. Even small actions can bring huge profit. Shopkeepers have thousands of things in their shop, big and small, expensive and cheap, but they value them all. They know that they might sell a big item occasionally, but they are always selling small things like candy. The tiny profit made from a bit of candy wouldn't even get a cup of tea, but by slow and constant accumulation they can make great profit from those small things. Similarly, we can make a big profit from reciting mantras every day, whereas we might only be able to go on a long retreat once every few years. And if we can recite the mantras with a bodhichitta motivation, we can make a *huge* profit out of even a few mantras.

The Benefits of the Mantra

Reciting the Buddha's mantra has great benefits. Even if we have experienced many problems in this life, that does not mean that all of the nonvirtuous karma we have collected in all previous lifetimes has been used up and we no longer have to experience the suffering that is their result. Reciting this mantra, however, has the power to purify all that negative karma. Reciting it once has the power to purify the nonvirtuous karma produced by disturbing negative thoughts that we have collected in forty thousand previous lifetimes. If, by reciting it, we could stop even one negative karma ripening, making it impossible to bring a result, that would be wonderful, but here we are saying it purifies *all* negative karmas accumulated for forty thousand lifetimes!

What prevents us from attaining the ultimate happiness of nirvana and full enlightenment? We are blocked by our obscurations, triggered by our karma and delusions, so what we most need to do is eliminate those obscurations. When we can do that, it becomes easy to attain all the realizations on the path. Because this was revealed by the Buddha, when we make a connection with him through reciting his mantra or his holy name (which we will look at with the Thirty-Five Buddhas), we establish within our mindstream the potential to destroy all our delusions.

Each time we recite the Buddha's mantra, it plants a seed, an imprint, which is left on the mental continuum, and which results, sooner or later, in being able to fully understand the teachings of the path. Understanding the full meaning of the mantra, we understand all the teachings of the Buddha. In that way, we are able to have the realizations of the path, and that gradually leads to enlightenment.

Even if we don't yet have realizations, with compassion we can use the Buddha's mantra to benefit ourselves or others. The fundamental thing is to have strong faith in whatever meditations or mantras we are using. Lama Tsongkhapa explained the essential importance of three factors: strong faith in the guru's instructions, some experience of emptiness, and the good heart, bodhichitta. To the extent that we have these qualities, we will be able to do whatever activities are needed to help and serve others.

Patients have recovered from heart attacks and other diseases by reciting Shakyamuni Buddha's mantra many thousands of times. A *geshe*[28] at one of our centers in Spain advised a student with serious heart problems to do this. The doctors thought she would die soon, but she recited the Buddha's mantra one or two hundred thousand times and visualized nectar coming and purifying her, and her heart returned to its normal size and she was cured.

Many problems can come from self-cherishing, attachment, and the other disturbing thoughts, which make actions become negative. For instance, when we harm other beings; they then become the conditions for harming us. The main cause of receiving harm, however, is our own ignorance, anger, and attachment, and the harmful actions we do to others because of these delusions. When we recite Guru Shakyamuni Buddha's mantra, we counteract all this.

How to Practice with
Shakyamuni Buddha's Mantra[29]

After sitting down and calming yourself with some breathing meditation, visualize Guru Shakyamuni Buddha in front of you (as described above).

Then, do some preliminary practices, such as saying the refuge prayer, the four immeasurable thoughts, and the seven-limb prayer.[30] You can also offer a mandala.[31]

Expand the visualization of the Buddha to include all sentient beings surrounding you.

Then think, "I have received this perfect human rebirth and have met both the infallible teachings and the infallible teachers who can lead me on the path to enlightenment, releasing me from all suffering and allowing me to attain ultimate happiness. This is not so with all these other kind mother sentient beings, who have been my mother countless times and have been so kind to me. In order to help them be free from their terrible suffering, I will do this meditation and attain the state of buddhahood myself."

Purifying Delusions
Request from your heart, "Please purify me and all sentient beings from the delusions, obscurations, sicknesses, and afflictions caused by external harmful spirits."

Visualize a stream of *rays of white nectar* coming from Guru Shakyamuni Buddha's heart, flowing into you, entering through the crown of your head. As it flows into you, repeat this prayer three times.

To the guru, founder, bhagavan, tathagata, arhat, perfectly completed buddha, glorious conqueror,[32] Shakyamuni

Buddha, I prostrate, make offerings and go for refuge. Please grant me your blessings.

Now recite Guru Shakyamuni Buddha's mantra, for one or more malas, or at least seven times.

TADYATHA OM MUNE MUNE MAHA MUNEYE SVAHA

As you recite the mantra, feel the radiant rays of white nectar slowly fill your body, completely purifying all your delusions. Feel they are pouring strongly into you, like when you stand under a strong shower. As soon as the rays touch and flow into your body, a sensation of infinite mental and physical bliss fills you.

Feel your body is completely full of radiant white light. Think, "All my delusions and sickness as well as all the afflictions caused by the external spirits are completely purified."

Accumulating Merit

Visualize a stream of *rays of golden nectar* coming from Guru Shakyamuni Buddha's heart, flowing into you, entering through the crown of your head. This light is the essence of the Buddha's holy body, holy speech, and holy mind. As your body fills with this light, feel infinitely blissful, mentally and physically. Again, say the mantra.

TADYATHA OM MUNE MUNE MAHA MUNEYE SVAHA

At the end of the mantra recitation, feel you are completely filled with the Buddha's radiant golden light and you have attained the qualities of the Buddha's holy body, holy speech, and holy mind.

Then, the snow lions dissolve into the throne, the throne dissolves into the lotus, and the lotus dissolves into the sun and moon. They dissolve into Guru Shakyamuni Buddha, who comes to the crown of your head, melts into light, and dissolves into your body. Feel that all wrong conceptions are completely destroyed, and everything becomes completely empty. Your mind becomes the blissful omniscient mind of the Buddha. Feel that you *are* the Buddha.

Light beams radiate from your holy body. At the tip of each light beam is a tiny Shakyamuni Buddha. All these Shakyamuni Buddhas enter and absorb into each and every sentient being, purifying all their sufferings and its causes, delusion and negative karma. Then the light beams with Shakyamuni Buddhas at their tips return and absorb into you.

Rejoice by thinking, "How wonderful it is that I have enlightened all sentient beings."

Finish by making this dedication.

> By the merits of having done this meditation practice, may I attain the enlightened state of Guru Shakyamuni Buddha and lead all other sentient beings to that enlightened state.

2. CHENREZIG

I N THE BLISSFUL WESTERN realm called Having Lotus,[33] there was a kind wheel-turning king, King Supreme Goodness,[34] who didn't have a son. He dedicated everything in his life to the Dharma, including his great wealth and all his activities. Every day the king would make an offering of a lotus flower taken from a nearby lake to the Buddha, Dharma, and Sangha. One day the servant who went to pick the lotus saw growing from the lake a lotus stem with leaves as huge as an eagle's wings and an unopened bud in the center. When the servant reported this, the king said, "Inside that lotus bud there will definitely be a holy nirmanakaya that has taken spontaneous birth."[35]

King Supreme Goodness, his ministers, and the rest of his entourage went to the lake to see the lotus. When they opened the flower to check what was inside, they saw a sixteen-year-old youth with a radiant, white, holy body, adorned with the holy signs and exemplifications. He had a white scarf wrapped around his waist and an antelope skin over his left shoulder. (Antelopes are so compassionate that it is said an antelope will stand between a hunter and his prey and offer itself to the hunter in place of the other animal.) From his holy mouth, the youth exclaimed over and over, "How pitiful sentient beings in the six realms[36] are!" He kept repeating this.

The king and all his entourage prostrated to the youth, who was actually Chenrezig manifested in this form and taken birth in the lotus. The king then spread a special cloth on the ground, asked the boy to sit on it, and invited him to the palace, where he abided as an object of devotion for the king and all his family.

Thinking to benefit sentient beings, Chenrezig, in the aspect of this sixteen-year-old boy, generated bodhichitta. He then made requests to all the buddhas and bodhisattvas of the three times,[37] saying, "I will lead each and every single sentient being to peerless full enlightenment." He then added, "Until I have done this, if any thought seeking my own happiness arises, may my head crack into ten pieces like an *azarka*." (Perhaps this is some kind of fruit—the meaning is to crack into small pieces.)

When Chenrezig made this prayer, Amitabha, Buddha of Infinite Light, said, "I will help you accomplish your work for sentient beings." Chenrezig's holy body then emitted six beams, with one beam going to each of the six realms, where it worked to liberate sentient beings.

Later, Chenrezig went to the top of Mount Meru[38] and looked around with his wisdom eye. Even though he had liberated so many sentient beings from the six realms, when he looked, there still seemed to be the same number of them as before. So, he again sent beams to the six realms and liberated sentient beings. With his compassion and wisdom, Chenrezig liberated beings in this way three times, but still the sentient beings did not seem to become fewer in number. Chenrezig then thought, "It seems that this samsara has no end. Therefore I will abide in the blissful state of peace for myself."

Because thinking this broke his bodhichitta commitment, Chenrezig's head cracked into ten pieces. The pain was so unbearable that he screamed and wept. Amitabha then came and collected the pieces of Chenrezig's shattered head from the ground, put the pieces together, and blessed them as eleven faces. (As you know, one form of Chenrezig has a thousand arms and eyes and eleven faces.) To end samsara, which is beginningless, Amitabha blessed all but one of the faces in a peaceful aspect to subdue sentient beings. For the sentient beings unable to be subdued by peaceful means, Amitabha blessed one face in a wrathful aspect. The face of Amitabha Buddha on the very top of the other heads signifies that Chenrezig achieved enlightenment by depending on the kindness of his guru, Amitabha, and even after enlightenment he still had great devotion for his guru.

After Amitabha Buddha had blessed him, Chenrezig prayed, "In order to work for sentient beings until samsara ends, may I have a thousand arms and a thousand eyes." Right at that moment, the thousand arms and thousand eyes manifested. This is just one version of how Chenrezig came to have a thousand arms and a thousand eyes.[39]

Just as there are many manifestations of Chenrezig, there are many stories about him. In another one, Amitabha had a thought to benefit transmigratory beings. From his right eye, he sent a beam of white light, which transformed into Chenrezig; and from his left eye, he sent a beam of blue light, which transformed into Tara.

CHENREZIG LOOKS ON ALL SENTIENT BEINGS

In Tibet, we call the Buddha of Compassion *Chenrezig*, which is *Avalokiteshvara* in Sanskrit. For Tibetans, Chenrezig is in a male aspect, but that seems to be due to karma. A buddha will manifest in whatever way is most beneficial for sentient beings, as a male or a female, a child, an animal, a king, or a beggar. In China, the Buddha of Compassion is in the female aspect of Kuan Yin and in Japan she is called Kannon. Whatever the aspect, Chenrezig is the embodiment of the compassion of the numberless buddhas of the past, present, and future, here to guide and liberate us from all suffering and the causes of suffering, and to lead us to liberation and enlightenment.

Chenrezig is always guiding us. He is the special deity karmically connected to the people of the Snow Land, Tibet, and manifesting in the form of His Holiness the Dalai Lama. Guru Shakyamuni Buddha made predictions about the Dalai Lamas being Chenrezig and about how they would particularly guide sentient beings in Tibet, bringing them refuge and spreading the Dharma. Now, because His Holiness is vital to the people of the entire planet, Chenrezig is also the special deity for the whole world.

In the *White Lotus Sutra*, there is a story of a king called Golden Rim[40] who had a son named Unblinking Eyes.[41] Guru Shakyamuni Buddha predicted, "You, Unblinking Eyes, will pacify the delusions of sentient beings, liberating them from not only the lower realms but from samsara itself. Having generated the compassionate thought, you will achieve enlightenment and be called Chenrezig. You will draw many sentient beings into the Dharma and bring them to enlightenment. In particular, you will become the protector, the object of refuge, the savior, of the Snow Land. You will spread the Dharma like a shining sun in the Snow Land, this outlying land that no other buddha of the thousand buddhas of the fortunate eon[42] has been able to benefit."

Chenrezig looks at all transmigratory beings with compassion and never gives up on anyone, no matter how evil they are. Because he is constantly looking at us and guiding us, he is given the particular name, *Chenrezig*, which means "the one who continuously looks at the world with compassionate eyes."[43]

King Songtsen Gampo and King Trisong Detsen of Tibet were manifestations of Chenrezig, as were the great scholars who translated the Dharma from Sanskrit into Tibetan. Showing unimaginable kindness, Chenrezig manifested in these various forms and then spread the Dharma in Tibet. Now that Tibetan Buddhism, which encompasses the entire Buddhadharma, has spread to the rest of the world, you can see that we are completely in the care of and completely guided by Compassion Buddha.

According to *The Flower Garland Sutra* (*Avatamsakasutra*):

> When the moon rises, numberless reflections appear wherever there is water in this world. That is how Chenrezig manifests. Effortlessly, naturally, Chenrezig manifests in all kinds of forms, even as medicine, a bridge, or water. Chenrezig, manifesting to sentient beings in whatever form benefits them, does inconceivable work for sentient beings.

There is only one moon, but when the moon rises, every body of water reflects it. The moon's reflection comes effortlessly everywhere there is water, whether ocean, lake, river, or pond, even on a drop of dew. Since Chenrezig manifests as medicine, bridges, water, and other things, there is no doubt that Chenrezig manifests as our virtuous friend to guide us and give us the opportunity to learn Dharma. And Chenrezig manifests in the six syllables OM MANI PADME HUM to purify our negative karma and enable us to collect extensive merits, fulfilling all our wishes and bringing us to enlightenment in the quickest, easiest way.

VISUALIZING CHENREZIG

The Many Different Aspects of Chenrezig

A text by Gomo Rinpoche[44] begins with a verse of prostration to Chenrezig:

> Your thousand arms signify a thousand wheel-turning kings;
> Your thousand eyes signify the thousand buddhas of the fortu-
>   nate eon;
> You manifest in whatever aspect is needed to subdue sentient
>   beings:
> To you, pure Compassionate-Eyed One, I prostrate.[45]

While the four-arm Chenrezig is the simplest and most common form seen in Tibetan Buddhism, the thousand-arm, thousand-eye Chenrezig is also a very common aspect. But these two are not the only ones; there are many forms of Chenrezig within Tibetan Buddhism, such as the secret Chenrezig, Gyalwa Gyatso; or Chenrezig Singhanada, three-faced and two-armed, who protects from disease; Ganapati,[46] who protects from poverty; and Dzambhala, who grants wealth.

As the embodiment of all the buddhas' compassion, one aspect is simply not enough to lead all sentient beings—each with their different propensities and personalities—to enlightenment. Some beings are able to subdue their minds more quickly through the outer manifestations of Chenrezig with four arms, whereas for others the thousand-arm Chenrezig is more effective. It is said there are 108 names for Chenrezig, which means there are that many aspects. Depending on a sentient being's karma, the aspect that suits that being will manifest to help them generate compassion, wisdom, and all the other realizations of the path to enlightenment.

Chenrezig is special to so many sentient beings, and not only in

countries where the Mahayana is the main form of Buddhism. Because compassion is the foremost attitude to develop, the Buddha of Compassion is naturally the most popular buddha, the one in most people's hearts. Whether they simply recite his mantra or undertake *nyungné* retreats,[47] through their connection with Chenrezig people are able to purify many eons of negative karma and accumulate a great deal of merit.

Four-Arm Chenrezig

A form of Chenrezig we often see is white in color and has four arms. The first two arms are together at his heart, his hands in the prostration mudra and holding a wish-granting jewel; the second two arms are at the level of his shoulders, the right hand holding a crystal mala and the left a white lotus. His face is peaceful and smiling, and he gazes at us and all beings with infinite compassion. He wears exquisite silks and is beautified with jewel ornaments. He is seated in the vajra position on an open lotus and a white moon disk.

Thousand-Arm Chenrezig

In a more complex manifestation of Chenrezig, he has a thousand arms, a thousand eyes, and eleven faces.

Unlike the four-arm Chenrezig, who is seated, the thousand-arm Chenrezig is standing on a lotus and moon disk. His two principal hands are together at his heart in the mudra of prostration, holding a wish-granting jewel. His next two right hands hold a crystal mala and a Dharma wheel, while the last one, without implement, is in the mudra of granting sublime realizations; his three left hands hold a lotus, a bow and arrow, and a vase. The other 992 hands are arranged in a circle around the body, all in the mudra of granting sublime realizations. In the palm of each of the thousand hands there is an eye.

He has eleven faces. The first three are white in the center, green on the right, and red on the left; the three above that are green in the center, red on the right, and white on the left; the three above that are red in the center, white on the right, and green on the left. Above that is a face

in wrathful aspect, deep blue in color, and on the crown is Amitabha's beautiful holy face. The different colors of the faces signify the four actions of a buddha: pacifying (white), increasing (green), controlling (red), and wrathful (blue).

He is beautifully adorned with jewel ornaments and loose-fitting, divine clothes.

The Mantra

There are different versions of the Chenrezig mantra, although the two you will mostly hear are the long mantra and the short, six-syllable mantra. The six-syllable mantra is very easy to recite. Even those not particularly interested in Buddhism, especially children, love to recite it. Because Chenrezig is the manifestation of all the buddhas' compassion, his mantra is everywhere in Tibet and Nepal, and the practice is done by so many people. Trekkers in Nepal hear it so much they just naturally start to say it.

The long mantra is this:

NAMO RATNA TRAYAYA / NAMAH ARYA JNANA SAGARA VAIROCHANA VYUHA RAJAYA / TATHAGATAYA / ARHATE / SAMYAKSAM BUDDHAYA / NAMAH SARVA TATHAGATEBHYAH / ARHATEBHYAH SAMYAKSAM BUD-DHEBHYAH / NAMAH ARYA AVALOKITESHVARAYA / BODHISATTVAYA / MAHASATTVAYA / MAHAKARUNIKAYA / TADYATHA / OM DHARA DHARA / DHIRI DHIRI / DHURU DHŪRU / ITTE VATTE / CHALE CHALE / PRACHALE PRA-CHALE / KUSUME / KUSUME VARE / ILI MILI / CHITI JVA-LAMAPANAYA SVAHA

ན་མོ་རཏྣ་ཏྲ་ཡཱ་ཡ། ན་མཿཨཱཪྻ་ཛྙཱ་ན་སཱ་ག་ར་བཻ་རོ་ཙ་ན་བྱཱུ་ཧ་རཱ་ཛཱ་ཡ། ཏ་ ཐཱ་ག་ཏཱ་ཡ། ཨ་རྷ་ཏེ། སམྱཀྶཾ་བུ་དྡྷཱ་ཡ། ན་མཿསརྦ་ཏ་ཐཱ་ག་ཏེ་བྷྱཿ། ཨ་རྷ་ཏེ་བྷྱཿ སམྱཀྶཾ་བུ་དྡྷེ་བྷྱཿ། ན་མཿཨཱཪྻ་ཨ་བ་ལོ་ཀི་ཏེ་ཤྭ་རཱ་ཡ། བོ་དྷི་སཏྭཱ་ཡ། མ་ཧཱ་སཏྭཱ

ཡ། མ་ནྡུ་ཀུ་ རུ་ ཏི་ཀུ་ཡ། ཏ་ཐུ་ སྒྲ། ཨོཾ་ རུ་ར་རུ་ར། རི་རི་རི་རི། རུ་རུ་རུ་རུ།
ཨིནྜི་མིནྜི། ཚ་ལི་ཚ་ལི། པ་ཚ་ལི་པ་ཚ་ལི། ཀུ་སུ་མེ་ཀུ་སུ་མེ་ལ་རེ། ཨི་ལི་མི་ལི།
ཙི་ཏི་རྡོ་ལ་མ་པ་ནད་ཡེ་སྭ་ཧཱ།

The short mantra is this:

OM MANI PADME HUM

ཨོཾ་མ་ཎི་པ་དྨེ་ཧཱུྃ།

There is a story about how the great mantra of Chenrezig came about. Once, in the presence of Shakyamuni Buddha, Chenrezig stood up and, prostrating with his hands, said to the Buddha, "I have a mantra, the essence of which is great compassion. Please, O Tathagata, give me permission to explain this mantra in order to cause all sentient beings to abide in happiness, to remove disease, to cause long life and wealth, to purify all the negative karmas and obscurations, to increase all knowledge, to make all good actions succeed, to free from all fears, and to fulfill all wishes." Shakyamuni Buddha assented to his request.

Chenrezig then explained that in a former time, numberless eons before, a buddha called Kashyapa[48] descended in the world. After explaining the essence of this mantra of vast compassion, Kashyapa placed his golden-colored hand on Chenrezig's crown and said, "Son of the buddhas, the essence of this mantra should be your mantra. Use it to bring great benefit and happiness to sentient beings in the future."

If a sentient being who has much devotion to Chenrezig recites this mantra or always keeps it with them, at the time of their death, all the buddhas will come to wherever they are and guide them to whichever buddha's pure realm they wish to be born in.

Chenrezig prayed,

If any sentient being who always recites this mantra is reborn
in the realm of suffering transmigratory beings, may I never
receive enlightenment.

If any sentient being who always recites this mantra is not born
in a buddha's pure land, may I never receive enlightenment.

If any sentient being who always recites this mantra does not
achieve realizations of the various concentrations, may I never
receive enlightenment.

If any sentient being who always recites this mantra does not
have their wishes of this life fulfilled, may I never receive
enlightenment.

If all the wishes of a person who always recites this mantra are
not fulfilled, it cannot be called the heart mantra of the Great
Compassionate One.

Chenrezig received enlightenment numberless eons ago, long before
this world came into existence. Even though he prayed not to receive
enlightenment if sentient beings who recited this mantra were born in
the lower realms rather than the pure realms and so forth, he *did* receive
enlightenment. That means the mantra does not betray—it has the
power to bring all those benefits.

The Meaning of the Six-Syllable Mantra

The six-syllable mantra of Compassion Buddha, OM MANI PADME
HUM, contains the entire Buddhist path, including the paths of the
four levels of tantra: kriya tantra, charya tantra, yoga tantra, and highest
yoga tantra. These six syllables have the power to completely close the
door of the six realms, meaning we will cease the continuity of taking
birth in the six realms.

The main body of the mantra is MANI PADME. MANI, which means
"jewel," signifies the method side of the path to enlightenment—the
development of bodhichitta, which is the jewel of our practice. PADME,
which means "lotus," signifies the wisdom side, the understanding of

the nature of reality. Just as a lotus grows out of the mud yet is unstained by it, Chenrezig transcends the dualistic mind of ignorance, the concept of true existence, and directly perceived emptiness. In the illustrations of Chenrezig, you will see he holds a white lotus. Therefore these two syllables combined contain both the Hinayana and the Mahayana, with its two divisions of Paramitayana, or bodhisattva's path, and Vajrayana, or tantric path.

Everything in Buddhism is contained within the base of the two truths: conventional truth and ultimate truth. MANI refers to conventional truth, which is also called all-obscuring truth because, although it is true on one level, it obscures the ultimate nature of reality, which is the ultimate truth. PADME refers to this ultimate truth.

So, MANI PADME contains the whole of the Buddhadharma: the base (the two truths), the path (method and wisdom), and the goal to be achieved (the rupakaya, or form body, and dharmakaya, or truth body of a buddha). MANI leads us to the rupakaya; PADME leads us to the dharmakaya.

The last syllable of the mantra is HUM. It establishes the root of the blessing in our heart and enables us to actualize the method and wisdom contained in MANI and PADME. It's a bit like saying, "Hey!" when we are calling out to somebody, getting them to pay attention to us. By saying HUM, we are requesting the Buddha's compassionate holy mind to pay attention to us and grant us this.

In our practice, we purify our ordinary body, speech, and mind, transforming them into the vajra holy body, the vajra holy speech, and the vajra holy mind of Compassion Buddha. This is signified by the OM, its three sounds—*a*, *o*, and *ma*—signifying Compassion Buddha's holy body, holy speech, and holy mind. In that way, we are able to do perfect work for all sentient beings. OM, which we have already looked at with Shakyamuni Buddha's mantra, appears in many mantras and means just this.

Each of the six syllables has the power to stop us taking birth in any of the six realms: the hell, hungry ghost, animal, human, demigod, and god realms. Each of the six syllables destroys the continuity of the six root delusions: attachment, anger, ignorance, pride, doubt, and wrong view. Each creates the conditions to attain the six perfections of the bodhisattva: charity, morality, patience, perseverance, concentration, and wisdom.

Reciting the six-syllable mantra allows us to achieve the highest realizations and progress through the five paths necessary to attain enlightenment: the paths of merit, preparation, seeing, meditation, and no more learning, which is enlightenment.

This is just a fraction of what OM MANI PADME HUM means. It encompasses all the 84,000 teachings of the Buddha and integrates in one essence the intentions of all the buddhas of the ten directions.[49] It is the origin of all the collections of virtue and all the collections of happiness. Why? Because the particular benefit of reciting this mantra is to generate compassion for each and every sentient being whose mind is obscured and who is suffering. We not only wish them to be free from all their suffering and defilements, we take on that responsibility ourselves.

Everybody Needs the Chenrezig Mantra

Compassion is not just for those with faith in the Buddha, Dharma, and Sangha. It is not just for those who are Buddhist, for those who seek enlightenment. Everyone needs compassion. No matter what style of life we have, the compassionate life is the best life. With that, our life is totally transformed. Before it was like kaka,[50] but now it is transformed into gold. Before there was just ego, the self-cherishing mind, but now there is compassion. Compassion brings a huge difference in our life, like the difference between the earth and the sky.

Everybody needs to recite OM MANI PADME HUM to develop compassion. We are so fortunate that with our human body we are able to communicate and to chant Chenrezig's mantra. Ants need to recite it, whales need to, monkeys need to, but they can't.

In many areas in Tibet and Nepal, especially along trails, there are a lot of stupas[51] and stones carved with the Chenrezig mantra. You can see big piles of these stones, called "MANI stones," as you leave the airport at Lukla.⁵² Sometimes a whole text, such as the *Heart Sutra*, is carved on a stone. One of my uncles, my teacher who first taught me the alphabet when I was four, carved MANI stones like this. Because of the mantra's great benefit, you can see it everywhere, adorning prayer flags and stones, and you can hear people reciting the mantra as they pass.

Just seeing mantras on stones purifies our obscurations by leaving impressions on the mind. As with prayer flags, when the wind touches these mantras and then touches a human being or animal, it purifies the negative karmas and obscurations of that sentient being.

Just like Westerners like to recite their mantra "Oh when can I be happy," Tibetans like to recite OM MANI PADME HUM. They recite it while they are working, cooking, or doing any of the chores they need to do. When they are not serving customers, shopkeepers recite OM MANI PADME HUM. As they walk, Tibetans will invariably have a small prayer wheel full of MANI mantras, which they spin clockwise as they recite.

Prayer wheels are my hobby; they offer so many benefits. The huge prayer wheels I ask the FPMT centers to build bless all the insects on the ground and in the area, besides all the people who turn them. They are such a great blessing for the area and a quick way to liberate sentient beings from the lower realms and enlighten them. Any person who circumambulates and turns the prayer wheel receives unbelievable purification. If a prayer wheel has one hundred million MANI's, one turn is equivalent to saying one hundred million OM MANI PADME HUM mantras.

And that is true even of the small, hand-held prayer wheels you always see Tibetans spinning as they walk. Because of methods such as microfiche printing, they can have millions of MANI's in a small wheel, so one turn creates incredible merit, no matter what they are doing. Reciting OM MANI PADME HUM makes the most mundane activity highly meaningful.

The old mothers in Solu Khumbu chant OM MANI PADME HUM so much. They have almost no intellectual understanding of the Dharma, and they can't even understand it if a lama comes to teach, because he teaches in Tibetan, not Sherpa, the only language they speak. Being illiterate, they can't even open a Dharma book and read it, and so they have no opportunity to learn the Dharma. But by reciting OM MANI PADME HUM, somehow their hearts become so much more compassionate. They may not understand why other beings are suffering so much, but they have a strong natural feeling of compassion for others and the wish to pray for them.

This was true of my mother, who would simply recite OM MANI PADME HUM when a lama was giving teachings. Because of reciting the MANI mantra, she had a hundred thousand times more compassion than I have. I can read all the texts but still my compassion is like clouds in the sky: utterly unstable, never lasting. Just before she passed away, she told me that for most of her life she recited fifty thousand MANI's a day, but as she became older she was no longer able to do that many. Still, I am certain the great power of her compassion came from reciting OM MANI PADME HUM. It gave her a happy, meaningful life and a happy, meaningful death.

There is a tantra called *Zung of the Eleven-Face Arya Avalokiteshvara.* In it Chenrezig is said to mention,

> By reciting my heart mantra, sentient beings receive the bodhisattvas' holy deeds, the heart of all the Victors, called the heart of transcendental wisdom. In short, for sentient beings tormented by various sufferings, my heart mantra will abide and become a guide for them. Also, this heart mantra hooks the harm-givers, such as the flesh-eaters and other violent spirits, and causes them to generate loving-kindness and compassion. It then brings them to enlightenment.

Furthermore, he says,

> Any sentient being who holds my name will abide in nonreturning. They will be completely liberated from all sicknesses and from all the defilements, all the vices collected with the body, speech, and mind.

"My name" here means the six-syllable mantra, and "nonreturning" means our life will never degenerate but always progress toward enlightenment.

When a doctor tells us we have cancer, what they are actually saying is that now is the time to cut all meaningless thoughts and only think about and practice the Dharma. We should understand such advice to mean just that, and we should do whatever is necessary to bring the Dharma into our life.

It is not enough just to be able to say the words of the mantra; we should first cultivate as positive a motivation as we can—and the bodhichitta motivation is the best—and then recite it. Whoever recites the mantra with a bodhichitta motivation is somebody who really knows how to recite it. It is said in the teachings that the greater devotion we have for Chenrezig, the more power and benefit the mantra has.

The Benefits of Reciting the Chenrezig Mantra

Although there are innumerable benefits whether we recite the six-syllable Chenrezig mantra or the long one, if we can have a clear idea of what those benefits are, we will have more energy to recite it. The teachings often mention fifteen:

1. We will always be born in a country where there is a Dharma king, a ruler who works according to the Dharma.
2. We will always be born in a virtuous country, one where everybody has freedom to create virtue.
3. We will always be born in fortunate times.
4. We will always meet a virtuous friend. Here "virtuous friend" does not necessarily mean a teacher, but rather a Dharma friend, one who helps us in our Dharma practice. Their influence will help us to continue our Dharma practice.
5. We will receive a perfect body, having perfect limbs and senses.
6. Our actions will become subdued.
7. Our moral conduct will not degenerate. We will be able to increasingly keep our morality purely.

8. We will live in a good environment, surrounded by people we have a good relationship with.

9. Our material possessions will not be stolen by others.

10. We will always be respected by others and receive help from them. People will make offerings to us.

11. We will receive whatever possessions we need.

12. We will quickly attain whatever we wish for.

13. We will become a guide for others, an object of refuge for worldly gods, demigods, and the *nagas*.[53]

14. We will always be born in a country where a buddha is present. Just as those who were disciples of Shakyamuni Buddha are reborn in whatever country he manifests, many have the good fortune to always see His Holiness the Dalai Lama and receive teachings from him.

15. We will not only hear the teachings but also be able to realize the profound meaning of them.

Furthermore, a principal way the mantra benefits is by the protection it offers. The texts say if we recite a mala of the six-syllable mantra when we get up in the morning with the proper Dharma motivation, we will be protected in these ten ways:

1. We will never fall ill; our body will always be healthy.

2. We will always be protected by gods and buddhas.

3. We will never lack a means of living but will easily be able to gain material needs, such as wealth, food, clothing, and so forth.

4. We will have no fear of enemies because we will be able to subdue their minds.

5. We will never be disrespected, not only now but also in the future.

6. We will never fall into a lower caste, but always achieve a higher caste by living in ethics.

7. We will be free from the danger of poisons, spirit harm, and spirit possession.

8. We will never have an unpleasant odor; our body will always have

a scented smell. This does not mean a scented smell from bought perfume but a natural fragrance coming from the body.

9. We will never encounter the enmity of others. Nobody will harbor bad thoughts about us or say hurtful or displeasing words. Everybody will be happy with us.

10. We will be free from chronic or contagious diseases and be liberated from untimely death.

The Chenrezig Mantra Purifies and Transforms Our Mind

Reciting the Chenrezig mantra can bring all these incredible benefits because the act of reciting it with a strong, pure motivation has the power to transform our mind in two ways: by diminishing our negative minds and thus purifying our delusions, and by increasing our positive minds and thus accumulating great merit.

When we do even one prostration to Compassion Buddha or recite his name or his mantra even once, we collect the same amount of merit as having offered service to the buddhas equaling not just the number of grains of sand of the River Ganges but the number of grains of sand there would be in sixty-two River Ganges.

Any powerful delusions that arise, such as strong desire or hatred, are naturally pacified by chanting this mantra. By reciting it seven times, the negative karma accumulated from one hundred past lifetimes is purified. Reciting it twenty-one times purifies a thousand eons of negative karma. If we recite it 108 times, which means one mala, it has the power to purify forty thousand eons of negative karma. Of course, this depends on having strong faith in the benefit of the mantra and reciting it with a bodhichitta motivation, and so forth. The purer our motivation is, the greater the power of purification.

It is said that reciting it even once can purify the four root downfalls of a fully ordained monk or nun—killing a human being; telling great lies, such as boasting they have realizations when they don't; taking things not given to them; and having sexual intercourse—actions that bring about rebirth in the very lowest of the hot hells.

For both lay people and sangha, it purifies the five immediate neg-ativities, the very heavy negative karmas that cause rebirth in the hell realm immediately after death. These are killing our mother; killing our father; killing an arhat, a being who has achieved the arya path and who is free from samsara; maliciously drawing blood from a buddha; and causing disunity within the sangha. This last one carries the heaviest negative karma we can commit, along with heresy, holding incorrect views about the guru.

There are many stories of people who incurred different heavy nega-tive karmas and were advised by Chenrezig to recite his mantra. Then, rather than going to the lower realms, where they were destined, they were able to be born in a pure land.

By purifying our mind with this mantra, we are able to solve all our own problems and to solve others' problems, bringing so much peace and happiness not only to our family and friends but to the whole world and all living beings, both human and nonhuman.

Generally, the motivation for what we do is self-cherishing, working only for the happiness of this life. It keeps our life so busy and causes us stress and anxiety, not to mention the attachment and anger it gen-erates, which cause us to create nonvirtuous actions and harm ourselves and others. It is possible, however, to turn that attitude around and cherish others rather than ourselves, developing the powerful minds of loving-kindness and compassion.

When we see that all the problems in our life come from ego, from the self-cherishing mind, and that every happiness comes from a mind that cherishes others, we naturally look for a method that will bring that transformation about. The fundamental step in that is connecting with Compassion Buddha, Chenrezig, and we can easily do that by reciting his mantra.

If we were able to continuously recite the Chenrezig mantra, or even do ten malas a day, we would not only transform our own mind, but our mere presence would benefit others greatly. Those who saw or touched us, let alone spoke to us, would be somehow benefited, absorbing some of our positive energy. It is even said in the texts that, when we die and are cremated, the smoke from our burning body will have the power to purify those it touched.

Once, when I was in Malaysia, some people who worked in a hospice there told me they often felt dejected when the patient they were attending didn't have any reaction or didn't show any signs of getting better. I told them there was no reason to feel discouraged; even if there was no response, what they were doing was still very worthwhile, and I encouraged them to recite Chenrezig's mantra to the patients as they were working. Being with a dying person after having recited the Chenrezig mantra is highly meaningful. They might not be able to see or hear us, but simply touching them, such as if we massage them, purifies their negative karma.

It is said in the tantric text *Padme Chöpen gyi Gyü* that if we recite ten malas of the mantra every day, our children, their children, and so on, up to seven generations, will never be reborn in the lower realms.[54] How is that possible? It is the power of the mantra. When we recite the Chenrezig mantra that many times every day, our body becomes a relic. The mantra blesses everything; everything becomes a relic, including the blood and sperm, which is passed from generation to generation.

If we recite six million OM MANI PADME HUM, even our spit has so much power. By spitting on something, or blowing on it, we are able to heal somebody so easily. For instance, if we spit or blow on some cream or butter and then rub it over a place of pain on the body, we will stop the pain. Whatever type of activity we do will be most beneficial. Whether it is a pacifying, increasing, controlling, or wrathful activity, it will be successful because of the power of the mantra. These things are not the main goal, however. The main goal is to achieve enlightenment in order to liberate sentient beings from suffering and bring them to enlightenment, but these other benefits come as a byproduct.

How to Practice with Chenrezig's Mantra [55]

Anyone can do this practice, called *The Welfare of Living Beings That Pervades Space* by the great yogi Thangtong Gyalpo. However, you are only permitted to generate yourself as Four-Arm Chenrezig if you have received a great initiation (*wang*) of any deity of performance (*charya*), yoga, or highest yoga tantra and the subsequent permission (*jenang*) of Four-Arm Chenrezig, or an action tantra great initiation of any deity of the tathagata or lotus families and the subsequent permission of Four-Arm Chenrezig. Otherwise, you should visualize Four-Arm Chenrezig above your head or in front of you.

> I take refuge until I am enlightened
> in the Buddha, the Dharma, and the Supreme Assembly.
> By my generosity and so forth,
> may I become a buddha in order to benefit living beings. *(3x)*

> On the crowns of myself and all sentient beings pervading space
> is a white lotus and moon.
> On top of it, from HRIH ཧྲཱིཿ arises the Supreme Arya Chenrezig,
> white and clear, radiating five-colored light rays;
> smiling and looking with eyes of compassion.

> Of your four arms, the palms of the first two are joined
> and the lower two hold a crystal rosary and a white lotus.
> You are adorned with silk and precious jewelry
> and wear a deerskin upper garment.

> Amitabha adorns your head.
> You are seated with your legs in the vajra posture.
> A stainless moon is your back rest.
> In nature, you encompass all objects of refuge.

Think that you and all sentient beings are making the following request as if in one voice:

Lord, your body is white in color, unsoiled by faults;
a complete buddha adorns your head;
you look at living beings with eyes of compassion;
to you, Chenrezig, I prostrate.

Recite that request three times, seven times, and so forth—however
many times you are able.

Through having made requests one-pointedly in that way,
lights radiate from the body of the Arya
and purify impure karmic appearances and mistaken minds.

The environment becomes Sukhavati Pure Land,
and the body, speech, and mind of its inhabitants—living
   beings—
become the body, speech, and mind of powerful Chenrezig—
appearance, sound, and awareness, inseparable from emptiness.

Reflecting on the meaning of this, recite as many times as you can:

OM MANI PADME HUM

At the end, place your mind in equipoise on its own essence of the
nonconceptualization of the three circles.[56]

The bodies of myself and others appear as bodies of the Arya,
the resonance of sounds is the melody of the six syllables,
and thoughts and conceptualizations are the expanse of great
   exalted wisdom.

Due to this virtue,
may I quickly become powerful Chenrezig
and lead all living beings
without exception to that state.

3. MANJUSHRI

ONCE, A VERY LONG time ago, a pilgrim to Wutai Shan, the holy place of Manjushri in China, was asked to take a letter to a particular village and give it to a particular bodhisattva. When he reached the village and asked a pig farmer there about the bodhisattva, the man replied that there was no human bodhisattva there by that name but that he had a pig of that name.

The pilgrim then read the message to the pig, which said, "Your time to be in this world is now finished. It is time for you to benefit other sentient beings in another world." As soon as the message was read, the pig made a huge noise and passed away. He was actually a bodhisattva pig, protecting all the other pigs. When leading the other pigs, he would always check ahead for danger, and when it was safe, he would let the other pigs go first; he was always the last pig.

The man who gave the pilgrim the letter was actually Manjushri. It is said that everybody who goes on pilgrimage to Wutai Shan sees Buddha Manjushri. They don't however necessarily see him in his usual aspect, with a sword and so forth, like in the paintings. To see Manjushri in the pure aspect of a buddha you must have a pure mind, and a pure mind is very rare, so most people see Manjushri as an ordinary person (or pig!). When you go to Wutai Shan you will definitely see Manjushri, but it doesn't mean you will recognize him.

I heard this story from Kirti Tsenshab Rinpoche,[57] the great lama who is one of my gurus. There are many other stories about Wutai Shan and how Manjushri emanates to benefit beings. Although we traditionally see Manjushri sitting in a vajra posture with a flaming sword—the manifestation of all the buddhas' wisdom—he appears in many aspects, as do all buddhas.

MANIFESTATIONS OF MANJUSHRI

Manjushri and Shantideva

Shantideva was born with the name Shantivarman in the eighth century in India, near Bodhgaya, where the Buddha was enlightened. He was highly intelligent. When he was six, he meditated on Manjushri and not only saw Manjushri but also had a realization of him. Manjushri himself gave the young Shantivarman many teachings, passing down the lineage of the profound path—the wisdom teachings—to him.

Because Shantivarman was a prince, he was obliged to become king when his father died, but the night before his enthronement he had a dream. Manjushri was sitting on the king's throne, and he said to Shantivarman, "The one son, this is my seat and I am your guru, leading you to enlightenment. We can't both sit on the same seat." When he awoke from the dream, he realized that he could not accept the crown, and so he escaped, going to Nalanda Monastery, where the abbot ordained him, naming him Shantideva.

Nalanda was a vast and wonderful place, the greatest seat of Buddhist knowledge in the world. Thousands of scholars studied, debated, and meditated there, and great pandits wrote incomparable treatises and developed incredible tenets on logic, as well as studied the sciences, art, medicine, and so forth.

Shantideva was a hidden yogi who already had great realizations, but he didn't reveal these in Nalanda at first. He had secretly composed two texts, *Condensed Advice* and *Compendium of Sutras*, but the other monks thought Shantideva was extremely lazy. It was only when they challenged him to recite a sutra, thinking this would shame him into leaving, that he recited the complete *Guide to the Bodhisattva's Way of Life*, his most famous work, like water pouring from a clear spring. The other monks immediately realized he was a great master.

Manjushri and Sakya Pandita

When the great Tibetan yogi, Sakya Pandita,[58] was only twelve, his guru, Drakpa Gyaltsen, told him that, because he was the spiritual son of Lama Atisha and Lama Dromtönpa, he should study well and do a retreat on Manjushri. Because all the buddhas' wisdom is manifested in this special aspect, those who practice Manjushri can receive all seven wisdoms, which are attainments such as *great wisdom* to comprehend and memorize both the meanings and the words of the extensive teachings, *clear wisdom* to be able to understand the subtle meaning of any subject, and *quick wisdom* to be able to immediately understand any difficult points and immediately eliminate wrong conceptions.[59]

Before Sakya Pandita was able to do the retreat his guru advised him to do, there were some hindrances. However, after six months, during a meditation session, he saw Manjushri sitting in front of him on a throne with two bodhisattvas beside him. Then, with his holy mouth, Manjushri gave him this short teaching on the four clingings:

- If you cling to this life you are not a Dharma practitioner.
- If you cling to the three realms of samsara that is not renunciation.
- If you cling to cherishing the self that is not bodhichitta.
- If you cling to the self as truly existing that is not right view.

Because Sakya Pandita realized that the importance of all the Buddha's teachings was contained in this advice, he kept it in his heart, meditating on it and putting it into practice.

Lama Tsongkhapa Is Manjushri

Lama Tsongkhapa, the great fourteenth-century teacher who founded the Geluk tradition,[60] is said to be a manifestation of Manjushri. Very often, Lama Tsongkhapa is called Jamgon, which is one of the names for Manjushri, meaning the savior who has purified all obscurations. Tsongkhapa is the savior from Tsongkha in Amdo, the place he was born.

The story is that his mother gave birth to him on the road as she was leading her cows out to the mountains for the day. Because of her work, she had no choice but to leave the baby there on the road, though she was afraid he would be eaten by animals. But when she came back, she found he was protected, lying under the wings of ravens that had crowded around him. Happy, she took the baby back home alive. The blood that had come out during his birth covered the road, and at that place a sandalwood tree grew. On the leaves of the tree were images of Manjushri's vajra body and the syllable DHI, Manjushri's seed syllable.[61] This is a sign that Lama Tsongkhapa is a manifestation of Manjushri. He is also the embodiment of Chenrezig, all the buddhas' compassion, and Vajrapani, all the buddhas' power. It was near that place that the Third Dalai Lama founded Kumbum monastery, where one hundred thousand statues of Manjushri have been built. Kumbum means "one hundred thousand enlightened bodies."

Manjushri often advised Lama Tsongkhapa, especially on how to quickly actualize the realizations of the graduated path to enlightenment. He told him, "To train your mind in the actual lamrim, you should purify your obscurations with a Vajrasattva practice and so forth and accumulate merit. Then, you should make a single-pointed request to the guru in order to receive the blessing within your heart. If you attempt to strongly and continuously practice in this way every day, realizations will come without any difficulty."

Because of his connection with Manjushri, Lama Tsongkhapa was able to check directly with him and clarify all the subtle and profound points within the sutra and tantra teachings, especially the Prasangika view of dependent arising and emptiness.

One day, while Lama Tsongkhapa was giving teachings to hundreds of disciples, offering several different teachings in a single day, Manjushri advised him to go into retreat immediately. Lama Tsongkhapa objected, saying he couldn't leave the teachings in the middle, but Manjushri asked him, "Don't you have to benefit numberless sentient beings?" The point of Manjushri's advice was that the people who were taking teachings from him at that time were limited in number, but sentient beings are numberless. By doing the practice he could complete the realizations on the path to enlightenment and, in that way, benefit more sentient beings. So, Lama Tsongkhapa stopped his teachings and went off to practice. Whatever work Lama Tsongkhapa had to do, whatever teachings he gave, he always asked Manjushri.

THE SOFT GLORIFIED ONE

Manjushri is *Jampalyang* in Tibetan. The first part of the name, *manju* (*jam* in Tibetan), means "soft," "pacified," and *shri* (*pel* in Tibetan) means "glorified." So, Manjushri is the "soft glorified one." What does that mean? Manjushri's holy mind has become soft or pacified by having eliminated all delusions, both the disturbing-thought obscurations (*nyöndrip*) that block liberation and the subtle obscurations to knowledge (*shedrib*) that block full enlightenment.

What are these subtle defilements? They are the subtle negative imprints left on the mental continuum by the concept of inherent existence. This concept is something we sentient beings hold until we become enlightened. When we become an arya being and are in meditative equipoise, single-pointedly concentrating on emptiness, these obscurations are not manifest, but when we arise from meditation, the dual view naturally reasserts itself. As an arya being, we have achieved nirvana, but we are still blocked from full enlightenment by these subtle obscurations. Therefore we need to combine the wisdom side that realizes emptiness with the method side of bodhichitta and enter the Mahayana, then work through the six perfections of a bodhisattva and achieve full enlightenment.

Only when we have eliminated all the subtle obscurations will we become fully enlightened, which is what the second part of Manjushri's name—*shri* or *pel*, "glorified"—refers to. Therefore *Manjushri*, and *Jampalyang*, refers to the holy mind that is free from all mistakes of the mind, all the defilements, and has completed all the realizations.

Visualizing Manjushri

Like most deities, there are many aspects of Manjushri, such as Black Manjushri, a wrathful deity very powerful in preventing and curing illnesses, and Yamantaka, a particularly fearful deity. Usually, however, Manjushri is depicted as youthful, in the peaceful *sambhogakaya* or enjoyment body aspect,[62] orange in color, with one face and two hands. He is seated on a lotus and moon disk in a vajra posture, with

his legs crossed. He looks at us and all sentient beings with eyes full of loving-kindness and with a compassionate smile. He is adorned with an underskirt and divine scarves and wears many ornaments.

His left hand is at his heart in the mudra of expounding the Dharma, with thumb and ring finger touching, and holds the stem of a lotus that blooms by his ear. The lotus has a *Prajnaparamita*, or *perfection of wisdom*, text resting in it, radiating light. His right hand holds a flaming sword of wisdom. You shouldn't think of Manjushri's sword as a physical one made of steel. Its nature is ultimate wisdom, the dharmakaya. Just as a material sword cuts the body, Manjushri's wisdom sword cuts through all delusions.

There is a prayer to Manjushri which describes him well.

> Obeisance to my guru and protector Manjushri, who holds to his heart a scriptural text symbolic of his seeing all things as they are. Whose intelligence shines forth as the sun, unclouded by delusion or trace of ignorance.

> Who teaches in sixty ways, with the loving compassion of a father for his only son, all creatures caught in the prison of samsara, confused in the darkness of their ignorance, overwhelmed by their suffering.

> You, whose dragon-thunder-like proclamation of Dharma arouses us from the stupor of our delusion and frees us from the iron chains of our karma, who wields the sword of wisdom hewing down suffering wherever its sprouts appear, clearing away the darkness of ignorance.

> You, whose princely body is adorned with the one hundred and twelve marks of Buddha, who has completed the stages achieving the highest perfections of a bodhisattva. Who has been pure from the beginning, I bow down to you, O Manjushri.

You will often see images in Tibetan shrine rooms or read descriptions of what is called a "merit field." This is a vast collection of buddhas, bodhisattvas, protectors, and so forth, grouped around a central figure, usually the Buddha or the guru. We can most easily collect the most extensive merit from meditating on this "field." When you see an extensive merit field, such as for the Guru Puja,[63] you will notice there are different lineages depicted there. The Buddha's entire teachings are often divided into two aspects, the *extensive conduct* (*zabmö tawa*) and *profound view* (*gyachen chö gyü*). The teachings of the steps of the extensive conduct, focusing on the method side of the path, were handed down from the Buddha to Maitreya Buddha and Asanga, whereas the teachings of the steps of the profound view, focusing on the wisdom side of the path, were handed down from the Buddha to Manjushri and from Manjushri to Nagarjuna and then to Aryadeva and the other pandits.[64] From this, we can see that Manjushri is the source of all the wisdom teachings of the Buddha.

The Mantra

Manjushri's mantra is this:

OM AH RA PA CHA NA DHI

ཨོཾ་ཨ་ར་པ་ཙ་ན་ཧྲཱིཿ

For this reason, Manjushri in this more common aspect, is often called Arapatsana Manjushri. Manjushri's mantra is an especially quick way to attain wisdom and develop a sharp memory. If you recite this mantra many times, you will be able to memorize hundreds of pages of texts. It is said if you recite this mantra a hundred thousand times, you will be able to see Manjushri.

Because Manjushri is the embodiment of all the buddhas' wisdom, even the young monks and nuns in the monasteries recite the Manjushri mantra and do the Manjushri practice to purify defilements and receive wisdom. Many get up very early, around four or five o'clock, and memorize part of a text before going to the daily puja. They then chant the Manjushri mantra as they run outside, repeating the last syllable, DHI as many times as possible in one breath. You will hear them in monasteries like Kopan in Kathmandu, running to their breakfast, shouting DHI DHI DHI DHI DHI DHI! His Holiness the Dalai Lama said he used to do that, and it helped him to develop wisdom.

As you repeat the DHI, imagine Manjushri in front of you and his wisdom in the form of the flaming syllable DHI, like a blazing fire. This comes from Manjushri and absorbs into a similar DHI visualized at the back of your tongue. From this, wisdom flames arise, eliminating the darkness of ignorance. You can imagine the flame filling your whole body, fully developing your wisdom. Imagine all your pores completely fused with the syllable DHI, causing you to attain nonforgetfulness.

How to Practice with Manjushri's Mantra[65]

Having sat down and calmed yourself with some breathing meditation, visualize Manjushri in front of you (as described above). Visualize all sentient beings in the form of human beings surrounding you.

Then, do some preliminary practices, such as saying the refuge prayer three times, the four immeasurable thoughts, and the seven-limb prayer.[66] You can also offer a mandala.

Visualization

From the DHI 🕉 syllable at your heart, light radiates out and invokes from their natural abodes Arya Manjushri surrounded by the assembly of buddhas and bodhisattvas.

Praise

I prostrate to Manjushri,
who possesses the holy body of youth,

who radiates the lamp of wisdom,
and who dispels the darkness of the three worlds.

Mantra Recitation

On top of the moon cushion at Manjushri's heart there appears a yellow wheel with six spokes. At the central hub is a syllable DHI and on the spokes are the six syllables of the root mantra. On the wheel's rim is the mantra of increasing wisdom.

Light radiates from the mantras, pouring into you and all sentient beings surrounding you, dispelling the darkness of ignorance of yourself and others. It hooks back all the wisdom of samsara and nirvana, which dissolves into you and all other beings.

With this visualization recite the mantras:

Mantra of Increasing Wisdom:

NAMO MANJUSHRIYE KUMARA BHUTAYA BODHISAT-
TVAYA MAHASATTVAYA MAHAKARUNIKAYA TADYATHA
OM ARAJE BIRAJE SHUDDHE VISHUDDHE SHODHAYA
VISHODHAYA AMALE BIMALE NIRMALE JAYA VARE RUJALE
HUM HUM HUM PHAT PHAT PHAT SVAHA

Root mantra:

OM AH RA PA CHA NA DHI

After the recitation of mantras, make offerings and praise as before and stabilize with the hundred-syllable Vajrasattva mantra, as follows:

Offerings

OM SARVA TATHAGATA ARYA MANJUSHRI SAPARIVARA
ARGHAM [PADYAM, PUSHPE, DHUPE, ALOKE, GANDHE,
NAIVIDYA] PRATICCHA YE SVAHA

OM SARVA TATHAGATA ARYA MANJUSHRI SAPARIVARA
SHAPTA AH HUM SVAHA

Praise

I prostrate to Manjushri,
who possesses the holy body of youth,
who radiates the lamp of wisdom,
and who dispels the darkness of the three worlds.

Vajrasattva Mantra to Purify Mistakes

OM VAJRASATTVA SAMAYA MANUPALAYA / VAJRASATTVA
TVENOPATISHTHA / DRIDHO ME BHAVA / SUTOSHYO ME
BHAVA / SUPOSHYO ME BHAVA / ANURAKTO ME BHAVA
/ SARVA SIDDHIM ME PRAYACCHA / SARVA KARMA SU
CHAME / CHITTAM SHRIYAM KURU HUM / HA HA HA HA
HO / BHAGAVAN SARVA TATHAGATA / VAJRASATTVA MAME
MUNCHA / VAJRA BHAVA MAHA SAMAYA SATTVA AH HUM
PHAT

At the root of your tongue is a syllable DHI. The top of the DHI is facing down toward your windpipe. With this visualization, recite DHI
108 times in one breath. Visualize that the whole body turns into the
syllable DHI.

Dedication

> Due to these merits,
> May I quickly attain the state of Arya Manjushri
> And place all migrating beings, without exception,
> In that very state.
>
> May the day be auspicious
> May the night be auspicious
> May all the day and night be auspicious
> May there be the auspiciousness of the Three Jewels.

Then recite dedication prayers and auspicious verses.

4. TARA

BEFORE SHE BECAME ENLIGHTENED, Tara promised to liberate all migratory beings from the two extremes: the extreme of samsara and the extreme of peace, meaning the peace of lower nirvana. That means she promised to lead all beings to full enlightenment.

From the very beginning, before she even generated bodhichitta, she vowed to attain enlightenment in a woman's body.[67] So, here we are talking about women's liberation happening eons ago! Initially, she attained bodhichitta in a woman's body; in the middle, she attained the paths of merit, preparation, seeing, and meditation in a woman's body; and in the end, she also became fully enlightened in a woman's body.

I heard the story of Tara from one of my gurus, Pabongka Dechen Nyingpo. Inconceivable eons ago, during the time of the Drum Sound Buddha (Dundubhisvara, Ngé Dra),[68] there was a highly respected princess called Wisdom Moon (Jnanachandra, Yeshe Dawa). She studied the Dharma and made offerings to that Buddha for millions of years until she attained bodhichitta.

At that time, some fully ordained monks, knowing of her great merits, told her that she could do superb work for the Dharma if she attained a man's body. When they urged her to pray for this, she answered them by making this vow: "There are many who desire enlightenment in a man's body, but few who work for the benefit of sentient beings in the body of a woman. Therefore, until samsara is empty, I shall work for the benefit of sentient beings in a woman's body."

She then lived for millions of years in the king's palace, achieving the patience of the unborn Dharma and the concentration called the *all-liberating concentration*. With the power of that concentration, she vowed that each morning she would liberate millions of sentient beings from delusions and cause them to attain renunciation, and that she would not eat until she had done that. Then, in the afternoon, she again led that many sentient beings on the path. Because her function was to give extensive benefits to sentient beings each day like this, she became known as Tara the Liberator.

In the eon called Perfect Victory (Vishuda, Nampar Gyalwa), she promised in front of the Buddha Amoghasiddhi that she would protect sentient beings from the eight fears. Then she entered in the meditative equipoise called the *concentration of destroying the harms*. For ninety-five eons, every day during that time, she led millions of sentient beings in the path of concentration, and every night she subdued millions of maras.

During the eon called Unobstructed (Apratibaddha, Thokpa Mäpa), all the buddhas initiated a monk called Glow of Immaculate Light (Vimala Jyotis Prabha, Drima Mäpa Ökyi Nangwa)[69] with a great beam that was the essence of all their compassion. That monk became Chenrezig. After that, he was again initiated by all the buddhas with a great beam that was the essence of all their transcendental wisdom. Those two beams became the father and mother, and the mixing of the two caused Tara to arise from Chenrezig's heart to fulfill the wishes of all the buddhas and continuously work for migratory beings.

Whenever and wherever pitiful sentient beings are in danger and afraid, if they pray to Tara, she immediately guides them from the eight external and internal fears, such as lions, fire, pride, and hatred. As soon as beings unable to obtain their wishes pray fervently to Tara, she appears. She takes infinite forms and performs inconceivable actions to fulfill the hopes and wishes of sentient beings.

Pabongka Dechen Nyingpo said that there are so many stories about Tara, it is impossible to recount them all.

TARA THE LIBERATOR

Tara means "star" in Sanskrit, and hence "that which guides us." Her Tibetan name, *Dolma*, means "she who saves" or "liberator." Tara, the embodiment of all the buddhas' compassionate actions, is the one who liberates us from all the inner and outer obstacles that cloud the development of our mind and guides us to successfully accomplish both our temporal and ultimate happiness. Therefore, to succeed in actualizing the graduated path to enlightenment, we must rely upon a buddha such as Tara.

Many Indian yogis relied upon Tara. By taking refuge in Tara, they completed the path and did great works for the teachings and for living beings, leading uncountable numbers on the path. For example, the great pandit Lama Atisha attained the entire graduated path to enlightenment by relying upon Tara.

Atisha was invited by the religious king of Tibet, Yeshe Ö, to reestablish Buddhadharma in Tibet. At that time, many wrong views had spread, and the king didn't know what to do. When a minister mentioned Atisha's name, the hairs on the back of the king's neck stood up and tears came to his eyes. He had so much devotion for Atisha, just hearing his name. While he was collecting gold to offer Atisha to invite him to travel from Nalanda Monastery in India to Tibet, he was captured by an irreligious king who demanded his body weight in gold as a ransom. His nephew had almost collected enough—the weight of his head was still missing—when King Yeshe Ö told him to not use the gold for him but to use it instead to invite Atisha, saying he would give up his life for the Dharma.

When he received the invitation, Atisha consulted Tara, who told him going to Tibet would be very beneficial for the Dharma, but his life would be shortened by many years. After a long and dangerous journey, he reached Tibet. When he arrived at court, the king's nephew explained that Tibetans were an ignorant people and asked him to therefore write something simple for them.

Atisha wrote *Lamp for the Path to Enlightenment*, which was the very first lamrim text. By listening to it and reflecting and meditating on it, so many people have achieved enlightenment. The light of this lamrim teaching has dispelled so much ignorance, even in the minds of many thousands of people living in the West, because it integrates all the teachings of the Buddha into a step-by-step practice that allows anyone to achieve enlightenment.

Even though Lama Atisha passed away a long time ago in Tibet, he is still benefiting us by giving us the opportunity to understand the teachings of the graduated path to enlightenment. He was able to offer extensive benefit to living beings and the teachings through depending upon Tara. As many stories attest, throughout Lama Atisha's life, Tara always gave him advice.

That Tara is in female form is significant. Even though there are more and more female heads of state emerging these days, there are still far more male leaders, but that has no bearing on the qualities of women. There is no difference in the potential of either sex. If a man doesn't practice the Dharma, his mind is not transformed, and it is exactly the same for a woman. Conversely, when they practice the Dharma their minds are transformed. Both men and women can attain enlightenment in exactly the same way. Just as there have been innumerable male yogis who have gone on to attain enlightenment, there have also been innumerable female yoginis who have done the same thing.

Tara is probably the most prominent example of a person who attained enlightenment in a female aspect, but there are many others. It depends on our own motivation. If we see that we can benefit others more in a female body than a male one, we can ensure that we get one. And vice versa, of course.

The English nun Venerable Tenzin Palmo is a great inspiration. Like the wonderful stories we hear of French and Spanish Christian nuns living in isolated places, or the great Tibetan yoginis, for twelve years she lived in an extremely remote place, in a cave high in the Himalayas, sacrificing her life to practice the Dharma and facing great hardships.[70] We need inspiring stories like that. The main thing we must cultivate to get results from our practice is continual renunciation, so she is a wonderful example for us. Just as the places in India and Nepal where yogis and yoginis achieved the path hundreds of years ago are to this day places that inspire others to practice, by being a living example, she is an inspiration to the Western world.

Mother Tara

The benefits of practicing Tara are uncountable. By reciting the *Praises to the Twenty-One Taras* with devotion, at dawn or dusk, and remembering Tara and reciting her mantra at any time of the day or night, we are protected from fear and danger, and all our wishes are fulfilled. If we pray to Tara, Tara will grant help quickly.

She is especially quick in granting us success in obtaining the ultimate happiness of enlightenment, but there are also many temporal benefits of reciting the Tara mantra or the *Praises to the Twenty-One Taras* prayer. Tara can solve many problems in life: liberating us from untimely death, helping us recover from disease, bringing us success in business. Somebody with a serious problem, such as a life-threatening disease, who relies on Tara will very commonly be freed from that problem. For instance, His Holiness the Dalai Lama encouraged us to recite Tara's mantra as a protection for ourselves and others against the coronavirus COVID-19.

Pabongka Dechen Nyingpo tells a story of one of his students who didn't know much Dharma but had faith in Tara and so received help from her, but not as much as he might have. One day during his journey to Mongolia, while walking along reciting Tara prayers, he heard a dog barking and saw a tent. Because he needed some water to quench his thirst, he went there, where he saw a young girl, alone, tending many yaks. Seeing the monk was weak and hungry, she insisted he stay with her for a few days and she fed him. When it was time to leave, she gave him some *tsampa* and other food. Because he was completely lost, she gave him very explicit directions on how to get to his destination and, as he was leaving, she gave him a large bunch of grass. She explained that when he awoke each morning, he should drop some grass on the ground and head in whichever direction it fell.

He only had a little food, enough for a day or two, but each day, when he opened the sack, his food was never depleted. Following the directions the girl had given him, he managed to find his way to his destination. When he looked in his sack at the very end of his journey, there was not one speck of food left. He was so surprised with this that he sent a letter to his guru, Pabongka Rinpoche, in Lhasa. Rinpoche wrote back and said that it was a pity he hadn't followed the girl's instructions completely. If he had, he would have been in a pure realm already. That yak herder was a manifestation of Tara, but he was unable to see this. Tara manifests in many aspects, not just the green and white forms that are commonly depicted.

Tara is like our mother. Take my mother as an example. She did all the work while the rest of us—there were three of us—were useless. One day, she had to go into the forest to get the firewood. Because none of us could make food, we waited outside the door for her to return so we could eat. When she came back very late with a very heavy load of firewood, she could not make a fire because she was sick. She lay down next to the fireplace in so much pain. There was no fire in the stove and no food. She was screaming, calling for her mother: "Ama! Ama!" (My grandmother, who was still alive at that time, lived quite near.) Because none of us could make one, there was no fire; we just sat and watched our mother. Even adults call for their mother when they have bad pain or a serious problem. However, Tara is much closer to us than a mother, and she is quick to grant us help and protect us from danger.

The best way we can become close to Tara, what pleases her the most, is when we fervently try to develop the mind of bodhichitta. The more we are able to practice bodhichitta and cherish others more than ourselves, the closer we will be to Tara, and the easier it will be for her to offer us help quickly.

The *Praises to the Twenty-One Taras* begins, "I prostrate to the noble transcendent liberator." That means that Tara herself is completely liberated from the whole of samsara and the cause of samsara through having completed the both the method and wisdom sides of the practice. Not only that, by having overcome the two obscurations, gross and subtle, she is also free from being bound to lower nirvana. Liberated from both samsara and the peace of lower nirvana means she is fully enlightened. And because she in turn liberates all of us, allowing us to attain full enlightenment, she is called Tara the Liberator, the mother who liberates.

The Mother of the Victorious Ones

Tara is also called Mother of the Victorious Ones because, just as a mother gives birth to her children, Tara gives birth to all the buddhas. The ultimate meaning of Tara is the transcendental wisdom of nondual bliss and emptiness, the culmination of both the method side of the path and the wisdom side, fused in one mind. This is synonymous with the clear light—the dharmakaya or truth body of the buddha. This transcendental wisdom is called "nondual bliss and emptiness" because it is characterized by three things: it has realized emptiness; it experiences great bliss; and it has the feeling of vastness or being empty. This is the omniscient mind that sees both the absolute and conventional truth of all existence simultaneously.

This dharmakaya is the absolute guru, the real meaning of "guru." It is important we understand that the word "guru" means much more than a human being who teaches us. Even though the buddhas have different aspects and different names, they are all born from the dharmakaya. In reality, every buddha is the embodiment of this absolute guru: one manifests in many forms; many manifest in one form. When this manifests in an ordinary aspect as the conventional guru, this is the absolute guru appearing as the lama we directly receive teachings from.

As Khedrup Sangye Yeshe[71] explained: "Before the guru, there is not even the name 'Buddha.'" First we meet the guru externally and separately. After receiving teachings, we listen, reflect, and meditate on the path that is revealed by this guru. On the basis of correct devotion to the guru, we gradually actualize the complete path and remove our obscurations. When that happens, we meet the guru mentally. By gradually actualizing the path and achieving the dharmakaya, we achieve the absolute guru.

So, all the buddhas are born from the absolute guru, the dharmakaya, the transcendental wisdom of nondual bliss and emptiness, which is the actual meaning of "Mother." This transcendental wisdom, this completely pure subtle mind, manifests in this female aspect that is labeled "Tara."

Green Tara

Although there are many different aspects of Tara, the one we most often see in images is Green Tara.[72] The extremely vivid green color of Tara's holy form symbolizes the granting of wishes and the symbolic purification of the defilements of envy and jealousy, as well as the purification of the ordinary impure aggregate of form. Of the five transcendental wisdoms,[73] hers is the all-accomplishing wisdom. Her green color also symbolizes success in action.

With one face and two arms, she is in the aspect of a very beautiful sixteen-year-old girl. Her face is very peaceful, with a slight smile. Her eyes are not opened widely but are fine and a little rounded, very loving and compassionate. When we look at Tara, her eyes express compassion toward us, like the look a loving mother gives her only child. Her hair is very dark, half down and half tied up. The center of her hair has an utpala flower[74] as a crown. A tiara fastened in her hair is adorned with jewels, the central one being a ruby, symbolizing Amitabha, the principal buddha of her buddha family, the padma or lotus family.

Her right hand rests on her right knee, palm outward, in the mudra of granting sublime realizations, indicating her ability to provide beings with whatever they desire. Her left hand, at her heart, holds the stem of an utpala flower, with her thumb and ring finger together, symbolizing the unification of method and wisdom, and the other three fingers raised, symbolizing the Buddha, Dharma, and Sangha.[75] In some depictions, the stem she holds has three utpala flowers—a bud, a flower that is opening, and a fully opened flower—indicating that Tara is the mother of all the buddhas: past, present, and future.

Tara has fully developed breasts, is dressed in the silken robes of royalty, and wears rainbow colored stockings, with a white half-blouse. She is adorned with a necklace, bracelets, armlets, anklets, and so forth, as well as various scarves and jewel garlands, symbolizing her attainment of the six perfections.

Her right leg is extended, showing she is always ready to rise up and come to the aid of those who need her, while her left leg is drawn up, showing her renunciation of worldly desire. She has a moon disk behind her. She is adorned with the complete holy signs and exemplifications of a buddha.

The Mantra

Tara's mantra is this:

OM TARE TUTTARE TURE SVAHA

ༀ་ཏུ་རེ་ཏུཊ་རེ་ཏུ་རེ་སྭ་ཧཱ།

There is no way to receive enlightenment without realizing the meaning of Tara's mantra. As with many mantras, Tara's mantra starts with OM and finishes with SVAHA (pronounced *soha*), with the main part of the mantra being TARE TUTTARE TURE.

TARE *Liberates from Samsara*

TARE denotes liberating us from samsara, which means we are liberated from our five contaminated aggregates: the aggregates of form, feeling, discrimination, compositional factors, and consciousness. These aggregates are the basis on which the nominal sense of self, the I, is labeled. Because they are caused by the contaminated seed of karma and delusions, when we encounter desirable and undesirable objects, the different disturbing thoughts such as attachment and anger arise. Then, because of *that*, we again create karma. At the time of death, attachment to corporeal existence means our consciousness joins with the sperm and egg of our future parents and we take another samsaric life. Hence, the cycle of contaminated existence is perpetuated.

So, TARE shows that Mother Tara liberates living beings from true suffering, from the problems of samsara. The truth of suffering is the first of the four noble truths, the initial teaching of the Buddha after he became enlightened. We can relate this to the particular sufferings of human beings: birth, old age, sickness, death, meeting undesirable objects, not finding desirable objects, or finding them but gaining no satisfaction. No matter how much pleasure we enjoy, no matter how much we follow desire, there is no satisfaction at all. Furthermore, nothing in samsara is definite. We must leave the body again and again and take another body again and again.

Our present-life mother came from her mother, our grandmother; our grandmother came from another mother; and so on. It is the same with our father. We can see that this body we have now, which is a product of the conjoining of our parent's sperm and egg, is a collection of all the conjoinings of sperm and egg that have continued from parent to child for inconceivable generations since human beings began. Because of that, there is no essence to cling to; there is no reason to get attached to this body, this samsara.

Through all of these births, we experience problems again and again. If we have high status, we fall to low status. When we are born, we are born alone without any companion; when we die, we also die alone, our consciousness leaving the dead body and taking another rebirth. All these are the problems of true suffering.

If we rely upon Tara, by taking refuge in her and doing Tara practices, when we recite her mantra, with TARE Tara liberates us from all these true sufferings.

TUTTARE *Liberates from the Eight Fears*

If the first word, TARE, frees us from true suffering, the first of the four noble truths, the second word, TUTTARE, corresponds to the second noble truth in that it frees us from the true cause of suffering: karma and delusions.

We can all see how much the world is suffering now. There are more and more dangers. Glaciers are sliding into the ocean, causing the sea level to rise and endangering many coastal cities; there are more tsunamis and typhoons, more floods and fires. The dangers of the four elements of earth, fire, water, and air are increasing every year, with the potential to kill and harm millions of people. Just like the earthquake that ruined so much of Nepal years back, these disasters mean that people's survival is becoming more precarious. This is all a result of the mind. It is not a result of the subdued mind but the unsubdued mind, of the disturbing emotions such as greed, anger, ignorance, and so forth.

TUTTARE also frees us from the eight fears or dangers. There are eight fears related to external dangers from the elements, such as fire and water, and from such things as thieves and dangerous animals. However, the main dangers are not external but internal, coming from our delusions, such as ignorance and attachment. Relying on Tara liberates us from these eight internal dangers, these eight disturbing thoughts, and, as a consequence, frees us from the external dangers that arise from these disturbing thoughts. To guide us from these eight different fears, there are eight different aspects of Tara.

The eight external and internal fears:

1. fear of the danger of fire and fear of hatred
2. fear of the danger of water and fear of attachment
3. fear of the danger of lions and fear of pride
4. fear of the danger of elephants and fear of ignorance
5. fear of the danger of hungry ghosts and fear of doubt
6. fear of the danger of imprisonment and fear of miserliness
7. fear of the danger of thieves and fear of wrong views
8. fear of the danger of snakes and fear of jealousy

The first of the eight Taras[76] is the Tara who saves from the fear of the danger of fire and the fear of hatred. Hatred is the unsubdued mind that wishes to harm another being. Because it is such a violent, intense mind, it has the power to destroy all our virtue. It is compared to fire, which can destroy everything in its path.

Living with anger is like having a burning coal in the heart. Just as a tiny spark can set off a grass fire that can destroy a city, a spark of hatred can lead to creating harm that brings retaliation and then counterretaliation. In this way, it can destroy lives. Like a fire, hatred can rage through our life and kill our relationships and destroy any pleasure we might have. Anger can destroy everything, and therefore it is often referred to as the most destructive negative mind. By taking refuge in Tara, we can be protected from the danger of both hatred and the external fire element. It can be understood in both ways.

Then, there is the Tara who saves from the fear of the danger of water and the fear of attachment. Attachment is like water. Some dirt on a dry cloth can be brushed off easily, but when the cloth is wet, the dirt soaks right into it and it becomes incredibly difficult to clean. The wet cloth and the dirt sort of become inseparable. In the same way, it is almost impossible to separate the attached mind from the object of attachment. This Tara can protect us from all the outside dangers caused through water, such as floods and tsunamis, as well as the danger of attachment.

During the early Kopan courses, when we were still in the old tent, we would often do an all-night Tara practice,[77] which was a very power-ful purification practice, extremely effective in developing wisdom and protecting from black magic and so forth. Very often, while we were doing the practice, it would start raining heavily.

There is also the Tara who saves from the fear of the danger of lions and of pride. The snow lion exemplifies pride because it lives in very high places and thinks itself the most powerful and magnificent of all the animals.

Then there is the Tara who saves from the fear of the danger of ele-phants and of ignorance. The elephant is used as an example of igno-rance because when it is untamed, the harm it can do is enormous.

The next Tara is the one who saves from the fear of the danger of hungry ghosts and of doubt. This is also translated as spirits, meaning flesh-eating spirits. Just as they can consume us, so can doubt, making it impossible to make correct, virtuous choices.

Next is the Tara who saves from the fear of the danger of impris-onment or enchainment and of miserliness. Miserliness ties us to the object, making us cling to it. Further, it ties us to the whole of samsara through desire for the samsaric perfections we are attached to. Like a chain that imprisons us, where each link holds the next, our miserliness has us always grasping at one object of desire after the other.

There is also the Tara who saves from the fear of the danger of thieves and of wrong views or heresy. Whenever heresy arises toward the Three Rare Sublime Ones—the Buddha, Dharma, and Sangha—such as denying the teachings on karma and reincarnation, it robs us of the merits that have been collected within our mindstream for countless eons. Because heresy postpones for an incredible length of time the ripening of the result of even the merits we have dedicated, it is very dangerous.

Finally, there is the Tara who saves from the fear of the danger of snakes and of jealousy. Just as a snake can creep up on us unobserved and bite us, jealousy can bite into us and cause us such pain.

Because Tara is said to be able to save people from the eight fears, Tibetans naturally take refuge in her when they face any danger.

TURE *Liberates from Disease*

TURE liberates us from disease and corresponds to the third noble truth, the cessation of suffering. Our fundamental disease is ignorance, not knowing the absolute nature of the I. Relying on Tara, we can realize emptiness easily, which frees us from the ignorance that keeps us trapped in samsara.

Before that, Tara can save us from all the disturbing thoughts that arise from that ignorance, all of our delusions, such as anger, jealousy, miserliness, and so forth. As we develop on the path, these deluded aspects of mind lessen and then cease. This relates to the fourth noble truth, that of the path that leads to cessation.

In that way, TARE, which frees us from the truth of suffering, and TUTTARE, which frees us from the cause of suffering, relate to the method side of the path. TURE, corresponding to the cessation of suffering, relates to the wisdom side of the practice.

The Meaning of the Whole Mantra

Tara, Mother of the Victorious Ones, guides us and other living beings from the danger of falling into both samsara and lower nirvana and leads us to the perfect state of enlightenment.

The rough meaning of TARE TUTTARE TURE is "To you, embodiment of all the buddhas' actions, I always prostrate with my body, speech, and mind, no matter what my circumstances, happy or unhappy."

All the *yanas* or paths are contained in TARE TUTTARE TURE: the Hinayana, the Mahayana Paramitayana, and the Mahayana Vajrayana. The cessation of both the gross and subtle obscurations is contained in TARE TUTTARE TURE. Relating to the lamrim, TARE is the graduated path of the lower capable being, TUTTARE of the middle capable being, and TURE of the higher capable being.

As we have seen, with the final word, SVAHA, we ask that the blessings of the deity are firmly rooted in us. In other words, by taking refuge in Tara, reciting her mantra, and doing her practice, we receive the blessings of Tara and establish the path of the three capable beings in our heart. Through this, we can purify all obscurations of our body, speech, and mind and achieve Tara's pure vajra holy body, holy speech, and holy mind, which are signified by OM.

Whenever we recite or even just hear Tara's mantra, because it contains the four noble truths and the path to enlightenment in its entirety, it leaves an imprint on our mental continuum to actualize the whole path. Then, sooner or later, this imprint will manifest. At that time, we will not only be able to meet the Dharma again, but to actualize the complete meaning of the mantra, which is nothing less than attaining all the realizations and becoming enlightened, allowing us to do perfect work for all sentient beings.

THE TWENTY-ONE TARAS

Although there are innumerable aspects of Tara, there are twenty-one main ones, which are usually visualized as surrounding the central green Tara when we recite the *Praises to the Twenty-One Taras*. Each has a different function and can bring a particular benefit to sentient beings. Whether we are troubled with illness, poverty, an impending court case, or any other difficulty, there is one specific Tara we can address to help us with our problem.

The fact that so many holy beings have been able to offer extensive benefit to the world is due to Tara. The success that many common people enjoy is also due to Tara. In Tibet, it is very common to do a Tara puja for success or for overcoming obstacles such as sickness, where the *Praises to the Twenty-One Taras* is recited many times.

The first text I ever learned was the *Praises to the Twenty-One Taras*. There was an elder monk at Domo Geshe's monastery in Tibet who took care of me and helped me become a monk. Even though the *Twenty-One Taras* was all he ever taught me, when I asked Kirti Tsenshab Rinpoche whether I should regard him as my teacher, he said yes.

Every day we had to do pujas in peoples' homes. There were four or five monks, one who played cymbals, one who played the drum, and one who played the bell and *damaru*. Once I played the flute with him, copying what he did with his fingers. Sometimes we did all-night pujas, chanting the *Praises to the Twenty-One Taras*. My teacher had a long stick with a needle on top. There was a young monk who fell asleep and got the needle, right in the shoulder blades, but somehow I didn't get it. I don't know whether I slept or not.

The texts on Tara mention that it is very effective if we do the *Praises to the Twenty-One Taras* twice in the morning, three times around noon, and seven times in the evening, but, of course, even if we can only recite it once, that is very effective. Because we become closer to Tara and therefore more easily receive Tara's guidance, it helps us succeed in whatever we wish for. Naturally the best way to practice is with a bodhichitta motivation.

There are different traditions regarding the twenty-one Taras, so you might see images of them that differ slightly. There is one tradition, according to the great translator Phari Lotsawa, where there are peaceful-looking Taras and wrathful-looking ones, and some have many arms. There is also a tradition from Lama Atisha where each only has one face and two arms, but some have different colors and one or two are wrathful. I will describe the twenty-one Taras found in Lama Atisha's tradition.

A simple way to visualize the twenty-one Taras as you recite the praises is to visualize Green Tara in the center with the twenty-one Taras surrounding her clockwise on a twenty-one-petaled lotus, each on a petal and moon disk. One tradition says that as you recite the praise to each Tara, you imagine that Tara sending out an emanation that absorbs into you, giving you that quality—in the case of Tara the Swift Lady of Glory, the first Tara, the ability to influence sentient beings. If you have taken a Tara initiation, you can visualize that you become that Tara; otherwise, you can just feel that you now have that Tara's qualities. Then, in the same way, as you say the next praise, the next Tara sends an emanation that absorbs into you, and you receive that quality, and so on for all the twenty-one Taras.

If you find it too difficult to imagine each Tara absorbing into you, you can just imagine the principal Tara sitting at the center of the lotus on a moon disk, and as you say the praises with your hands in the prostration mudra, you imagine purifying beams coming from the principal Tara's heart and entering your heart. Then, at the end, imagine that a replica of Tara absorbs into your heart and your body, speech, and mind become one with Tara's holy body, holy speech, and holy mind.

Visualizing the Twenty-One Taras

According to the tradition of Lama Atisha, the color of each of the twenty-one Taras corresponds to the four types of enlightened activities of a buddha: white for pacifying; yellow for increasing positive qualities; red for power, such as the power to overcome external forces; and black for wrath, using forceful means to accomplish enlightened activities that cannot be accomplished by other means.

Each Tara has one face and two hands. In the palm of her right hand is a flask that accomplishes the activity of that Tara, while in her left hand is an utpala flower. Each sits on a throne of lotus and moon in the same position as the principal Tara—with right leg extended and left leg drawn up—and is adorned with silks and precious ornaments.

1. Swift Lady of Glory

> Homage! Tara, swift, heroic!
> Eyes like lightning instantaneous!
> Sprung from op'ning stamens of the
> Lord of three world's tear-born lotus![78]

On the first petal is Tara the Swift Lady of Glory (Nyurma Palmo),[79] red in color. She is the quick one, holding in her right palm a red flask for controlling. She grants the ability to influence sentient beings so that they will listen to you and you can lead them to the Dharma. Her mantra is this:

OM TARE TUTTARE TURE WASHAM KURU SVAHA

ཨོཾ་ཏུ་རེ་ཏུཏྟ་རེ་ཏུ་རེ་སྭ་ཤཾ་ཀུ་རུ་སྭ་ཧཱ།

2. Lady of Supreme Peace

> Homage! She whose face combines a
> Hundred autumn moons at fullest!
> Blazing with light rays resplendent
> As a thousand-star collection!

On the second petal is Tara, Lady of Supreme Peace (Shiwa Chenmo), white in color, holding a white flask containing nectar for pacifying disease. Her mantra is this:

OM TARE TUTTARE TURE SHANTIM KURU SVAHA

ཨོཾ་ཏུ་རེ་ཏུཏྟ་རེ་ཏུ་རེ་ཤཱནྟིཾ་ཀུ་རུ་སྭ་ཧཱ།

3. Lady of Golden Yellow Color

> Homage! Golden-blue one, lotus
> Water born, in hand adorned!
> Giving, effort, calm, austerities,
> Patience, meditation her sphere!

On the third petal is Golden-Colored Tara, Giver of Supreme Virtue (Serdok Chen), yellow-gold in color, holding in her hand a yellow flask containing nectar for increasing life and fortune. Her mantra is this:

OM TARE TUTTARE TURE PUSHTIM KURU SVAHA

ༀ་ཏུ་རེ་ཏུཏྟ་རེ་ཏུ་རེ་པུཥྚིཾ་ཀུ་རུ་སྭཱ་ཧཱ།

4. Lady of Complete Victory, Embodying All Positive Qualities

> Homage! Crown of tathagatas,
> Actions triumph without limit!
> Relied on by conquerors' children,
> Having reached ev'ry perfection!

On the fourth petal is Tara Completely Victorious, Embodying All Positive Qualities (Tsuktor Nampar Gyalma), yellow in color, holding a yellow flask containing nectar for increasing the lifespan. Her mantra is this:

OM TARE TUTTARE TURE AYUR-JYANA PUSHTIM KURU SVAHA

ༀ་ཏུ་རེ་ཏུཏྟ་རེ་ཏུ་རེ་ཨཱ་ཡུ་ཛྙཱ་ན་པུཥྚིཾ་ཀུ་རུ་སྭཱ་ཧཱ།

5. She Who Proclaims the Sound of Hum

Homage! Filling with TUTTARE,
HUM, desire, direction, and space!
Trampling with her feet the seven worlds,
Able to draw forth all beings!

On the fifth petal is Tara Proclaiming the Sound of HUM (Hung Dradrokma), red-yellow in color, holding a red flask containing nectar with the function of enchanting other sentient beings, causing them to be attracted to you. Her manta is this:

OM TARE TUTTARE SHTRI AKARSHAYA HRIH SVAHA

ཨོཾ་ཏཱ་རེ་ཏུཏྟཱ་རེ་ཏུ་རེ་ཧྲཱི་ཨཱ་ཀརྵ་ཡ་ཧྲཱིཿསྭཱ་ཧཱ།

If there is somebody you need to influence, such as somebody who is extremely deluded and tries to harm you and others and to harm the Dharma, in order to help that person transform their mind into the Dharma, then you can recite this mantra and insert that person's name between the *tuttare shtri* and the *akarshaya*, so the mantra becomes OM TARE TUTTARE SHTRI [the name of the person] AKARSHAYA HRIH SVAHA.

6. She Who Is Completely Victorious Over the Three Worlds

Homage! Worshipped by the all-lords,
Shakra, Agni, Brahma, Marut!
Honored by the hosts of spirits,
Corpse-raisers, gandharvas, yakshas![80]

On the sixth petal is Tara Completely Victorious Over the Three Worlds (Jikten Sumle Nampar Gyalma), red-black in color, who is victorious over the three realms. She holds a blue flask containing nectar that intoxicates the spirits. Her mantra is this:

OM TARE TUTTARE TURE SHATRUN UCCHATAYA SVAHA

ༀ་ཏུ་རེ་ཏུཏྟ་རེ་ཏུ་རེ་ཤ་ཏྲུན་ཨུ་ཙྪ་ཏ་ཡ་སྭཱ་ཧཱ།

By intoxicating the spirits, they become unable to function and so unable to cause harm to others. I guess it's a bit like taking a business client to dinner and getting them drunk, making it a lot easier to get them to agree to any deal you have to make.

7. She Who Conquers Others

> Homage! With her TRAD and PHAT sounds
> Destroying foes' magic diagrams!
> Her feet pressing, left out, right in,
> Blazing in a raging fire-blaze!

On the seventh petal is Tara Who Conquers Others (Shen Jom-Ma), black in color, destroying those possessing black magic. She has a slightly wrathful appearance—her forehead is wrinkled—and she holds a black flask containing nectar that averts mantras and black magic sent against you. Her mantra is this:

OM TARA TUTTARE TURE SARVA VIDYA APARA VARANAYA SVAHA

ༀ་ཏུ་རེ་ཏུཏྟ་རེ་ཏུ་རེ་སཪྦ་བི་ཛྱ་ཨ་པ་ར་སྶ་ར་ཉ་ཡ་སྭཱ་ཧཱ།

8. She Who Conquers Maras and Enemies

> Homage! TURE, very dreadful!
> Destroyer of Mara's champion(s)!

She with frowning lotus visage
Who is slayer of all enemies!

On the eighth petal is Tara Who Conquers Maras and Enemies (Dru Dra Jom-Ma), red-black in color. Her right hand holds a red flask containing nectar whose function is to defeat maras and enemies. Her mantra is this:

OM TARE TUTTARE TURE SARVA MARA SHATRUN MARAYA
PHAT SVAHA

ༀ་ཏུ་རེ་ཏུཏྟ་རེ་ཏུ་རེ་སཪྦ་སྨ་ར་ཤཏྲུན་སྨ་ར་ཡ་ཕཏ་སྭ་ཧཱ།

9. She Who Protects from All Fears

Homage! At the heart her fingers,
Adorn her with Three Jewel mudra!
Light-ray masses all excited!
All directions' wheels adorn her!

On the ninth petal is Tara Who Protects from All Fears (Jikpa Kunkyob Ma), white in color, her gesture signifying the Three Rare Sublime Ones. She holds a white flask containing nectar whose function is to protect all sentient beings from fear and dangers. Her mantra is this:

OM TARE TUTTARE TURE MAM UPAKRAMA RAKSHA RAK-
SHA SVAHA

ༀ་ཏུ་རེ་ཏུཏྟ་རེ་ཏུ་རེ་སྨཾ་ཨུ་པ་ཀྲ་མ་རཀྵ་རཀྵ་སྭ་ཧཱ།

If there are dangers such as earthquakes, floods, typhoons, or the like, you can take strong refuge and recite this mantra, or visualize Tara in front of you.

10. She Who Brings Maras and the World Under Her Power

> Homage! She so joyous, radiant,
> Crown emitting garlands of light!
> Mirthful, laughing with TUTTARE,
> Subjugating maras, devas!

On the tenth petal is Tara Who Brings Maras and the World Under Her Power (Dudang Jikten Wangdu Dema), red in color, holding a red flask containing nectar whose function is to destroy Mara and to control the world. Her mantra is this:

OM TARE TUTTARE SARVA MARA PRAMARDHANI SVAHA

ཨོྃ་ཏུ་རེ་ཏུཏྟ་རེ་ཏུ་རེ་སརྦ་མཱ་ར་པྲ་མར་ཧྲ་ནི་སྭཱ་ཧཱ།

11. She Who Eradicates Poverty

> Homage! She able to summon
> All earth-guardians' assembly!
> Shaking, frowning, with her HUM sign
> Saving from every misfortune!

On the eleventh petal is Tara Who Eradicates Poverty (Ponpa Selma), red-yellow in color, like refined gold. She holds a yellow flask containing nectar whose function is to eliminate poverty. Her mantra is this:

OM TARE TUTTARE TURE VASUDHARINI SVAHA

ཨོྃ་ཏུ་རེ་ཏུཏྟ་རེ་ཏུ་རེ་བ་སུ་དྷ་རི་ཎི་སྭཱ་ཧཱ།

This is the Tara you use when you make a Tara wealth vase for prosperity. When you put a statue or drawing of this Tara in a wealth vase, to eliminate either your poverty or that of others, you take strong refuge and recite this mantra in front of the vase.

12. She Who Grants All That Is Auspicious

Homage! Crown adorned with crescent
Moon, all ornaments most shining!
Amitabha in her hair-knot
Sending out much light eternal!

On the twelfth petal is Tara Who Grants All that Is Auspicious (Trashi Tamche Jinma), golden in color, performing auspicious activities. She holds a white flask containing nectar that performs auspicious actions. Her mantra is this:

OM TARE TUTTARE TURE MANGALAM SVAHA

ཨོཾ་ཏུ་རེ་ཏུཏྟ་རེ་ཏུ་རེ་མངྒ་ལཾ་སྭཱ་ཧཱ།

13. She Who Blazes Like Fire

Homage! She 'mid wreath ablaze like
Eon-ending fire abiding!
Right stretched, left bent, joy surrounds you
Troops of enemies destroying!

On the thirteenth petal is Tara Who Blazes Like Fire (Metar Barma), red in color and blazing like fire. She holds a red flask containing nectar that destroys enemies and protects from obstacles. Her mantra is this:

OM TARE TUTTARE TURE BHAYA BHASMIM KURU SVAHA

ཨོཾ་ཏུ་རེ་ཏུཏྟ་རེ་ཏུ་རེ་བྷ་ཡ་བྷ་སྨྀ་ཀུ་རུ་སྭཱ་ཧཱ།

There are wrathful actions you can do to destroy enemies, but whatever meditations or recitations you do, if you do them with anger, they don't become Dharma; they just become negative karma. It has to be done with the thought of bodhichitta—the wish to benefit other sentient beings, especially the harmful being, to stop them engaging in negativities.

14. She Who Is Frowning Wrathfully

Homage! She who strikes the ground with
Her palm, and with her foot beats it!
Scowling, with the letter HUM the
Seven levels she does conquer!

On the fourteenth petal is Tara Who Is Frowning Wrathfully (Tronyer Chen), having a slightly wrathful appearance, black in color. She holds a dark blue flask containing nectar that controls and subdues interferences. Her mantra is this:

OM TARE TUTTARE TURE VAJRA MAHA PADA BHASMIM
KURU SVAHA

ༀ་ཏུ་རེ་ཏུཏྟ་རེ་ཏུ་རེ་བཛྲ་མ་ཧྭ་པ་ད་བྷྰ་སྨིཾ་ཀུ་རུ་སྭ་ཧྭ།

15. She of Supreme Peacefulness

Homage! Happy, virtuous, peaceful!
She whose field is peace, nirvana!
She endowed with OM and SVAHA,
Destroyer of the great evil!

On the fifteenth petal is Tara the Supremely Peaceful One (Shiwa Chenmo), white in color. She holds a white flask containing nectar whose function is pacifying and purifying negative karma. Her mantra is this:

OM TARE TUTTARE TURE SARVA PAPAM PRASHAMANAYA SVAHA

ཨོཾ་ཏ་རེ་ཏུཏྟཱ་རེ་ཏུ་རེ་སརྦ་པཱ་པཾ་པྲ་ཤ་མ་ན་ཡ་སྭཱ་ཧཱ།

Reciting her mantra pacifies sickness, spirit harm, obscurations, and negative karma.

16. Tara Who Arises from the HUM of Intrinsic Awareness

> Homage! She with joy surrounded
> Tearing foes' bodies asunder,
> Frees with HUM and knowledge mantra,
> Arrangement of the ten letters!

On the sixteenth petal is Tara Who Arises from the HUM of Intrinsic Awareness (Rikpa Hungle Drölma), red in color. She holds a red-yellow flask containing nectar whose function is to increase wisdom. Her mantra is this:

OM TARE TUTTARE TURE SARVA DHARMAH PRATI-PARISHODHAYA SVAHA[81]

ཨོཾ་ཏ་རེ་ཏུཏྟཱ་རེ་ཏུ་རེ་སརྦ་དྷརྨཿ་ཏི་པ་རི་ཤོ་དྷ་ཡ་སྭཱ་ཧཱ།

17. She Who Causes the Three Realms to Tremble

> Homage! TURE! With seed letter
> Of the shape of syllable HUM!
> By foot stamping shakes the three worlds,
> Meru, Mandara, and Vindhya![82]

On the seventeenth petal is Tara Who Causes the Three Realms to Tremble (Drölma Jikten Sumyowa), red-yellow in color. Pacifying maras and obstacles, shaking the triple world, she holds a yellow flask containing nectar whose function is to control the power of mantras, which means controlling those who try to harm you using mantras. Her mantra is this:

OM TARE TUTTARE TURE SARVA STAMBHANI TARE SVAHA

ༀ་ཏུ་རེ་ཏུཏྟ་རེ་ཏུ་རེ་སཱརྦ་སྟཾབྷ་ནི་ཏུ་རེ་སྭཱ་ཧཱ།

18. She Who Neutralizes Poison

Homage! Holding in her hand the
Hare-marked moon of deva-lake form!
With twice spoken TARA and PHAT,
Totally dispelling poison!

On the eighteenth petal is Tara Who Neutralizes Poison (Dukselma), white in color. She holds a white flask containing nectar whose function is to eliminate all sicknesses and poison. Her mantra is this:

OM TARE TUTTARE TURE NAGA VISHA SHANTIM KURU SVAHA

ༀ་ཏུ་རེ་ཏུཏྟ་རེ་ཏུ་རེ་ན་ག་བི་ཧ་ཤཱུ་ཧྟི་གུ་རུ་སྭཱ་ཧཱ།

If somebody poisons you or you have taken some poison by mistake, this is the mantra you can chant to eliminate it.

19. She Who Alleviates All Suffering

Homage! She whom gods and their kings,
And the kinnaras[83] do honor!

Armored in all joyful splendor,
She dispels bad dreams and conflicts!

On the nineteenth petal is Tara Who Alleviates All Suffering (Duk-Ngal Tamche Selwé Drölma), white in color. She holds a white flask containing nectar that eliminates disputes, bad dreams, and other suffering. Her mantra is this:

OM TARE TUTTARE TURE MOCANA SVAHA

ༀ་ཏུ་རེ་ཏུཏྟ་རེ་ཏུ་རེ་མོ་ཙ་ན་སྭཱ་ཧཱ།

Because this Tara eliminates quarrels and bad dreams, if you are having persistent nightmares or quarrels in the family or in the office, this is the mantra to recite.

20. She Who Removes Pestilence

Homage! She whose two eyes bright with
Radiance of sun and full moon!
With twice HARA and TUTTARA
She dispels severe contagion!

On the twentieth petal is Tara Who Removes Pestilence (Rimne Selwé Drölma), red in color. She holds a red flask containing nectar whose function is to eliminate all epidemics and contagious diseases. Her mantra is this:

OM TARE TUTTARE TURE VISARATA SVAHA

ༀ་ཏུ་རེ་ཏུཏྟ་རེ་ཏུ་རེ་བི་ས་ར་ཏ་སྭཱ་ཧཱ།

If there is a contagious disease or epidemic in the country, this is the specific Tara to be practiced.

21. She Who Completely Perfects All Enlightened Activities

Homage! Full of liberating
Pow'r by the set of three natures!
Destroys hosts of spirits, yakshas,
And raised corpses! Supreme! TURE!

On the twenty-first petal is Tara Who Completely Perfects All Enlightened Activities (Trinle Tamche Yongsu Dzokpar Jepé Drölma), white in color and radiating varicolored lights. She holds a green flask containing nectar that accomplishes various magical attainments. Her mantra is this:

OM TARE TUTTARE TURE SARVA SIDDHI SADHANAM SVAHA

ཨོཾ་ཏུ་རེ་ཏུཏྟཱ་རེ་ཏུ་རེ་སརྦ་སིདྡྷི་སཱ་ཧྣཾ་སྭཱ་ཧཱ།

Generally, we recite all the Twenty-One Taras within the *Praises to the Twenty-One Taras*, but sometimes when you recite each praise, if you like, you can stop and recite the mantra for that Tara a number of times.

As you can see, each Tara relates to a specific problem, so you can focus on the Tara that deals with whatever problem you have. Of course, this also applies to anybody you are doing the practice for. For instance, if a friend is sick and you want to help them with the Twenty-One Taras, you can focus on that particular Tara and recite her mantra, while imagining beams of nectar emitting from her heart and entering the heart of the sick friend, purifying them completely. Whatever wishes you want to succeed, or whatever problems you want to overcome, you can focus on that particular Tara and chant more of that mantra.

WHITE TARA

White Tara resembles Green Tara in most aspects, besides, of course, that her color is white, symbolizing having overcome the two obscurations.

She has seven eyes: a third eye on her face in the middle of her fore-head, and one on each of her palms and on the soles of her feet. These symbolize her realization of the three doors of liberation (emptiness, signlessness, and wishlessness)[84] and the realization of the four immea-surable thoughts (loving-kindness, compassion, joy, and equanimity). Unlike Green Tara, who has her right leg extended, White Tara sits in the full vajra posture.[85]

White Tara's long-life mantra is this:

OM TARE TUTTARE TURE MAMA AYUR PUNYE JNANA PUSHTIM KURU SVAHA

ༀ་ཏུ་རེ་ཏུཏྟ་རེ་ཏུ་རེ་མ་མ་ཨཱ་ཡུར་པུཉྫེ་ཛྙཱ་ན་པུཥྚི་ཀུ་རུ་སྭཱ་ཧཱ།

Although we all have a certain lifespan determined by the karma cre-ated in previous lives, that lifespan can be cut short through the ripen-ing of negative imprints caused by having committed a heavy negative action motivated by self-cherishing or one of the other delusions. This creates an obstacle to our life, which can result in death.

Reciting the mantra of White Tara is especially effective for elimi-nating life obstacles, helping us to have a long life. It is also a powerful healing mantra. However, as I have mentioned, if the motivation is only for relief from this temporal suffering and to enjoy this life's pleasures, the recitation does not become virtuous, even though it may help alle-viate the immediate problem.

Along with the practices of Namgyalma and others that help us have a long life, a White Tara practice is considered very effective when we liberate animals. Prolonging the lives of the animals by saving their lives naturally prolongs our own life. By planting a particular seed, we get a particular result. If we plant a potato, a potato grows; if we plant a chili seed, a chili plant grows. In the same way that the plant depends on the seed, the result depends on the cause, and a positive action that prolongs the life of another creates the cause for our own long life. We can not only liberate animals for our own long life, however; we can also dedicate the practice to members of our family or to other people. We can actually dedicate it to all living beings.

A very simple way to practice White Tara is to visualize the sick person you are trying to help in front of you with White Tara above them. You then visualize beams of white nectar entering the crown of their head, totally filling their body, purifying all their defilements and negative karmas, their sickness, and the threat of untimely death. As you do this, you can recite White Tara's long-life mantra for them at least twenty-one times and then the Tara mantra, OM TARE TUTTARE TURE SVAHA.

Then, when you have finished the mantra recitation, really feel that their body is filled with white nectar like milk from White Tara and envision they have achieved all of Tara's qualities: perfect power, the ability to benefit sentient beings, great compassion, and especially immortality.

How to Practice with Green Tara's Mantra[86]

There are many ways of practicing Tara—and many different aspects of Tara to practice—from a simple Green Tara sadhana[87] to the highest yoga tantra aspect of Chittamani Tara. Even if you don't do a formal practice, it is very good to visualize Tara when you recite her mantra.

Visualize Tara as described above in the space in front of you, level with your forehead, at a comfortable distance of about one body length. (If you wish, you can visualize Tara on your crown.)

First, think of the transcendental wisdom of nondual bliss and emptiness of all the buddhas, which fully sees all existence. This is the holy mind of the dharmakaya, the absolute guru. Just as sentient beings act under the control of anger and attachment, buddhas work for all living beings under the control of compassion. At this time, the holy mind of all the buddhas, the absolute guru, manifests in this particular female form of Tara.

On her forehead is a white OM ༀ, the essence of the vajra holy body; at her neck, a red AH ཨཱཿ, the essence of vajra holy speech; and at her heart, a blue HUM ཧཱུྃ, the essence of the vajra holy mind.

From the OM at Tara's forehead, white nectar beams are emitted and enter you through your forehead, completely purifying all the obscurations and negative karmas you have accumulated with the body from beginningless rebirths until now. From the AH at Tara's throat, red nectar beams are emitted and enter through your throat, completely purifying all the obscurations and negative karmas accumulated with your speech from beginningless rebirths until now. From the HUM at Tara's heart, blue nectar beams are emitted and enter your heart, completely purifying all the obscurations and negative karmas accumulated with your mind from beginningless rebirths until now. Out of compassion for you and all living beings, Mother Tara has purified you.

Concentrate on this as you recite the mantra:

OM TARE TUTTARE TURE SVAHA

When you finish the meditation, pray to Tara:

> Without delay of even a second, may I become Tara and, in each second, free uncountable numbers of living beings from all their sufferings and lead them to full enlightenment.

Pray that, through generating bodhichitta, you will achieve your wish to achieve Tara for the sake of other living beings.

The essential Mahayana practices of loving-kindness, compassion, morality, and, ultimately, bodhichitta are the best offerings you can make to Tara; they are the practices that please her the most. They bring you closer to Tara, so that she quickly helps all your actions to succeed.

Because, rather than following the selfish mind, you are using your life to serve others—because of your attitude of bodhichitta—Tara is extremely pleased with you. She melts into green light, enters through your forehead, and absorbs into your heart.

Think:

> My body, speech, and mind have been blessed to become Tara's vajra holy body, holy speech, and holy mind

By receiving the blessings of Tara with a calm, devoted mind, you plant the seed to develop your mind and actually achieve Tara.

After the absorption, if you wish, one-pointedly concentrate on the nature of Tara's holy mind. Then conclude your practice by dedicating the merits to the generation of bodhichitta and to your achievement of Tara, in order to lead every living being as quickly as possible to Tara's enlightenment. You can finish with the standard dedication prayers.

5. MEDICINE BUDDHA

W^HEN THE MEDICINE BUDDHA was a bodhisattva called Stainless Star, one of the many prayers he made for us sentient beings was this:

> When I become the Medicinal King, the King of Lapis Light, may any sentient being who recites my mantra or hears my name or sees, hears, touches, or remembers me, or does the recitation-meditation never have any sickness or harm. May they have a long life, the Dharma, and wealth.
>
> There is no doubt that for any sentient being who makes a statue of Medicine Buddha or does concentration, or meditation, on Medicine Buddha, but even for somebody who doesn't concentrate on Medicine Buddha but simply expresses my name or even makes seven steps in my direction [which means toward a Medicine Buddha statue or to do a puja], the door to the evil-gone realms [which means the lower realms] and to samsara will be closed. May they be born in the higher realms, have all the seven qualities, and achieve peerless enlightenment.
>
> May the power of my prayers be equal to that of all the buddhas of the fortunate eon, especially in regard to profundity, extensiveness, and power.[88]

The above prayer was just one that the Medicine Buddha made when he was a bodhisattva. He and all seven of the Medicine Buddhas did so many prayers for us sentient beings, that in these degenerated times—which is now—all our wishes might succeed.

Reciting the Medicine Buddha's mantra or the names of the seven

Medicine Buddhas every day purifies whatever karma we have to be reborn in the lower realms. That was guaranteed by the main Medicine Buddha and the other Medicine Buddhas when they made extensive prayers for the sentient beings of these degenerate times. They promised that if we do the Medicine Buddha practice, they will actualize our prayers, allowing us to quickly be able to accomplish everything we wish for.

THE SEVEN MEDICINE BUDDHAS

In the Medicine Buddha practices, such as the one called the *Wish-Fulfilling Jewel*,[89] there are seven Medicine Buddhas, but generally when we visualize the Medicine Buddha to recite the mantra, we visualize the main Medicine Buddha: Medicine Guru, King of Lapis Light.

In the center of a lotus is a white moon disk. Seated on the moon disk is the Medicine Buddha. He has one face and two arms. He is blue in color, like a very clear, very blue sky, radiating blue light from his body. In the past we translated *bendurya*, the color of the Medicine Buddha, as lapis lazuli, but that seems incorrect. Although there doesn't seem to be an exact translation in English, we can take it to be sapphire.

His right hand rests on his right knee, palm up, in the mudra of granting sublime realizations. He holds the stem of an arura plant between his thumb and index finger. Arura is the special plant that heals both the sickness of the mind and sickness of the body, destroying all suffering and its causes. His left hand is in the mudra of concentration. In it, he holds a lapis lazuli bowl filled with immortal nectar that destroys death and pacifies the chronic disease of the delusions.

He is seated in the full lotus position and is wearing the three red-colored robes of a monk. He has all the signs and holy exemplifications of a buddha.

Even though he appears to us as truly existent, every part of Medicine Buddha's holy body is merely labeled by the mind: the head, the hands, the legs, the begging bowl, the arura plant.

Besides the main Medicine Buddha, there are the other six Medicine

Buddhas. Generally, we visualize them all above our head. From the top to the bottom they are like this:

The first buddha is Renowned Glorious King of Excellent Signs. He is golden in color and is making the mudra of granting refuge, his right hand at his heart, palm outward, and his left hand on his lap, palm upward, as in the meditation mudra.

Below him is King of Melodious Sounds, Brilliant Radiance of Skill, Adorned with Jewels, Moon, and Lotus. He is yellow in color and is making the mudra of granting the supreme, with his right hand on his right knee, palm outward, similar to Tara's mudra, and his left hand in the meditation mudra.

Then there is Stainless Excellent Gold, Great Jewel Who Accomplishes All Vows. He is golden in color and is making the Dharma teaching mudra, both hands at his heart, with his right palm outward and raised and his left palm inward and raised and partly in front of the right.

After that is Supreme Glory Free from Sorrow. He is light red in color and is making the mudra of meditative equipoise, with both hands on his lap, the right resting on the left and the thumbs touching.

Next there is Melodious Ocean of Proclaimed Dharma. He is pink in color and is making the Dharma teaching mudra.

Then there is Delightful King of Clear Knowing, Supreme Wisdom of an Ocean of Dharma. He is coral colored[90] and is making the mudra of granting the supreme.

The last of the seven Medicine Buddhas is Medicine Guru, King of Lapis Light. As we have seen, he is sapphire colored, with his right hand in the mudra of granting the supreme realizations and his left in the mudra of concentration.

All of these buddhas are sitting on a lotus and moon disk and wearing the three robes of a monk, as in the description of the main Medicine Buddha. The differences are their colors and their mudras.

THE MANTRA

There is a long and a short Medicine Buddha mantra. The long one is this:

OM NAMO BHAGAVATE BHAISHAJYE / GURU BAIDURYA /
PRABHA RAJAYA / TATHAGATAYA / ARHATE SAMYAKSAM
BUDDHAYA / TADYATHA / OM BHAISHAJYE BHAISHAJYE
MAHA BHAISHAJYE [BHAISHAJYE] / RAJA SAMUDGATE
SVAHA

ཨོཾ་ན་མོ་བྷ་ག་ཝ་ཏེ་བྷཻ་ཥ་ཇྱེ། གུ་རུ་བཻཌུརྻ། པྲ་བྷ་རཱ་ཛཱ་ཡ། ཏ་ཐཱ་ག་ཏཱ་ཡ།
ཨརྷ་ཏེ་སོ་མྱུ་མྐྲ་བུཧྲ་ཡ། ཏ་དྱ་ཐཱ། ཨོཾ་བྷཻ་ཥཛྱེ་བྷཻ་ཥ་ཛྱེ་མ་ཧཱ་བྷཻ་ཥ་ཛྱེ་[བྷཻ་ཥ་
ཛྱེ།] རཱ་ཛཱ་ས་མུངྒ་ཏེ་སྭཱ་ཧཱ།

Common pronunciation:

*Om namo bagawatay bekanzay guru baidurya / praba radza
ya / tatagataya / arhatay samyaksam buddhaya / ta ya ta /
om bekanzay bekanzay maha bekanzay [bekanzay] / radza
samudgatay soha*

The short Medicine Buddha mantra is this:

TADYATHA / OM BHAISHAJYE BHAISHAJYE MAHA BHAISHA-
JYE [BHAISHAJYE] / RAJA SAMUDGATE SVAHA

ཏ་དྱ་ཐཱ། ཨོཾ་བྷཻ་ཥ་ཛྱེ་བྷཻ་ཥ་ཛྱེ་མ་ཧཱ་བྷཻ་ཥ་ཛྱེ་[བྷཻ་ཥ་ཛྱེ།]རཱ་ཛཱ་ས་མུངྒ་ཏེ་སྭཱ་ཧཱ།

Common pronunciation:

*Ta ya ta / om bekanzay bekanzay maha bekanzay [bekanzay] /
radza samudgatay soha*

The bracketed BHAISHAJYE (*bekanzay*) is optional.

The Meaning of the Mantra

In the Medicine Buddha mantra, BHAISHAJYE means the elimination of pain and MAHA BHAISHAJYE means the great elimination of pain. In one explanation of the mantra, the first BHAISHAJYE refers to eliminating the pain of true suffering, the pain not just of disease but of all the problems of body and mind. It also eliminates the pain of death and rebirth, that which is caused by karma and delusions.

The second BHAISHAJYE refers to eliminating all the true causes of suffering, which are not external but within the mind. This refers to the karma and delusions themselves, the inner causes that enable external factors to become conditions for disease.

The third BHAISHAJYE, MAHA BHAISHAJYE, or the great elimination of pain, refers to eliminating even the subtle imprints left on the consciousness by the delusions.

The fourth BHAISHAJYE is optional. Some texts have it, others don't, but His Holiness the Dalai Lama recites the mantra with the fourth BHAISHAJYE.

The Medicine Buddha mantra actually contains the remedy of the whole graduated path to enlightenment, from the beginning up to the peerless happiness of full enlightenment. The first BHAISHAJYE contains the graduated path of the lower capable being; the second BHAISHAJYE, the graduated path of the middle capable being; and MAHA BHAISHA-JYE, the graduated path of the higher capable being. Reciting the mantra leaves imprints on our mind so that we are able to actualize the path contained in the mantra.

As we have seen, the initial word of the mantra, TADYATHA, means "this contains," and the OM, composed of *a*, *o*, and *ma*, signifies the pure holy body, holy speech, and holy mind of the buddha, here referring to those of the Medicine Buddha. Actualizing the whole path to enlightenment purifies our impure body, speech, and mind and transforms them into the Medicine Buddha's pure holy body, holy speech, and holy mind.

We can then become a perfect guide for living beings. With our omniscient mind, we are able to effortlessly, directly, and unmistakenly see the level of mind of every living being and all the methods that fit them, in order to lead them to the peerless happiness of full enlightenment. We also have the perfect power to manifest in various forms to suit every living being and reveal the necessary methods to guide them, whether giving material help, secular education, or Dharma teachings. Whenever an imprint left by a sentient being's past positive actions ripens, without the delay of even a second, we can reveal the various means to guide them to enlightenment.

The Power of the Mantra in These Degenerate Times

It is explained in the sutras that reciting the Medicine Buddha mantra, doing his practice, or making offerings to him are extremely effective ways to bring peace and success to a whole country, especially in these degenerate times. In a country where there is untimely rain, hailstorms destroying the crops, earthquakes, and various contagious diseases, the Medicine Buddha helps. Also, wherever there are wars, famines, and natural disasters, the texts say that if the king of the country, with a mind of loving-kindness, makes offerings to the Medicine Buddha, the crops will grow well, wars will cease, and the sentient beings of that country will be happy and healthy, enjoying greater wealth, long life, and power.

When Manjushri, in the presence of all seven Medicine Buddhas and Shakyamuni Buddha, requested the Medicine Buddha to grant his mantra, they all in one voice granted it and explained its benefits. Because of that, when we recite this mantra, all the buddhas and bodhisattvas will pay attention to us and protect us.

The text called *Mengyu Rinchen Bumpa* says,

> Reciting Medicine Buddha's name and mantra once equals having recited the names and mantras of all the tathagatas of the past, present, and future.

It also says,

> Remembering, seeing, hearing, touching, or meditating on
> Medicine Buddha includes remembering, seeing, hearing,
> touching, or meditating on all the buddhas and bodhisattvas,
> all the Triple Gem. Therefore, Medicine Buddha's holy name
> is "All-Encompassing of Those Gone to Bliss."[91]

Reciting this mantra as a daily practice purifies all our negative karmas
and quickly pacifies diseases and harm from spirits. Furthermore, just as
a mother pays attention to her beloved child, all the buddhas and bodhisattvas always pay attention to us, guide us, and protect us. Because of
that, the mantra has the power to immediately pacify all our inner sicknesses and harm from spirits. We will no longer be controlled by others,
and all the harms and quarrels caused by our enemies will be pacified.

Because of the extensive prayers the seven Medicine Buddhas made
when they were still bodhisattvas to actualize all the wishes of living
beings when the teachings of Shakyamuni Buddha were in decline,
whatever we wish for will happen when we rely on them. Therefore, of
all the many different deities that can be practiced, to really progress
quickly in the Dharma in these degenerate times, my suggestion is that
everybody should practice the Medicine Buddha.

We are living in a time when the five degenerations are flourishing:
the degenerations of mind, lifespan, sentient beings, time, and view.
All the other degenerations basically come from the first, the *degeneration of mind*. Because we sentient beings have not developed our minds
in spiritual paths, ignorance, anger, desire, and other delusions have
increased and become very gross. This has resulted in the *degeneration of
lifespan*, with the average life expectancy becoming progressively shorter
than when human beings first appeared in this world system.[92] It has
also led to the *degeneration of sentient beings*, whose minds have become
very stubborn and difficult to subdue. It is increasingly difficult for us to
practice patience, loving-kindness, compassion, and so forth. The *degeneration of time* is shown by the escalation of wars and natural disasters

such as earthquakes, droughts, famines, and epidemics. Finally, there is the *degeneration of view*, with fewer people believing the truth and more people believing lies and wrong explanations, such as believing that virtue is not the cause of happiness and nonvirtue is not the cause of suffering.

Just as Guru Padmasambhava predicted more than a thousand years ago, because of the flourishing of the five degenerations, new diseases are emerging all the time, doctors are becoming less able to recognize and treat them, and the power of medicine to cure them is decreasing. Food is becoming less nutritional and air and water pollution are causing more and more illnesses. Everything is degenerating, including success in both worldly concerns and the Dharma.

Because our minds are degenerating, practicing the Dharma is becoming harder and whatever practice we do seems to have less effect. Even our ability to connect to the power of most mantras has degenerated, which is why when we do a deity practice now, we generally have to recite many more mantras than in previous times.

On the other hand, because of the power of the promises made in the past by the Medicine Buddhas, the Medicine Buddha mantra actually becomes *more* powerful as times degenerate. So, you can see why it is important to recite the Medicine Buddha's mantra. By doing so, the wishes we have for our Dharma practice are quickly achieved, as well as, along the way, worldly matters such as success, health, and long life. The main success we should aim for, of course, is success on the path to enlightenment, to liberate ourselves from the oceans of samsaric suffering forever and achieve enlightenment so we can enlighten all sentient beings.

I often recommend that for anybody interested in Buddhist practice—in fact for anybody who wants happiness—the fundamental practice should not only be to recite OM MANI PADME HUM but also the mantra of the Medicine Buddha. I also recommend that centers do Medicine Buddha pujas in addition to their regular Tara pujas. If you normally do a Tara puja in the evening of the Tibetan eighth[93] as part of your center's activities, it is very good to do a Medicine Buddha puja in the morning before breakfast.

The Mantra That Saves from the Lower Realms

When we recite the Medicine Buddha mantra, any being who hears us—not just humans but also animals, birds, and insects—will never be born in the lower realms again. In that way, not only do we take care of ourselves each day by reciting the Medicine Buddha mantra and doing the practice, we are also able to take care of others.

When the texts talk about the benefits of reciting the Medicine Buddha mantra and the names of the Medicine Buddhas, we can take these as definitive teachings, not interpretive. It's not that they say such-and-such, but we must try to understand that there is another meaning there. When the texts tell us that chanting the mantra saves from the lower realms, they mean exactly that. Therefore when I recite mantras for animals or human beings, one of the mantras I always recite is the Medicine Buddha mantra, to prevent them from ever being reborn in the lower realms. Whenever we meet somebody, we should do this.

If you have your own pets, you should recite the Medicine Buddha mantra to them every day. Really, the mantra is so short it takes almost no time to recite, so it would be a great loss if you didn't recite it. Of course, there are many benefits to reciting it silently with the intention of benefiting that person or that animal, but here I'm talking about reciting it out loud in the ear of the being, not just quietly mumbling it.

Just providing your pets with food and comfort is not enough. This is not their only life, so it is essential that you help them attain a better rebirth, one where they will have less suffering and more happiness. When you recite the mantra to them, you leave a positive imprint on their mindstream, meaning they will be able to meet the Dharma in all future lifetimes, to be quickly liberated from the oceans of samsaric suffering, and to achieve enlightenment. That is the most important aim. To do anything less is kind of sad. Having a pet becomes more for your own selfish happiness.

Hearing or remembering the Medicine Buddha's mantra even purifies the five immediate negativities, karmas so heavy they cause one to immediately be born in the hell realm after death. It also says that even seeing, touching, or remembering the holy body of a statue of the

Medicine Buddha completely purifies the pollution that comes from taking food and other things that people have offered with devotion to the sangha community. Here *pollution* does not refer to external pollution, as in the Western sense; this is mental pollution.

In *Liberation in the Palm of Your Hand*, when Pabongka Dechen Nyingpo talks about the refuge practice, he mentions various negative karmas collected in relation to the sangha that have to be purified, including stopping somebody from making offerings to the sangha, criticizing the sangha, and causing disunity among the sangha. These are all very heavy negative actions, but they can all be purified by reciting the Medicine Buddha mantra, as can all the negative karmas collected in relation to the Buddha, Dharma, and Sangha.

The Mantra That Heals

The Medicine Buddha mantra is extremely effective at healing, whether we recite it for our own benefit or somebody else's. When we recite it 108 times and blow over the food, drink, or the medicine we are taking, the sickness will be pacified, we will have long and healthy life, and all our wishes will be fulfilled. By reciting the Medicine Buddha mantra, we can also increase the power of the medicine we are taking or giving to others.

Place the medicine in a bowl in front of you and visualize a moon disk above it. Standing on the moon disk is a blue OM surrounded by the syllables of the Medicine Buddha mantra, TADYATHA OM BHAISHA-JYE BHAISHAJYE MAHA BHAISHAJYE BHAISHAJYE RAJA SAMUDGATE SVAHA, in a clockwise direction. As you recite the mantra, visualize that nectar flows down from all the syllables of the mantra and absorbs into the medicine. The syllables and the moon then dissolve into the medicine, which becomes very powerful and able to cure all diseases and harm from spirits, as well as their causes: negative karma and delusions.

After Tibetan doctors have made medicine, they use Medicine Buddha meditation and mantras to bless it. The medicine is then more effective because, besides the power of all the medicinal plants and other substances it contains, it has additional power from their practice that can help bring purification of the mind and a quick recovery.

It is good for somebody who is a healer to do a Medicine Buddha retreat for one or two months, where the mantra and the Medicine Buddhas' names are recited every day. It is mentioned that if we do this, the medicinal goddesses and protectors will help us make correct diagnoses of our patients' illnesses and to prescribe the right treatments.

My relative Pemba is codirector of Chamtse Ling, the FPMT center in Hong Kong, with Esther Ngai, who helped to buy the place. Esther sometimes had unimaginable headaches and had to have major brain surgery. She usually recited one mala of Medicine Buddha mantras a day, and during the operation she was able to see the Medicine Buddha the whole time. That means the Medicine Buddha was guiding her, appearing to her during the operation when she needed help. There are so many stories I could mention about the healing abilities of reciting the Medicine Buddha mantra.

The Mantra That Benefits the Dying and Dead

When somebody such as a family member is dying, we must remember to recite the Medicine Buddha mantra with a bodhichitta motivation, not quietly to ourselves, but loudly in the person's ear. Then, even if they are unconscious, because they will still absorb the sound of the mantra, they will be saved from rebirth in the lower realms and get a higher rebirth.

The Medicine Buddha practice can even purify those who have already died and liberate them from suffering, and that includes animals. Anybody who eats meat should make it beneficial for the animal that has been killed by reciting a purifying mantra before eating. Reciting one (or all) of the mantras of Medicine Buddha, Mitrukpa, or Milarepa,[94] as well as the special mantra to bless the meat, OM AH BIRA KHE CHARA HUM, and blowing upon the meat about to be eaten purifies the being's karmic obscurations and allows it to be reborn in a pure land or in one of the upper realms, as a human or god.

This is even true of blowing on a dead body or old bones we find on the road. Even if the animal or human being died hundreds or even thousands of years ago and their consciousness is in the lower realms, reciting the Medicine Buddha mantra and blowing on their bones can transfer the consciousness to a pure land or an upper realm. At the very least, it will shorten the duration of their suffering in the lower realms.

By reciting the Medicine Buddha mantra, blowing over substances such as powder or sand grains, and then sprinkling that substance on the body of somebody who is dying or dead, we can benefit them. Although the texts specify sand grains, I usually mention powder or sesame seeds because people might find the thought of sprinkling sand over the head uncomfortable. If it is difficult to go to where the person is, the blessed substance can be sent there and somebody else can sprinkle the body for purification. I keep some black sesame seeds and some white powder for this purpose, and if there is somebody dying or dead, I do various mantras for them, including Medicine Buddha and Namgyalma, and then blow over these substances and sprinkle them on the body.

It is also very beneficial to do an elaborate Medicine Buddha puja, such as the *Wish-Fulfilling Jewel*, for those who are dying or have already died. The Medicine Buddha puja contains the dedicated purposes of each of the Medicine Buddhas and is often done for someone who is seriously ill.

There are many ways you can help somebody who is about to die.[95] One thing I would like to emphasize is that when you visit a dying person, the first thing you should do is recite the name of the Buddha Having a Jewel Ushnisha: Rinchen Tsugtor Chänla.[96] Because he is similar to the Medicine Buddha and Maitreya Buddha in that through the prayers he made, anybody who even hears his name will not be reborn in the lower realms, I would strongly recommend you recite the his name along with the mantras of the Medicine Buddha and Maitreya.

HOW TO PRACTICE WITH MEDICINE BUDDHA'S MANTRA[97]

When you do a practice for a sick or dying person or animal with all the seven Medicine Buddhas, you visualize them all piled up, one above the other, above the head of the being you are practicing for. Alternatively, for yourself or on behalf of the other being, you visualize them above your own head, as described here.

About four inches above the crown of your head is a lotus flower. In the center is a white moon disk, upon which is seated your root guru—the dharmakaya essence of all buddhas—in the form of the main Medicine Buddha.

Do some preliminary practices, such as saying the refuge prayer three times, the four immeasurable thoughts, and the seven-limb prayer.[98]

Request
Then, make this request:

> I beseech you, Bhagavan Medicine Guru, whose holy body signifies omniscient wisdom and compassion as vast as limitless space, please grant me your blessings.

> I beseech you, compassionate Medicine Guru, holding in your right hand the king of medicines symbolizing your vow to help all pitiful sentient beings plagued by the 424 diseases, please grant me your blessings.

> I beseech you, compassionate Medicine Guru, holding in your left hand a bowl of nectar symbolizing your vow to give the glorious undying nectar of the Dharma, which eliminates the degenerations of sickness, old age, and death, please grant me your blessings.

Visualization
Above the crown of Guru Medicine Buddha is a wish-granting jewel, the essence of which is the Guru.

Above that is Buddha Delightful King of Clear Knowing, Supreme Wisdom of an Ocean of Dharma, whose body is coral-colored. His right hand is in the mudra of bestowing sublime realizations and his left hand is in the mudra of granting the supreme.

Above him is Buddha Melodious Ocean of Proclaimed Dharma, with a pink-colored body and hands in the mudra of teaching the Dharma.

Above him is Buddha Supreme Glory Free from Sorrow, light red in color, with both hands in the mudra of meditative equipoise.

Above him is Buddha Stainless Excellent Gold, Great Jewel Who Accomplishes All Vows, golden in color, with his right hand in the mudra of expounding the Dharma.

Above him is Buddha King of Melodious Sound, Brilliant Radiance of Skill, Adorned with Jewels, Moon, and Lotus, yellow in color, with his right hand in the mudra of bestowing sublime realizations and his left hand in the mudra of concentration.

Above him is Buddha Renowned Glorious King of Excellent Signs, golden in color, with his right hand in the mudra of granting refuge and his left hand in the mudra of concentration.

Request

Repeat each verse seven times. After the seventh recitation, as you repeat "May your vow . . .," the Medicine Buddha of that request absorbs into the one below.

> To the bhagavan, tathagata, arhat, fully enlightened Buddha Renowned Glorious King of Excellent Signs I prostrate, offer, and go for refuge.

May your vow to benefit all sentient beings now ripen for myself and others.

To the bhagavan, tathagata, arhat, fully enlightened Buddha King of Melodious Sound, Brilliant Radiance of Skill, Adorned with Jewels, Moon, and Lotus I prostrate, offer, and go for refuge.

May your vow to benefit all sentient beings now ripen for myself and others.

To the bhagavan, tathagata, arhat, fully enlightened Buddha Stainless Excellent Gold, Great Jewel Who Accomplishes All Vows I prostrate, offer, and go for refuge.

May your vow to benefit all sentient beings now ripen for myself and others.

To the bhagavan, tathagata, arhat, fully enlightened Buddha Supreme Glory Free from Sorrow I prostrate, offer, and go for refuge.

May your vow to benefit all sentient beings now ripen for myself and others.

To the bhagavan, tathagata, arhat, fully enlightened Buddha Melodious Ocean of Proclaimed Dharma I prostrate, offer, and go for refuge.

May your vow to benefit all sentient beings now ripen for myself and others.

To the bhagavan, tathagata, arhat, fully enlightened Buddha Delightful King of Clear Knowing, Supreme Wisdom of an Ocean of Dharma I prostrate, offer, and go for refuge.

May your vow to benefit all sentient beings now ripen for myself and others.

To the bhagavan, tathagata, arhat, fully enlightened Buddha Medicine Guru King of Lapis Light I prostrate, offer, and go for refuge.

May your vow to benefit all sentient beings now ripen for myself and others.

Visualization

Granting your request, from the heart and holy body of Medicine Guru, infinite rays of white light pour down, completely filling your body from head to toe. They purify all your diseases and afflictions due to spirits and their causes, all your negative karma and mental obscurations. Your body becomes clean and clear as crystal.

The light rays pour down twice more, each time filling your body with blissful clean-clear light which you absorb. You become the essence of the Medicine Buddha's blissful and omniscient mind of wisdom and compassion.

At your heart appears a lotus and moon disk. Standing at the center of the moon disk is the blue seed syllable OM surrounded by the syllables of the mantra. As you recite the mantra, visualize rays of light radiating out in all directions from the syllable at your heart. The light rays pervade the sentient beings of the six realms, especially the being you are doing the practice for. Through your great love wishing them to have happiness, and through your great compassion wishing them to be free from suffering, they are purified of all diseases and afflictions due to spirits and their causes, all their negative karma and mental obscurations.

The Recitation of the Mantra

The long mantra, as commonly pronounced:

> *Om namo bagawatay bekanzay guru baidurya / praba radza*
> *ya / tatagataya / arhatay samyaksam buddhaya / ta ya ta /*
> *om bekanzay bekanzay maha bekanzay [bekanzay] / radza*
> *samudgatay soha*

The short mantra, as commonly pronounced:

> *Ta ya ta / om bekanzay bekanzay maha bekanzay [bekanzay] /*
> *radza samudgatay soha*

Feel great joy and think: All sentient beings are transformed into the aspect of the Guru Medicine Buddha. How wonderful that I am now able to lead all sentient beings into the Medicine Buddha's enlightenment.

The Guru Medicine Buddha melts into light and absorbs into your heart. Your mind becomes completely one with the dharmakaya, the essence of all the buddhas.

Finish with dedications prayers.

When you have finished, imagine that there is not even an atom of negative karma left in your mental continuum. If you have done this practice for somebody and have been imagining the Medicine Buddhas absorbing into that being, imagine the same for them. As the last Medicine Buddha, King of Lapis Light, absorbs into that being, their body becomes calm and clear, like crystal, and their body, speech, and mind become one with the Medicine Buddha's holy body, speech, and mind.

When this practice is done with stable concentration and strong compassion, you can definitely help that being to avoid birth in the lower realms. You don't have to be physically in the presence of that person or animal. You can be home while they are in the hospital, for instance; it is still as effective.

6. VAJRASATTVA

MANJUSHRI ADVISED LAMA TSONGKHAPA that meditation alone is not enough to quickly generate the realizations of the path. Just as a crop cannot grow in a rocky and barren field—the ground must be cleared and well watered before the seeds can grow into strong plants—so too the mind cannot develop on the path while it is clouded with negative thoughts and emotions. We must eliminate our negativities and actualize our positive potential to the fullest by not creating any more negative karma, accumulating positive karma, and purifying the negative karma we have in our mindstream. These three things are vital if we are to gain any realizations.

The sublime method to accumulate merit is the guru yoga practice within the Vajrayana, where we see our guru as inseparable from the deity we are practicing. The sublime method to purify the negative karma and obscurations that cloud our mind is the Vajrasattva practice. If we do a daily tantric practice, at the beginning of a higher tantric sadhana there are invariably the twin preliminaries of a guru yoga practice and a Vajrasattva meditation in order to create the cause for success in the main part of the practice.

At present, we have mental blocks that hinder our Dharma practice, obstacles that obstruct us and prevent us from generating realizations on the path. Unless we can remove those blocks, we will be unable to develop the mind. Our mind—our sleeping, ignorant mind—won't awaken. The practice of purification is therefore vital because it creates the space that allows the mind to have realizations. I would say that purification practice is *the* essential practice we can do.

There are many means of purifying the mind, many purification practices, but the Vajrasattva practice is one of the most powerful; it is the one that has the power to purify even the heaviest negative karma. It

is common to all schools of Tibetan Buddhism and is a crucial element of any *ngöndro*, the series of preliminary practices that are undertaken before beginning a long tantric retreat.

You might have seen that there are two main forms of Vajrasattva. One form is simpler and is just Vajrasattva on his own, whereas in another he is sitting in union with the wisdom mother. This form is often referred to as "with consort" or *yab-yum* or "father and mother."[99] This representation of a deity in union with the wisdom mother is common in highest yoga tantra and it is symbolic. In reality it is one being, but its manifestation as father and mother signifies the unification of method and wisdom—the dharmakaya.

Vajrasattva without a wisdom mother is white, with one face and two hands; he is in the aspect of a youth of sixteen. Half of his black hair is gathered on top of his head, the rest curls down his back. He is seated on a moon disk on a white lotus, his legs crossed in the vajra position. In his right hand he holds a gold vajra (*dorjé*) to his heart, symbolizing bliss, and in his left, at his hip, he holds an upturned bell, symbolizing emptiness.[100] He is dressed in lavish garments and adorned with gold and jewels, ornaments, earrings, bracelets, and so forth. His face is gentle and loving.

When we visualize Vajrasattva with the wisdom mother, both their bodies are white; each has one face and two arms. He holds a vajra and bell at his heart, she a curved knife and skull cup.[101] They are embracing each other. The father is adorned with six mudras, the mother with five.[102] He sits in the vajra posture, she in the lotus posture.[103]

The Vajrasattva mantra is effective no matter who does it, but it will be even more effective if we have taken a Vajrasattva initiation, either a great initiation in the lower kriyā tantra[104] or a highest yoga tantra initiation. With the highest yoga tantra, we are empowered to do all the meditations, visualizing ourselves alone or with consort.

However, it is not that we can only visualize Vajrasattva with the wisdom mother after we have taken a highest yoga tantra initiation.

As long as we have faith and we feel the need to purify, we can do the meditation, even visualizing the highest yoga tantra aspect.

There is nothing that cannot be purified with the Vajrasattva practice. Because Vajrasattva without the wisdom mother is a kriya tantra deity, reciting the mantra while visualizing him purifies broken *pratimoksha*, or individual liberation, vows, and bodhisattva vows. When we do the practice as a highest yoga tantra, with the aspect of Vajrasattva with wisdom mother, that purifies everything, including the heaviest karma of breaking the root tantric vows.

The Mantra

The long, hundred-syllable mantra is this:

OM VAJRASATTVA SAMAYA MANUPALAYA / VAJRASATTVA
TVENOPATISHTHA / DRIDHO ME BHAVA / SUTOSHYO ME
BHAVA / SUPOSHYO ME BHAVA / ANURAKTO ME BHAVA
/ SARVA SIDDHIM ME PRAYACCHA / SARVA KARMA SU
CHAME / CHITTAM SHRIYAM KURU HUM / HA HA HA HA
HO / BHAGAVAN SARVA TATHAGATA / VAJRA MAME MUN-
CHA / VAJRA BHAVA MAHA SAMAYA SATTVA AH HUM PHAT

ཨོཾ་བཛྲ་སཏྭ་ས་མ་ཡ་མ་ནུ་པཱ་ལ་ཡ། བཛྲ་སཏྭ་ཏེ་ནོ་པ་ཏིཥྛ་ དྲྀ་ཌྷོ་མེ་བྷ་
ཝ། སུ་ཏོ་ཥྱོ་མེ་བྷ་ཝ། སུ་པོ་ཥྱོ་མེ་བྷ་ཝ། ཨ་ནུ་རཀྟོ་མེ་བྷ་ཝ། སརྦ་སིདྡྷི་མྨེ་
པྲ་ཡ་ཙྪ། སརྦ་ཀརྨ་སུ་ཙ་མེ། ཙིཏྟཾ་ཤྲི་ཡཾ་ཀུ་རུ་ཧཱུྂ། ཧ་ཧ་ཧ་ཧ་ཧོཿ བྷ་ག་ཝཱན་
སརྦ་ཏ་ཐཱ་ག་ཏ། བཛྲ་མ་མེ་མུཉྩ། བཛྲཱི་བྷ་ཝ་མ་ཧཱ་ས་མ་ཡ་སཏྭ་ཨཱཿཧཱུྂ་ཕཊ།

The short mantra is this:

OM VAJRASATTVA HUM

ཨོཾ་བཛྲ་སཏྭ་ཧཱུྂ།

There is also a short mantra that goes OM VAJRASATTVA HA but when I wrote to my root guru, His Holiness Trijang Rinpoche,[105] and asked about both versions, he replied that it was better to recite OM VAJRA-SATTVA HUM.

It is recommended in many texts and by many great masters such as His Holiness Trijang Rinpoche that each day we recite either the long mantra twenty-one times or the short one twenty-eight times in order to stop the increase of any negative karma we have accumulated during that day, as well as purifying the negative karma accumulated during this life and from beginningless previous lives. The root tantra called *Adorned with the Vajra Essence* (*Dorjé Nyingpo Genki Gyü*) explains,

> According to the method of the hundred syllables, each rec-
> itation of the mantra twenty-one times stops you receiving
> the downfalls and increasing any negative karma. This is
> explained by the highly attained ones. You should also enjoy
> reciting it in the interval times.

Here, "downfalls" refers to the root vows we have broken. "Interval times" means in the breaks between meditation sessions.

Of course, reciting a full mala of the long mantra is more powerful than just twenty-one recitations, but even if we cannot do that before going to bed each day, a shorter recitation, with prostrations if possible, will still purify our negative karma.

The Meaning of the Mantra

The meaning of the short Vajrasattva mantra, OM VAJRASATTVA HUM, is this:

> Bhagavan, the Destroyer, the Qualified One Gone-Beyond,
> you who have the nature of possessing the vajra of all the
> tathagatas, great hero with your holy mind, in accordance
> with your samaya, please don't give up on me.

The Sanskrit *bhagavan* is *chom den dä* in Tibetan—*chom* "destroyer," *den* "having all the qualifications," and *dä* "having transcended the world"—meaning Vajrasattva has completely destroyed, or purified, the two obscurations and obtained all the qualities of a buddha, having gone beyond even the peace of lower liberation and attained highest enlightenment.

The "vajra of all the tathagatas" refers to the dharmakaya, the transcendental wisdom of nondual bliss and emptiness, the absolute guru. When we visualize Vajrasattva with the wisdom mother, the male deity represents bliss—the method side of the practice—the female deity represents the realization of emptiness, and being in union means that in tantra these two aspects of the path are combined. This is the definitive meaning of "vajra." It is the real meaning of the guru—the absolute guru, the dharmakaya. We should remember this whenever we see, hear, or remember the guru.

Vajrasattva, Dorjé Sempa in Tibetan, consists of vajra (*dorjé*) and sattva (*sempa*), which means "hero," so here we are asking—actually, demanding!—that Vajrasattva, this great hero, never forsakes us, in accordance with his samaya, referring to the pledge or commitment Vajrasattva made in the past.

The meaning of the long mantra is this:

Vajrasattva, you who have pledged (SAMAYA) to lead me on the path to enlightenment (MANUPALAYA), bring me to your vajra holy mind (VAJRASATTVA TVENOPATISHTHA), and grant me the firm and stable realization of the ultimate nature (DRIDHO ME BHAVA). Grant me the blessings of being extremely pleased with me (SUTOSHYO ME BHAVA) and bless me with the nature of great bliss (SUPOSHYO ME BHAVA).

Bless me with the love that leads to your state (ANURAKTO ME BHAVA), grant all powerful attainments (SARVA SIDDHIM ME PRAYACCHA), grant all virtuous actions (SARVA KARMA SU CHAME), and grant all your victorious qualities (CHITTAM

SHRITAM KURU), the vajra mind (HUM), and the five transcendental wisdoms (HA HA HA HA HO).

You who have destroyed every obscuration, attained all realizations, and passed beyond suffering (BHAGAVAN), you who have realized emptiness and know all things just as they are, inseparably (SARVA TATHAGATA VAJRA), do not abandon me (MAME MUNCHA), you who are in nature indestructible inseparability (VAJRA BHAVA), the great pledge being, the vajra holy mind (MAHA SAMAYA SATTVA), the vajra holy speech (AH), the transcendental wisdom of great bliss (HUM), clarifying the transcendental wisdom of inseparable bliss and emptiness and destroying the dualistic mind that obstructs it (PHAT).

The Power of the Mantra

Reciting the Vajrasattva mantra daily or in a long retreat—usually three months with one hundred thousand mantras—is considered the supreme method of purification. Through the practice we are able to not only purify our general nonvirtues but even the very heavy negativities, such as breaking the bodhisattva or tantric vows.

If negative karma is not purified with a practice such as Vajrasattva it continuously increases day by day, month by month, year by year. Even though we might not have killed any human beings or performed any other heavy negative actions, small negative actions become like huge mountains.

Therefore in order to stop that terrifying growth, everybody needs a powerful daily purification practice such as the Thirty-Five Buddhas or Vajrasattva.

It is said in the teachings,

> To the wise man, even a great negativity becomes small;
> to the fool, even a small negativity becomes huge.[106]

The wise are wise in the profound methods of purification and renunciation, wise in practicing bodhichitta, wise in meditating on emptiness. For such a person, even if they have created much heavy negative karma, it becomes weak because they have the means to purify it.

For example, in his early life, Milarepa used black magic to destroy the house where some enemies of his mother were enjoying a wedding feast, killing the many guests who were upstairs and the horses who were tied up downstairs. Afterward, repenting his act, he asked the lama who taught him the black magic what to do. The lama advised him to go to the great lama Marpa, who put him through a series of great hardships—such as building a nine-story house with his own hands, not once but three times—in order to overcome his negativities. Each time he had finished, Marpa had him tear it down and start again. Marpa scolded him and beat him many times, refusing to give him the teachings he wanted.

All these things became his preliminary practices, like doing many hundreds of thousands of Vajrasattva mantras and prostrations. Through this, Milarepa purified unimaginable obscurations and created unbelievable merit. By correctly following his guru Marpa's advice, he achieved the complete path to enlightenment in one lifetime.

On the other hand, even though the foolish person might not create many very negative actions, because they have no idea about purification, their karmic results become bigger and bigger. It is like a small amount of poison that has gone inside the stomach, spreading throughout the system, or like a small candle flame that can destroy a forest, a mountainside, or a whole city. Even though the negative karma is tiny, the harm is great.

If we examine the negative karmas we create in one day, even one hundred thousand rebirths in the animal, hungry ghost, and hell realms would not exhaust the suffering results of that one day's accumulation. The negative karmas that throw us into the lower realms don't need to be heavy ones. The Kadampa geshes[107] say, "While laughing and playing, just by moving our lips, we sink into the lower realms." This means that whatever we do thoughtlessly, frivolously, meaninglessly, even if it is just fooling around, becomes the cause to be reborn in the lower realms. Knowing this, when we have such a profound method of purification like Vajrasattva, how can we not think of using it?

We should all do the Vajrasattva practice every day, even if our Dharma understanding is limited or we are unable to do many retreats. In this way, we pacify the inner cause of our problems and experience more happiness and peace. If we live our life like this, when the day of our death comes, our negative karma will have become much weaker, causing much less distraction, and allowing us more chance of dying with a virtuous, happy mind, one that is free of worry and fear. Then we will more easily find a better body in our future life and be able to train our mind in the path.

To be able to do a three-month Vajrasattva retreat where we recite the mantra one hundred thousand times is truly incredible. It is stated that the Vajrasattva mantra is so powerful that reciting it that many times purifies any infraction of the root tantric vows, and even the five immediate and the five near-immediate negativities are purified. As we have seen, any of the five immediate negativities—killing your mother or father, killing an arhat, drawing blood from a buddha, and causing disunity in the sangha—causes us to be reborn in the lowest hell immediately after this life. The five near-immediate negatives are similar in having that result. They are killing a bodhisattva, killing an arya not yet an arhat, defiling our mother or a female arhat through sexual misconduct, stealing property from the sangha, and destroying a stupa. Vajrasattva purifies all negativities relating to the sangha, such as making a living through selling holy objects, as well as negativities relating to the Dharma. It purifies all the degenerated vows, such as criticizing the guru. To be able to purify whatever karma we have on our mindstream that brings such a result—can there be anything more worthwhile in life to do than this?

Purification does not depend solely on the number of mantras recited. As Pabongka Dechen Nyingpo explained, the effectiveness of the purification comes from both strong regret and strong determination not to commit the negative action again. These two factors make the purification extremely powerful. And, as I have said many times, a pure motivation is crucial and the best motivation is bodhichitta.

The most important reason for doing the practice of purification is to be able to generate the realizations of the path to enlightenment so we can do perfect work to bring all sentient beings to enlightenment. That's the main aim. Even if our life is so busy that there is not much time to do sitting practice, if we can live our life with the thought of benefiting all sentient beings, when we recite even one Vajrasattva mantra with bodhichitta, we receive the same benefit as having recited one hundred thousand Vajrasattva mantras.

But doing a Vajrasattva purification practice every day takes care of everything else by the way. It takes care of health, it ensures a long life, it overcomes obstacles to being successful, but most importantly, it overcomes obstacles to practicing the Dharma.

Vajrasattva Purifies Broken Vows

A lamrim text explains four ways to make our life most meaningful.

- The best way to live is to always live in the vows.
- The best way to act is to always act with a positive motivation.
- The best way to offer is to see all holy objects as embodiments of the guru.
- The best way to give is to give the Dharma.

The first way to make our life meaningful is to live in the vows. There are various levels of vows we can take to protect our karma, from the pratimoksha vows, such as the five lay vows and the vows of ordained sangha, up to the tantric vows,[108] and these vows are the tools we can use to most quickly accumulate merit. Unless we take and then keep our vows purely, enlightenment is impossible.

As Lama Tsongkhapa said in the *Foundation of All Good Qualities*,

> Even if I develop only bodhichitta, without practicing the three
>   types of morality
> I will not achieve enlightenment.

With my clear recognition of this,
please bless me to practice the bodhisattva vows with great
energy.[109]

If our morality degenerates, we become like a pot with no bottom—no matter how much delicious food we put in it, it runs straight through. We have no base for realizations. Although Lama Tsongkhapa mentions the bodhisattva vows here, this is true of all levels of vows. Without the morality of the pratimoksha vows, there can be no realizations. The more purely we keep the pratimoksha vows, the more quickly we are able to achieve the realizations of the lamrim topics, the three principal aspects of the path, and the two stages of highest yoga tantra: the generation stage and the completion stage.

Whether we are living in one, five, or a thousand vows, we accumulate an inconceivable amount of merit every second. On the other hand, when we break one of the vows we have pledged to keep in front of our guru, we create oceans of negative karma and have downfalls pour down on us like a tropical rain shower. The higher the vow we have taken, the heavier the karma we create by breaking it. The consequences of breaking a secondary bodhisattva vow are one hundred thousand times heavier than of breaking a pratimoksha root vow. And the consequences of breaking a secondary tantric vow are one hundred thousand times greater than of breaking a bodhisattva root vow.

Reciting the Vajrasattva mantra every day is vital if we have taken any level of vows, especially if we have taken a tantric initiation and have been given the bodhisattva and tantric vows. Because of their great subtlety, tantric vows can be very easily degenerated, and so we need to constantly purify whatever vows we have broken.

We might be quite daunted if we consider just this point, and the question might arise, "Since I seem to be incapable of keeping these vows purely, meaning negativities pour down on me like rainfall, how is it possible for me to achieve enlightenment?" Lama Atisha answered this question by explaining that the Vajrasattva practice is like throwing one stone to chase away a hundred birds. This means that doing the one practice of Vajrasattva can purify everything.

If we are put off taking initiations because we are scared of the vows, we will never get to plant the seed of the quick path to enlightenment. In one way it is difficult, because we do not have the very basic realizations, so our mind is very uncontrolled and we constantly break vows and receive downfalls. But on the other hand, we have the skillful means to purify all these negative karmas and infractions, especially with the highest yoga tantra aspect of Vajrasattva with the wisdom mother. Even the heaviest karmas can be purified with this aspect. Therefore, whoever has taken a highest yoga tantra initiation should visualize Vajrasattva with the wisdom mother in order to purify any tantric vows that have been broken.

How to Practice with Vajrasattva's Mantra

The Four Opponent Powers

If you recite the Vajrasattva mantra or do prostrations to the Thirty-Five Buddhas, in order to make the purification most effective, it is extremely important to incorporate it with the four opponent powers:

1. the power of dependence
2. the power of regret
3. the power of remedy
4. the power of the restraint

The first of the four powers is the power of dependence. This can also be called the "power of reliance on the holy object" or the "power of faculty of the holy object." It refers to taking refuge in the Three Rare Sublime Ones and generating bodhichitta. By taking refuge you save yourself from harm, and by generating bodhichitta you save others from harm.

The second power is the power of regret. Seeing you have created one specific negative action, or negative actions in general, you recognize that you have unwittingly created the cause for suffering. Understanding this, you naturally regret it. Thinking in this way takes very little time and it is easy and very effective for the mind. The more you understand the shortcomings of negative karma and the more you can regret having committed negative acts, the more powerful your purification will be.

Regret is not guilt; it is not living your life weighed down by guilt. Regret is the wisdom to see you have harmed yourself and others by doing that action. When you see that, the resolve not to repeat the action comes naturally. With regret comes the power to change the situation.

The third power is the power of the remedy. The texts often cite six ways of practicing the power of the remedy: reciting the names of the buddhas, reciting purifying mantras, making holy objects, reciting emptiness texts, meditating on emptiness or bodhichitta, and making offerings to the Three Rare Sublime Ones. Of these, the Vajrasattva practice is the perfect remedy.

Even when you purify very strongly, you can still suffer. People who do retreats such as Vajrasattva often have illnesses, pain, and even mental problems. That does not mean the purification is ineffectual or you are creating more negative karma. Far from it. Like a burst boil oozes pus, you are seeing the effects of purifying. Rather than experiencing eons in the lowest hells, you suffer a few days of stomach pains. Therefore that pain is a good sign that you are purifying, and that the practice is benefiting you.

The final power is the power of restraint, resolving not to do the action again. Pabongka Dechen Nyingpo said that this power means that you think, "From now on, even if it costs me my life, I won't commit this negative karma again." If you can do this strongly enough, you can completely destroy the negative karmic imprint of the action. Purifying less strongly will not completely destroy it but will lessen its effect. I often advise that if it is unrealistic to think you will never do that action again, then choose a feasible length of time you can restrain from doing it, such as a day, an hour, or even a minute, and then resolve to restrain from doing it for that period.

Ways to Visualize the Purification

Whether you do a formal Vajrasattva meditation or simply recite some mantras as you are walking along the road, as you recite you should visualize Vajrasattva (either with or without the wisdom mother) above your head and nectar flowing from his heart into you. I will describe various ways of doing this, but you can modify it to suit your circumstances.

Visualize Vajrasattva at whatever size suits you—small, the size of a person, or the size of Mount Everest. If Vajrasattva, the moon disk at his heart, and the mantra around the moon disk were all the same bright white color, your visualization might not be clear because you might be unable to differentiate the features. You can therefore visualize Vajrasattva's holy body as crystal, the moon disk at his heart as the color of a conch shell, and the mantras as silver. Although they are all white, making them slightly different shades aids clear visualization. The lotus is also white, as is the moon disk. Everything is white. The function of Vajrasattva is to pacify negative karmas, obscurations, disease, and harm from spirits, and the color white signifies the action of pacifying.

As you recite the mantra, there are three ways to visualize the nectar that flows from the heart of Vajrasattva (or the hearts of the deity father and mother) into your body.

The first way is called "chasing from above," which means purifying downward. It is like washing a bottle that is black with dirt under a tap, so that all the dirt flushes away and the bottle becomes sparkling clean and clear. Visualize nectar in the form of a white beam of light coming from Vajrasattva's heart and the heart of the wisdom mother, joining at the place of union and flowing in through the top of your head. It fills your body from above, causing all your negative karmas and obscurations to come out of the lower part of the body in the form of a dirty black liquid, like liquid coal sludge. In a more advanced visualization, you can imagine disease coming out in the form of blood and pus, spirit harm in the form snakes or other animals, and all negative karma and obscurations in the form of liquid smoke or sludge.

These flow out of you into a crack in the earth all the way to where the Lord of Death resides. You can visualize him as he appears in the illustration of the wheel of life, to signify impermanence and death. He is looking up, and the ocean of negativities, in whatever form you have visualized them, pour into his wide-open mouth. His mouth closes and is sealed with a golden double vajra. The crack in the earth closes up, making it impossible for the Lord of Death to return. In this way, you stop the danger of untimely death.

The second way is called "purifying from below," which is like pouring milk into a glass with some dirt in the bottom. As the milk fills the glass, the dirt is pushed to the top. Similarly, the nectar flows down into the body and pushes up all the negative karmas, in the form of liquid coal sludge, which goes out through the mouth and nose. You can imagine all the negative karmas blown straight out and away, like a hat blown by the wind.

Then, with the third way, called "purifying from the center," all the negative karmas and obscurations are chased away by the light pouring into the heart, like when you turn on a light and all the darkness in the room disappears immediately. Similarly, all the negative karmas and obscurations in the form of darkness at the heart become completely nonexistent as nectar flows into the heart.

A Short Vajrasattva Meditation[110]

Visualization

On your right side is your father; on your left side is your mother. Your enemies and those sentient beings who make you agitated are in front of you, and your friends and those you are attached to are seated behind you. All other universal living beings, in human form, are surrounding you, as far as you can imagine.

Visualize your object of refuge, the merit field, in the space in front of you, either elaborately or in the one aspect of Buddha Shakyamuni. As you recite the verse below, think that you and all sentient beings are together taking refuge in the Three Rare Sublime Ones.

The Power of Dependence: Taking Refuge

I forever take refuge in Buddha, Dharma, and Sangha, and in all
the three vehicles,
in the dakinis of secret mantra yoga, in the heroes and heroines,
in the empowering goddesses and the bodhisattvas.
But most of all, I take refuge in my holy Guru forever. *(3x)*

The Power of Regret

Think, "Almost every action I do, twenty-four hours a day, is motivated
by worldly concern, attachment to the comfort of this life. Nearly every
action I have ever created has been nonvirtuous, the cause of suffering.
Not only that, but I have also been continuously breaking my pratimoksha, bodhisattva, and tantric vows. Worst of all, I have created the
heaviest of negative karmas in relation to my virtuous friends—getting
angry at them, generating wrong views, having nondevotional thoughts
toward them, harming their holy bodies, and disobeying their advice.

"Having these negative imprints on my mental continuum is unbearable. It's as if I've swallowed a lethal poison. I must practice the antidote
right away and purify all these negative karmas immediately, without
a second's delay."

In this way, generate strong feelings of urgency and regret.

Remembering Impermanence and Death

Think, "Many people my age or younger have died. It's a miracle that
I'm still alive and have this incredible opportunity to purify my negative
karma. Death is certain but its time is most uncertain. If I were to die
right now, I would definitely be born in the lower realms. Because I
could not practice Dharma there, I would remain in the lower realms
for countless eons. Therefore, how unbelievably fortunate I am to be
able to purify my negative karma right now, without even a second's
delay, by practicing the Vajrasattva meditation-recitation."

The Power of Dependence: Generating Bodhichitta

Think, "But I am not practicing this Vajrasattva purification for myself alone—the purpose of my life is to release all hell beings, hungry ghosts, animals, humans, demigods, gods, and intermediate state[111] beings from all their suffering and its causes and lead them to unsurpassed enlightenment. In order to do this, I must first reach enlightenment myself. Therefore, I must purify all my negative karma immediately by practicing the Vajrasattva meditation-recitation."

Visualization

Above the crown of your head, seated upon a lotus and moon seat, are Vajrasattva father and mother. Their bodies are white; each has one face and two arms. He holds a vajra and bell, she a curved knife and skull cup. They are embracing each other. The father is adorned with six mudras, the mother with five. He sits in the vajra posture, she in the lotus.

Vajrasattva is your root Guru, the holy mind of all the buddhas, the dharmakaya, who, out of his unbearable compassion that embraces you and all other sentient beings, appears in this form to purify you and all others.

Thinking in this way, your mind is transformed into guru devotion— the root of all blessings and realizations of the path to enlightenment.

On a moon disk at Vajrasattva's heart stands a HUM encircled by a garland of the hundred-syllable mantra. A powerful stream of white nectar flows from the HUM and mantra garland and you are cleansed of all sickness, spirit harm, negative karma, and obscurations.

The Power of the Remedy: Mantra Recitation

OM VAJRASATTVA SAMAYA MANUPALAYA / VAJRASATTVA
TVENOPATISHTHA / DRIDHO ME BHAVA / SUTOSHYO ME

BHAVA / SUPOSHYO ME BHAVA / ANURAKTO ME BHAVA
/ SARVA SIDDHIM ME PRAYACCHA / SARVA KARMA SU
CHAME / CHITTAM SHRIYAM KURU HUM / HA HA HA HA
HO / BHAGAVAN SARVA TATHAGATA / VAJRA MAME MUN-
CHA / VAJRA BHAVA MAHA SAMAYA SATTVA AH HUM PHAT
(*Recite this 21x, 100x, or as many times as you can.*)

Generating Faith in Having Been Purified

From the crown of your head, Guru Vajrasattva says, "Child of the race,
your negativities, obscurations, and broken and damaged pledges have
been completely purified." Generate strong faith that all is completely
purified just as Guru Vajrasattva has said.

The Power of Restraint: Refraining from Creating Negativities Again

Think, "Before Guru Vajrasattva, I vow never again to commit those
negative actions I can easily abstain from and not to commit for a day,
an hour, or at least a few seconds those negative actions I find it difficult
to abstain from."

Absorption

Guru Vajrasattva is extremely pleased with your pledge. Vajrasattva
father and mother melt into light and dissolve into you. Your body,
speech, and mind become inseparably one with Guru Vajrasattva's holy
body, speech, and mind.

Meditation on Emptiness

In emptiness, there is no I, creator of negative karma; there is no action
of creating negative karma; there is no negative karma created.

Place your mind in that emptiness for a little while. In this way, look at
all phenomena as empty—they do not exist from their own side. With
this awareness of emptiness, dedicate the merits.

Dedication

Think, "Due to all these merits of the three times collected by all the buddhas, bodhisattvas, myself, and all other sentient beings, which appear to be real from their own side, but which are totally empty, may the I, which appears to be real but is totally empty, achieve Guru Vajrasattva's enlightenment, which appears to be real but is totally empty, and lead all sentient beings, who appear to be real but are totally empty, to that enlightenment, which appears to be real but is totally empty, by myself alone, who appears to be real but is also totally empty, nonexistent from my own side."

Now finish with your usual dedication prayers.[112]

7. THE THIRTY-FIVE CONFESSION BUDDHAS

T O CLIMB A FLIGHT of stairs, we naturally put our foot on the first stair, the one right in front of us. Unless we do that, we won't be able to step onto the second or the third stair, and so on, and finally get upstairs. Just wishing to be upstairs to enjoy that comfortable bed won't get us there. Likewise, attaining enlightenment happens step-by-step, but whether we progress quickly or slowly—whether we can achieve enlightenment in one, two, or many lifetimes—depends on how well we observe the vows we have taken. The importance of keeping the vows, and purifying the ones we have broken, is explained very clearly in the Vajrayana teachings.

Besides continually reciting the Vajrasattva mantra to purify the negativities accumulated from having broken our vows, another very powerful way to purify them is by prostrating while reciting the *Confession Prayer* within the prayers and prostrations to the Thirty-Five Confession Buddhas.[113] The prayer is incredibly beneficial, especially for those of us trying to live within the vows we have taken. Just saying it once purifies eons of negative karma.

Why is reciting the Thirty-Five Confession Buddhas' names so beneficial? Lama Atisha explained that when the Thirty-Five Buddhas were bodhisattvas engaging in the bodhisattvas' deeds, they each made a prayer: "If I become enlightened, for any sentient being who holds my name, who prostrates while reciting my name, may such and such of their negative karmas be purified." Each Confession Buddha specified which negativity would be purified. One of the powers of a buddha is that any prayer they made before buddhahood is actualized when they achieve enlightenment. This means that when we recite their names, by the power of that prayer, our recitation has unbelievable power to purify the different negative karmas.

Don't think you have ever purified enough. Even Lama Tsongkhapa, who actualized the graduated path to enlightenment and achieved the fully enlightened state, recited this prayer with prostrations, doing thirty-five sets of prostrations to the Thirty-Five Buddhas many hundreds of thousands of times. He practiced this so much and so intently during his retreats that the Thirty-Five Confession Buddhas actually appeared to him in his cave. (The visualization we use in our tradition is according to Lama Tsongkhapa's vision.) Due to this purifying practice, his Dharma work for sentient beings became as infinite as space. This is the power of purification.

I once asked one of my gurus, Denma Locho Rinpoche,[114] why Lama Tsongkhapa's life story talks about him doing many hundreds of thousands of prostrations to the Thirty-Five Confession Buddhas but doesn't mention Vajrasattva. Rinpoche explained that the Thirty-Five Buddhas practice, if done well even once, can purify even the five immediate negativities. That's why, although the practice of Vajrasattva is also incredibly effective, the Thirty-Five Buddhas practice is emphasized in Lama Tsongkhapa's biographies.

Just like Lama Tsongkhapa, many other yogis have purified by prostrating to the Thirty-Five Buddhas and doing the confession prayer. I generally encourage my students to do this practice every morning, reciting each name, if possible, three times while prostrating. That way, it becomes more than a hundred prostrations. It is also very good to do it again in the evening. Doing it in the morning purifies negative karmas broken during the night, and doing it in the evening stops the negative karmas of the day from increasing. If that is not possible, then do whatever you can. If you can even just recite each name once and then prostrate, that is very good. Of course, if you can do more than a hundred, no question that is excellent.

Whether you recite the Vajrasattva mantra or do prostrations to the Thirty-Five Buddhas, in order to make the purification completely effective, it is extremely important to incorporate it with the four opponent powers, as we have seen with the Vajrasattva practice above.

THE THIRTY-FIVE BUDDHAS

The Thirty-Five Confession Buddhas are visualized as a merit field, arranged in five rows below Guru Shakyamuni Buddha.

At Shakyamuni Buddha's heart sits Thousand-Arm Chenrezig, and at Chenrezig's heart is the syllable HRIH. Beams of light are emitted from the HRIH, forming five rows in the space below. At the end of each of the thirty-four beams is a throne supported by elephants and adorned with pearls. On each throne is seated one of the Thirty-Five Buddhas.

The thrones are supported by elephants rather than snow lions as usual because the elephant is stronger and more powerful than any other animal, meaning your negativities will be strongly purified. Pearls are specifically mentioned because they are white, symbolizing completely purifying all negativities.

In the first, top, row are six buddhas, blue in color and in the aspect of Akshobhya. Their hands are in the mudra of granting the supreme, with their right hand on their right knee in the earth-touching mudra (like Shakyamuni) and their left in their lap in the meditation mudra, holding a begging bowl. The exception is the third buddha (the fourth in the list below), King Lord of the Nagas, who has a blue-colored body but a white head. He holds his hands in a teaching mudra, with both hands at the heart.

In the second row are seven buddhas, white in color and in the aspect of Vairochana, their hands in the mudra of supreme enlightenment.

In the third row are seven buddhas, yellow in color and in the aspect of Ratnasambhava, their hands in the mudra of granting supreme realizations.

In the fourth row are seven buddhas, red in color and in the aspect of Amitabha, their hands in the lap in the mudra of concentration, holding a begging bowl.

In the fifth row are seven buddhas, green in color and in the aspect of Amoghasiddhi, their left hand in the mudra of concentration and their right in the mudra of giving refuge.

With Shakyamuni, these are the Thirty-Five Confession Buddhas. Each one is in the posture of the particular buddha of that buddha family.

THE BENEFITS OF RECITING THE NAMES

There are two main texts that explain the benefits of prostrating to each of the Thirty-Five Confession Buddhas. One is by Lama Atisha and the other is by Gyaltsap Jé, Lama Tsongkhapa's disciple. There is also another text by Ngulchu Dharmabhadra[115] that explains it a little bit differently.

The first of the Thirty-Five Confession Buddhas is the founder, Shakyamuni Buddha.

1. Shakyamuni Buddha

> *[Lama] tön pa chom den dä de zhin sheg pa dra chom pa yang dag par dzog päi sang gyä päl gyäl wa sha kya thub pa la chhag tshäl lo*[116]

To the founder, bhagavan, tathagata, arhat, perfectly completed buddha, glorious conqueror Shakyamuni Buddha, I prostrate.

With *lama tön pa chom den dä*, it says that the lama is the founder of the present Buddhadharma, the one who has been constantly guiding us from beginningless rebirths. For *chom den dä*, as we have seen with Vajrasattva, *chom* means "having destroyed," so he has destroyed the delusions. (I say "he" because we are talking about Shakyamuni Buddha, but if we are talking about Tara it's "she." Unlike English, Tibetan does not have this distinction.) *Den dä* means "having all the qualifications and transcended the world."

When you say *lama* at the very beginning, you reinforce that meaning of the ultimate guru. Everything is that quality. The meaning of just that very first word, *lama*, is unimaginable. It is like the limitless sky; everything refers to that. When you get ready to recite *lama tön pa chom den dä*, you can first think a little bit about the guru, what *lama* means, and then recite it. In that way, it becomes unbelievably rich.

When Lama Tsongkhapa first saw the Thirty-Five Buddhas while doing seven hundred thousand prostrations at Wolka Chölung in Tibet, he saw them without heads. This is because he recited the prayer without the words *de zhin sheg pa*, meaning "tathagata," which explains that quality of the buddhas. But afterward, when he recited *de zhin shek pa*, he saw them with heads.

Some texts say reciting Guru Shakyamuni Buddha's name purifies forty thousand eons of negative karma and some say eighty thousand eons, but in the Kangyur it says that reciting this name once purifies one hundred million eons of negative karma, and on top of that, hundreds and thousands more.

Reciting the names of the remaining thirty-four buddhas brings different benefits.

2. Thoroughly Destroying with Vajra Essence

De zhin sheg pa dor je nying pö rab tu jom pa la chhag tshäl lo

To Tathagata Thoroughly Destroying with Vajra Essence, I prostrate.

Thoroughly Destroying with Vajra Essence (Dor je nying pö) purifies ten thousand eons of negative karma. Also, by reciting it, you become enlightened.

3. Radiant Jewel

De zhin sheg pa rin chhen ö thrö la chhag tshäl lo

To Tathagata Radiant Jewel, I prostrate.

Radiant Jewel (Rin chhen ö thrö) purifies ten thousand eons of negative karma as well. For anybody who hears the name of this buddha, all their wishes succeed, and if a woman hears this name, she will become a wheel-turning king. That's what it says! I don't know. Also, hearing this name is the cause to receive a long life and help from the gods.

4. King, Lord of the Nagas

De zhin sheg pa lu wang gi gyäl po la chhag tshäl lo

To Tathagata King, Lord of the Nagas, I prostrate.

King, Lord of the Nagas (Lu wang gi gyäl po), also purifies a thousand eons of negative karma, as well as purifying harm from nagas. Because this buddha liberated so many nagas from suffering, benefiting and healing them, they are indebted to him. So, if you recite the name of the King, Lord of the Nagas, any sicknesses caused by nagas will be cured.

5. Army of Heroes

De zhin sheg pa pa wöi de la chhag tshäl lo

To Tathagata Army of Heroes, I prostrate.

Army of Heroes (Pa wöi de) purifies the negative karma of gossiping. Ngulchu Dharmabhadra says that it purifies all the negative karmas of speech.[117]

6. Delighted Hero

De zhin sheg pa päl gye la chhag tshäl lo

To Tathagata Delighted Hero, I prostrate.

Delighted Hero (Päl gye) purifies two thousand eons of negative karma.

7. Jewel Fire

De zhin sheg pa rin chhen me la chag tsäl lo

To Tathagata Jewel Fire, I prostrate.

Jewel Fire (Rin chhen me) purifies the negative karmas of the mind that have been stained by the pollution of the sangha. When people make offerings to the sangha, because they have delusions, the offerings are polluted, which can affect any sangha member who is not yet an arya being. Reciting this name protects against that.

According to Dharmabhadra, reciting the name once purifies a hundred thousand eons of causing disunity within the sangha or criticizing the arya sangha.[118] *The Preliminary Practice of Prostrations* also says this name purifies the five immediate negativities, especially that of causing disunity among the sangha.[119]

8. Jewel Moonlight

De zhin sheg pa rin chhen da ö la chhag tshäl lo

To Tathagata Jewel Moonlight, I prostrate.

Jewel Moonlight (Rin chhen da ö) purifies eight thousand eons of negative karma of the mind. It purifies having criticized the arya sangha. Ngulchu Dharmabhadra says that *all* the negative karmas collected with the mind are purified.[120]

9. Meaningful to See

De zhin sheg pa tong wa dön yö la chhag tshäl lo

To Tathagata Meaningful to See, I prostrate.

Meaningful to See (Tong wa dön yö) purifies a thousand eons of negative karma and the five immediate negativities—killing your father, mother, or an arhat, and so forth—which usually lead to being immediately reborn in the lowest hell after death without any intervening life. Even if you have committed one of these negative karmas, it is purified by reciting the name of Meaningful to See.

10. Jewel Moon

De zhin sheg pa rin chhen da wa la chhag tshäl lo

To Tathagata Jewel Moon, I prostrate.

With Jewel Moon (Rin chhen da wa), the five immediate negativities are purified, especially killing your father.

11. Stainless One

De zhin sheg pa dri ma me pa la chhag tshäl lo

To Tathagata Stainless One, I prostrate.

Stainless One (Dri ma me pa) purifies the five near immediate negativities. The *Preliminary Practice of Prostrations* also mentions it purifies the negative karma collected from stepping over the shadow of a stupa.[121]

12. Bestowed with Courage

De zhin sheg pa pä jin la chhag tshäl lo

To Tathagata Bestowed with Courage, I prostrate.

From the five immediate negativities, Bestowed with Courage (Pä jin) purifies the karma of having killed an arhat. It also purifies the negative karmas collected through becoming angry.

13. Pure One

De zhin sheg pa tshang pa la chhag tshäl lo

To Tathagata Pure One, I prostrate.

Pure One (Tshang pa) purifies the negative karmas collected through attachment. According to Ngulchu Dharmabhadra, the negative karma of malevolently causing a buddha to bleed is also purified.[122]

14. Bestowed with Purity

De zhin sheg pa tshang pä jin la chhag tshäl lo

To Tathagata Bestowed with Purity, I prostrate.

With Bestowed with Purity (Tshang pä jin), ten thousand eons of negative karma are purified, as well as the nonvirtue of causing disunity among the sangha.

15. Water God

De zhin sheg pa chhu lha la chhag tshäl lo

To Tathagata Water God, I prostrate.

With Water God (Chhu lha), a thousand eons of negative karma are purified, as well as the near immediate negativity of defiling your mother or a female arhat.

16. Deity of the Water God

De zhin sheg pa chhu lhäi lha la chhag tshäl lo

To Tathagata Deity of the Water God, I prostrate.

According to Ngulchu Dharmabhadra, with Deity of the Water God (Chhu lhäi lha), the negative karma of killing a bodhisattva is purified, as well as five thousand eons of negative karma.[123]

17. Glorious Goodness

De zhin sheg pa päl zang la chhag tshäl lo

To Tathagata Glorious Goodness, I prostrate.

Glorious Goodness (Päl zang) purifies five thousand eons of negative karma, as well as the negative karma of having killed the vajra master. The term used in the text is *lobpen*, which can mean guru or preceptor.

18. Glorious Sandalwood

De zhin sheg pa tsän dän päl la chhag tshäl lo

To Tathagata Glorious Sandalwood, I prostrate.

Glorious Sandalwood (Tsän dän päl) purifies seven thousand eons of negative karma, as well as having taken money, food, or offerings given to the sangha. If you have harmed the sangha by taking away what brings them together, those negative karmas are purified.

19. Infinite Splendor

De zhin sheg pa zi ji tha yä la chhag tshäl lo

To Tathagata Infinite Splendor, I prostrate.

Infinite Splendor (Zi ji tha yä) purifies seven eons of negative karma, as well as the negative karma of having destroyed stupas.

20. Glorious Light

De zhin sheg pa ö päl la chhag tshäl lo

To Tathagata Glorious Light, I prostrate.

Glorious Light (Ö päl) purifies seven eons of negative karma, as well as the negative karma collected through anger. You must relate this to your own life and see how often you get angry and how easy it is to do so. However, no matter how destructive anger is, by reciting the name of Glorious Light, you can purify all the negative karma you have created through anger.

21. Sorrowless Glory

De zhin sheg pa nya ngän me päi päl la chhag tshäl lo

To Tathagata Sorrowless Glory, I prostrate.

With Sorrowless Glory (Nya ngän me päi päl), the negative karma collected through attachment is purified. Gyaltsap Jé, Lama Tsongkhapa's older disciple, and Dharmabhadra both mention that.[124]

22. Son of Noncraving

De zhin sheg pa se me kyi bu la chhag tshäl lo

To Tathagata Son of Non-Craving, I prostrate.

With Son of Noncraving (Se me kyi bu), Ngulchu Dharmabhadra says ten thousand eons of negative karma are purified.[125] Gyaltsap Jé said whatever imprints left on the mind by having created negative karma are purified.[126]

23. Glorious Flower

De zhin sheg pa me tog päl la chhag tshäl lo

To Tathagata Glorious Flower, I prostrate.

Glorious Flower (Me tog päl) purifies the negative karma collected with the body, which means through physical actions. Gyaltsap Jé says one hundred thousand eons of negative karma are purified.[127] After Shakyamuni Buddha's verse, this purifies the greatest amount of negative karma.

24. Pure Light Rays Clearly Knowing by Play

De zhin sheg pa tshang päi ö zer nam par röl pä ngön par khyen pa la chhag tshäl lo

To Tathagata Pure Light Rays Clearly Knowing by Play, I prostrate.

Pure Light Rays Clearly Knowing by Play (Tshang päi ö zer nam par röl pä ngön par khyen pa) purifies negative karmas collected with speech. According to Ngulchu Dharmabhadra, one thousand eons of negative karma are purified.[128]

25. Lotus Light Rays Clearly Knowing by Play

De zhin sheg pa pä mäi ö zer nam par röl pä ngön par kyen pa la chhag tshäl lo

To Tathagata Lotus Light Rays Clearly Knowing by Play, I prostrate.

Lotus Light Rays Clearly Knowing by Play (Pä mäi ö zer nam par röl pä ngön par kyen pa) purifies seven eons of negative karma.

26. Glorious Wealth

De zhin sheg pa nor päl la chhag tshäl lo

To Tathagata Glorious Wealth, I prostrate.

Again, with Glorious Wealth (Nor päl), imprints left on the mind by committing negative karma are purified. It is also said that engaging in activities that pollute the sangha is purified.

27. Glorious Mindfulness

De zhin sheg pa drän päi päl la chhag tshäl lo

To Tathagata Glorious Mindfulness, I prostrate.

Glorious Mindfulness (Drän päi päl) purifies the negative karma of having criticized holy beings.

28. Glorious Name Widely Renowned

De zhin sheg pa tshän päl shin tu yong drag la chhag tshäl lo

To Tathagata Glorious Name Widely Renowned, I prostrate.

With Glorious Name Widely Renowned (Tshän päl shin tu yong drag), the negative karma collected with the body, through physical actions, is purified. It purifies the negative karma of being unhappy with a buddha descending to this world. Instead of rejoicing, you feel the opposite. Gyaltsap Jé also mentions that the negative karma collected through jealousy is purified.[129]

29. King Holding the Victory Banner of Foremost Power

De zhin sheg pa wang pöi tog gi gyäl tshän gyi gyäl po la chhag tshäl lo

To Tathagata King Holding the Victory Banner of Foremost Power, I prostrate.

King Holding the Victory Banner of Foremost Power (Wang pöi tog gi gyäl tshän gyi gyäl po) purifies having caused other sentient beings to collect negative karma and the negative karma you have collected by slandering others. *The Preliminary Practice of Prostrations* says the negative karma collected through pride and jealousy is purified.[130]

30. Glorious One Totally Subduing

De zhin sheg pa shin tu nam par nön päi päl la chhag tshäl lo

To Tathagata Glorious One Totally Subduing, I prostrate.

Glorious One Totally Subduing (Shin tu nam par nön päi päl) purifies subtle negative karmas, mainly to do with slander. Gyaltsap Jé says causing others to create negative karma is purified.[131]

31. Utterly Victorious in Battle

De zhin sheg pa yül lä shin tu nam par gyäl wa la chhag tshäl lo

To Tathagata Utterly Victorious in Battle, I prostrate.

For Utterly Victorious in Battle (Yül lä shin tu nam par gyäl wa), Gyaltsap Jé says reciting this name purifies all delusions and Dharmabhadra says it purifies the negative karma collected with pride.

By reciting this name, the negative karmas of rejoicing in others doing negative karma are purified. For example, rejoicing when there is a war. Let's say a Tibetan person rejoices when he hears that a hundred Chinese soldiers have been killed in a war. That person gets the same heavy karma as if he had killed those hundred human beings.

32. Glorious Transcendence through Subduing

De zhin sheg pa nam par nön pä sheg päi päl la chhag tshäl lo

To Tathagata Glorious Transcendence through Subduing, I prostrate.

Glorious Transcendence through Subduing (Nam par nön pä sheg päi päl) purifies the negative karmas collected by slandering others, as well as causing others to create negative karma.

33. Glorious Manifestations Illuminating All

De zhin sheg pa kün nä nang wa kö päi päl la chhag tshäl lo

To Tathagata Glorious Manifestations Illuminating All, I
prostrate.

Glorious Manifestations Illuminating All (Kün nä nang wa kö päi päl)
purifies having caused others to engage in negative karma and rejoicing
when others create negative karma.

34. All-Subduing Jewel Lotus

De zhin sheg pa rin chhen pä mäi nam par nön pa la chhag tshäl lo

To Tathagata All-Subduing Jewel Lotus, I prostrate.

With All-Subduing Jewel Lotus (Rin chhen pä mäi nam par nön pa),
you purify the very heavy negative karma of having abandoned the holy
Dharma, which means losing all respect for and reliance on any of the
Buddha's teachings.

For example, say that because you don't understand a teaching you
have heard, you reject it, thinking the fault lies with the teaching rather
than your lack of understanding. To think like that is to avoid the holy
Dharma, which is a heavier negative karma than having destroyed all
the temples, statues, stupas, and scriptures in this world. What you
must think in such a situation is that, although you can't appreciate
and understand the teaching now, you determine that you will be able
to do so in the future.

You also have to be very careful disposing of Dharma texts. Traditionally, damaged texts or texts that people can no longer keep are kept
in a stupa or a special house like a *tsatsa* house;[132] they are not burned.
When that isn't possible, you can respectfully offer fire to the Dharma
texts you can no longer keep. As the letters of the text are burned, you
can imagine them becoming empty, or imagine them absorbing into
your heart in the form of the syllable AH. You should never throw any
Dharma texts in the garbage because that's the equivalent of seeing
them as garbage, which is avoiding the holy Dharma.

35. King, Lord of the Mountains Firmly Seated on Jewel and Lotus

De zhin sheg pa dra chom pa yang dag par dzog päi sang gyä rin po chhe dang pä ma la rab tu zhug pa ri wang gi gyäl po la chhag tshäl lo

To Tathagata, arhat, perfectly completed buddha, King, Lord of the Mountains Firmly Seated on Jewel and Lotus, I prostrate.

King, Lord of the Mountains Firmly Seated on Jewel and Lotus (Dra chom pa yang dag par dzog päi sang gyä rin po chhe dang pä ma la rab tu zhug pa ri wang gi gyäl po) purifies the negative karma of having criticized the guru. It also purifies degenerated samaya vows. It is a good idea to recite this buddha's name three times. As criticizing the guru is the heaviest negative karma and something that happens very easily, if you can recite a mala of this name, that is excellent.

How to Practice with the Thirty-Five Confession Buddhas[133]

This is an abbreviated practice of prostrating to the Thirty-Five Confession Buddhas.

In the space in front of you, visualize your guru in the aspect of Shakyamuni Buddha, with Thousand-Arm Chenrezig at his heart.

At the heart of Thousand-Arm Chenrezig is the syllable HRIH ཧྲཱིཿ. Beams of light are emitted from the HRIH, forming five rows in the space below. At the end of each of the thirty-four beams is a throne supported by elephants and adorned with pearls and on each throne is seated one of the Thirty-Five Buddhas [as described above on page 137]. If you like, you can also visualize a row of the seven Medicine Buddhas below the Thirty-Five Buddhas and prostrate to them as well.

Think that each one of these buddhas is the embodiment of all the Buddha, Dharma, Sangha, and all statues, stupas, and scriptures of the three times and ten directions, whose essence is the Guru. Have complete faith that each one has the power to purify all your negative karma and imprints collected from beginningless time.

Now imagine that you emanate numberless bodies and that, as you prostrate, all these bodies—in all directions, covering every atom of the earth—prostrate along with you.

Then, before you start prostrating and saying the names of the Thirty-Five Buddhas, increase the merit by taking refuge:

> To Bhagavan, Tathagata, Arhat, Perfectly Complete Buddha, Precious Victory Banner, I prostrate. (*7x*)

> OM NAMO BHAGAVATE RATNA KETU RAJAYA / TATHAGA-TAYA / ARHATE SAMYAK SAMBUDDHAYA / TADYATHA / OM RATNE RATNE MAHA RATNE RATNA BIJA YE SVAHA (*7x*)

> OM NAMO MANJUSHRIYE / NAMAH SUSHRIYE / NAMA UTTAMA SHRIYE SVAHA (*3x*)

Homage to the *Confession of a Bodhisattva's Downfalls.*

> I, [say your name], throughout all times, take refuge in the Guru.
> I take refuge in the Buddha.
> I take refuge in the Dharma.
> I take refuge in the Sangha. (*3x*)

Then, while prostrating, recite the name of each buddha as many times as you can. At the end of reciting the names of the Thirty-Five

Confession Buddhas, you can also recite the name of the Medicine Buddhas once while prostrating.

> To the founder, bhagavan, tathagata, arhat, perfectly completed buddha, glorious conqueror Shakyamuni Buddha, I prostrate.

> To Tathagata Thoroughly Destroying with Vajra Essence, I prostrate.
> To Tathagata Radiant Jewel, I prostrate.
> To Tathagata King, Lord of the Nagas, I prostrate.
> To Tathagata Army of Heroes, I prostrate.
> To Tathagata Delighted Hero, I prostrate.
> To Tathagata Jewel Fire, I prostrate.
> To Tathagata Jewel Moonlight, I prostrate.
> To Tathagata Meaningful to See, I prostrate.
> To Tathagata Jewel Moon, I prostrate.
> To Tathagata Stainless One, I prostrate.
> To Tathagata Bestowed with Courage, I prostrate.
> To Tathagata Pure One, I prostrate.
> To Tathagata Bestowed with Purity, I prostrate.
> To Tathagata Water God, I prostrate.
> To Tathagata Deity of the Water God, I prostrate.
> To Tathagata Glorious Goodness, I prostrate.
> To Tathagata Glorious Sandalwood, I prostrate.
> To Tathagata Infinite Splendor, I prostrate.
> To Tathagata Glorious Light, I prostrate.
> To Tathagata Sorrowless Glory, I prostrate.
> To Tathagata Son of Noncraving, I prostrate.
> To Tathagata Glorious Flower, I prostrate.
> To Tathagata Pure Light Rays Clearly Knowing by Play, I prostrate.
> To Tathagata Lotus Light Rays Clearly Knowing by Play, I prostrate.

To Tathagata Glorious Wealth, I prostrate.

To Tathagata Glorious Mindfulness, I prostrate.

To Tathagata Glorious Name Widely Renowned, I prostrate.

To Tathagata King Holding the Victory Banner of Foremost Power, I prostrate.

To Tathagata Glorious One Totally Subduing, I prostrate.

To Tathagata Utterly Victorious in Battle, I prostrate.

To Tathagata Glorious Transcendence Through Subduing, I prostrate.

To Tathagata Glorious Manifestations Illuminating All, I prostrate.

To Tathagata All-Subduing Jewel Lotus, I prostrate.

To Tathagata, arhat, perfectly completed buddha, King, Lord of the Mountains Firmly Seated on Jewel and Lotus, I prostrate.

Then, either recite the confession prayer and general confession, and close the session with the mantra of pure morality and the prayer to keep pure morality, as in the practice in FPMT's *Confession of Downfalls: Prostrations to the Thirty-Five Buddhas*, or just finish with your normal dedications.

8. THE FIVE GREAT MANTRAS

The Mantras

There are five great mantras for liberating sentient beings from the lower realms:

1. The Kunrik Mantra
2. The Mitrukpa Mantra
3. The Namgyalma Mantras
4. The Stainless Pinnacle Deity Mantra
5. The Wish-Granting Wheel Mantra

Besides these mantras, there are other powerful mantras, such as the powerful mantras for benefiting beings at death and the four dharmakaya relic mantras, which are incredibly beneficial in protecting us in our life and helping us when we or somebody else is dying.[134]

The Benefits of the Mantras

These five great mantras are commonly used when an extremely powerful blessing is needed, such as when we bless water during an animal liberation practice or with a *jangwa* purifying puja when someone has died.

Generally, our next rebirth is determined by the final moment of the consciousness of this life, the mind we have right at the moment of death. The teaching on the twelve links of dependent origination explains that as we are dying, as our body ceases to function, the two links of craving and grasping cause us to seek another body. If the mind is dominated by negative thoughts such as anger or attachment, that ensures a rebirth in the lower realms. Due to anger, for instance, our grasping will lead us to a hellish intermediate state and then to rebirth in a hell realm. According to tantra, however, it is possible to change that while the person is in the intermediate state through the power of the tantric practice of *jangwa*, which includes reciting these mantras to the dying person, done by a powerful meditator with good concentration.

Of course, this type of practice is far too advanced for us, but we can make our life very meaningful with these mantras. Even our leisure time, such as going to the beach, can become meaningful, a cause for enlightenment, rather than just for our own pleasure and thus a cause for more samsara. By reciting these mantras over a container of sea water (or some water from our home already blessed) and then pouring it in the sea, we bless all the beings in the sea.

It's wonderful to help animals, but how can we *best* help them? On a very practical level, we can always be careful not to harm them, avoiding stepping on ants and so forth, but it would be so much better to bring them real peace and to make their lives meaningful, so sooner or later they can be reborn as a human being, meet the Dharma, and go on to attain liberation and enlightenment. One way we can do this is to say mantras to them whenever we encounter them. Although the animal has no logical understanding, there is power in the mantra that can help purify their delusions. Chenrezig's mantra, OM MANI PADME HUM, is especially good for this.

There is also the practice of animal liberation,[135] where we actively buy live animals from a place where they are going to be killed and sold for food, then release them in as safe a place as possible, somewhere where they can live without danger. Liberating animals is also a huge benefit to us humans. Prolonging the lives of the animals creates the cause for us to have a long life.

Much more beneficial than just saving their lives is to do it within the context of a Dharma event, thus giving them a Dharma imprint at the same time. When we are about to liberate an animal (or a million animals), we can say mantras and carry the animal while we circumambulate a stupa or other holy objects. The positive merit that the animal receives from such a practice is incalculable. On one level, we are saving that animal's life, and on another level, we are giving it the causes for full enlightenment. What more can anybody do for an animal?

Liberating animals can be a simple act or part of a ceremony involving many people and thousands of animals. In Singapore, Hong Kong, and Taiwan, they release animals by the tens of thousands, making an elaborate and wonderful ceremony of it. They set up an altar with many stupas filled with mantras, such as the four dharmakaya relic mantras, and many texts, such as teachings by Lama Tsongkhapa, prajnaparamita sutras, and so on. Then, they sprinkle the animals with water blessed by reciting the five great mantras as well as the names of the Thirty-Five Confession Buddhas and the Medicine Buddhas. While saying mantras over the animals, they circumambulate with them around an altar full of holy objects, each circumambulation creating the karma for the animals to achieve enlightenment. After that, they mindfully release them some place where they will be safe.

Placing the five great mantras on the body of a dying or dead being purifies their negative karma, meaning they are saved from rebirth in the lower realms. Kirti Tsenshab Rinpoche explains that the people of Amdo, in the lower part of Tibet, use a method where they print or write these mantras on paper and press them onto the person who is dying or dead to purify that person's negative karma.

If you drive, killing insects is unavoidable, and so having these mantras on your car is important. A long time ago, my attendant, Venerable Roger, decided we needed a car while we were in California, so he bought a red van. He was very excited. When I saw it, I thought, "This car belongs to all sentient beings," but the thought only lasted a couple of days.

Trying to think of how to protect the insects that were killed when they hit the windscreen, I decided to put some mantras on the car. Gradually, we added more and more—we made stickers of the mantras of the Thirty-Five Buddhas, Lama Tsongkhapa, Maitreya Buddha, White Tara, all the powerful mantras—and soon the car was covered. The idea is that the mantras that are on the car, especially these five very powerful mantras, have unbelievable power to purify the karma of any being that sees or touches them.

I often tell people in the West that having mantras such as Namg-yalma in the car is vital, because not only the sentient beings inside but also all beings who touch the car have their negative karma purified and they obtain a higher rebirth. When you drive, so many insects and ants are killed, especially at nighttime when so many insects fly into the windscreen or are crushed under the wheel, but with the powerful mantras inside, the negative karma of all those small insects is purified. Of course, that doesn't mean you should drive over rabbits or dogs or children! As a policeman drags you to prison, you can't really tell them you did it because you have a mantra in the car! I suspect that would be inadmissible in a court case.

The Kunrik Mantra

Kunrik's mantra is this:

OM NAMO BHAGAVATE / SARVA DURGATE PARI SHODHANI RAJAYA / TATHAGATAYA / ARHATE SAMYAKSAM BUD-DHAYA / TADYATHA / OM SHODHANI / SHODHANI / SARVA PAPAM BISHODHANI / SHUDHE BISHUDHE / SARVA KARMA AVARANA BISHODHANI SVAHA

ཨོཾ་ན་མོ་བྷ་ག་ཝ་ཏེ། སརྦ་དུརྒ་ཏེ་པ་རི་ཤོ་དྷ་ནི་རཱ་ཛཱ་ཡ། ཏ་ཐཱ་ག་ཏཱ་ཡ། ཨརྷ་ཏེ་སམྱཀྶཾ་བུདྡྷཱ་ཡ། ཏདྱ་ཐཱ། ཨོཾ་ཤོ་དྷ་ནི། ཤོ་དྷ་ནི། སརྦ་པཱ་པ་བི་ཤོ་དྷ་ནི། ཤུདྡྷེ་བི་ཤུདྡྷེ། སརྦ་ཀརྨ་ཨཱ་ཝ་ར་ཎ་བི་ཤོ་དྷ་ནི་སྭཱ་ཧཱ།

Kunrik is called the king of the deities purifying from the lower realms. He is white in color, with three faces; he holds a *dharmachakra* (Dharma wheel).

In Amdo, a customary preparation for death is receiving a Kunrik initiation, which completely purifies all the negative karma created during that life. This leaves the person very relaxed and without any worries, so they are prepared when death happens.

Although *jungwa*, the practice that is done when somebody has died, now incorporates practices such as Medicine Buddha or Vajrayogini,[136] it was originally done with Kunrik. If you do a Kunrik puja for somebody who has already been reborn in the lower realms, they are liberated from there.

The Mitrukpa Mantra

Mitrukpa's mantra is this:

NAMO RATNA TRAYAYA OM KAMKANI KAMKANI ROCHANI ROCHANI TROTANI TROTANI TRASANI TRASANI PRATI-HANA PRATIHANA SARVA KARMA PARAM PARA NI ME SARVA SATTVA NANCHA SVAHA

ན་མོ་རཏྣ་ཏྲ་ཡཱ་ཡ། ཨོཾ་ཀཾ་ཀ་ནི་ཀཾ་ཀ་ནི། རོ་ཙ་ནི་རོ་ཙ་ནི། ཏྲོ་ཊ་ནི་ཏྲོ་ཊ་ནི། ཏྲ་ས་ནི་ཏྲ་ས་ནི། པྲ་ཏི་ཧ་ན་པྲ་ཏི་ཧ་ན། སརྦ་ཀརྨ་པ་རཾ་པ་ར་ཎི་མེ་སརྦ་ སཏྭ་ནཉྩ་སྭཱ་ཧཱ།

Mitrukpa is Tibetan for Akshobhya, one of the five buddha families or Dhyani Buddhas. It is said that anybody who simply hears the Mitrukpa mantra can be saved from the lower realms. The mantra can even purify somebody who has created very heavy karma through doing the five immediate negativities or harming or criticizing the sangha. If you abandon the holy Dharma, this very heavy negative karma can be purified by just seeing the Mitrukpa mantra, so another powerful way of helping a dying person is to place this mantra next to their bed where they can see it. If simply seeing this mantra can do that, there is no need to mention the unbelievable benefits that come from reciting the Mitrukpa mantra.

When you recite the Mitrukpa mantra one hundred thousand times and blow on water, sand, or mustard seeds, and then sprinkle that blessed substance on the body of a person or animal that has died, if that being has been born in one of the lower realms, they will immediately be liberated from there. Even though the consciousness has been separated from the body and is somewhere else completely, because of its past connection with that body, the consciousness is still affected. It is said that that being will attain a higher rebirth within seven days.

His Holiness the Dalai Lama explained that in the past, when he ate meat, he kept all the bones, then recited the Mitrukpa mantra and blew on the bones. This kind of practice is unbelievably good to do. If you eat meat, you *must* do something for the animal who has died. Otherwise, it is very sad; that animal cherished its life as much as you cherish yours. If you don't know the Mitrukpa mantra or any of the other powerful mantras, you must at least recite one mala or half a mala of OM MANI PADME HUM or the Medicine Buddha mantra.[137] If that's not possible, you should at least recite it twenty-one or seven times. Reciting it with strong compassion, you blow on the meat before you eat it and make a strong dedication for that animal to immediately be liberated from the lower realms and to receive a perfect human body or rebirth in a pure land.

It is said in the texts that to recite the Mitrukpa mantra even once purifies the negative karma that continues from life to life. Therefore it is very good to have the Mitrukpa mantra somewhere in the house, especially above the door, where people can see it. If you recite the Mitrukpa mantra every day, there is no question that at the time of your death you will be saved from the lower realms.

The Namgyalma Mantras

Namgyalma's long mantra is this:

OM NAMO BHAGAVATE SARVA TRAILOKYA PRATIVISH-ISHTAYA / BUDDHAYA TE NAMA / TADYATHA / OM BHRUM BHRUM BHRUM SHODHAYA SHODHAYA / VISHODHAYA VISHODHAYA / ASAMA SAMANTA AVABHASA SPHARANA GATI GAGANA SVABHAVA VISHUDDHE / ABHISHINCHANTU MAM / SARVA TATHAGATA SUGATA VARA VACHANA AMRITA ABHISHEKARA / MAHAMUDRA MANTRA PADAI / AHARA AHARA / MAMA AYUS SAMDHARANI / SHODHAYA

SHODHAYA / VISHODHAYA VISHODHAYA / GAGANA
SVABHAVA VISHUDDHE / USHNISHA VIJAYA PARISHUDDHE /
SAHASRA RASMI SANCHO DITE / SARVA TATHAGATA AVALO-
KINI / SHAT PARAMITA PARIPURANI /SARVA TATHAGATA
MATE / DASHA BHUMI PRATISHTHITE / SARVA TATHAGATA
HRIDAYA / ADHISHTHANA ADHISHTHITE / MUDRE MUDRE
MAHA MUDRE / VAJRA KAYA SAMHATANA PARISHUDDHE /
SARVA KARMA AVARANA VISHUDDHE / PRATINI VARTAYA
MAMA AYUR / VISHUDDHE SARVA TATHAGATA / SAMAYA
ADHISHTHANA ADHISHTHITE / OM MUNI MUNI MAHA
MUNI / VIMUNI VIMUNI MAHA VIMUNI / MATI MATI MAHA
MATI / MAMATI SUMATI TATHATA / BHUTA KOTI PAR-
ISHUDDHE / VISPHUTA BUDDHE SHUDDHE / HE HE JAYA
JAYA / VIJAYA VIJAYA / SMRARA SMRARA / SPHARA SPHARA
/ SPHARAYA SPHARAYA / SARVA BUDDHA ADHISHTHANA
ADHISHTHITE / SHUDDHE SHUDDHE / BUDDHE BUDDHE
/ VAJRE VAJRE MAHA VAJRE / SUVAJRE VAJRA GARBHE
JAYA GARBHE / VIJAYA GARBHE / VAJRA JVALA GARBHE
/ VAJROD BHAVE / VAJRA SAMBHAVE / VAJRE VAJRINI /
VAJRAMA BHAVATU MAMA SHARIRAM / SARVA SATTVA
NANCHA KAYA PARISHUDDHIR BHAVATU / ME SADA SARVA
GATI PARISHUDDHISHCHA / SARVA TATHAGATASHCHA /
MAM SAMASHVAS YANTU / BUDDHYA BUDDHYA / SIDDHYA
SIDDHYA / BODHAYA BODHAYA / VIBODHAYA VIBODHAYA
/ MOCHAYA MOCHAYA / VIMOCHAYA VIMOCHAYA /
SHODHAYA SHODHAYA / VISHODHAYA VISHODHAYA /
SAMANTANA MOCHAYA MOCHAYA / SAMANTA RASMI PAR-
ISHUDDHE / SARVA TATHAGATA HRIDAYA / ADHISHTHANA
ADHISHTHITE / MUDRE MUDRE MAHA MUDRE / MAHA-
MUDRA MANTRA PADAI SVAHA

ཨོཾ་ན་མོ་བྷ་ག་ཝ་ཏེ་སརྦ་ཏྲེ་ལོ་ཀྱ་པྲ་ཏི་བི་ཤིཥྚཱ་ཡ། བུདྡྷ་ཡ་ཏེ་ན་མཿ ཏདྱ་ཐཱ།
ཨོཾ་བྷྲཱུཾབྷྲཱུཾ། ཤོ་དྷ་ཡ་ཤོ་དྷ་ཡ། བི་ཤོ་དྷ་ཡ་བི་ཤོ་དྷ་ཡ། ག་ག་ན་ས་ཧ་ཙ་ཝ
ཧྭ་བི་ཤུ་རྡྷ་ཧེ་ག་ཏི་ག་ག་ན་སྭ་བྷཱ་བ་བི་ཤུདྡྷེ། ཨུ་ཥྞཱི་ཥི་ཙ་སྨྱཱ། སརྦ་ཏྲེ་ག

ཏུ་སུ་ག་ཏུ་བ་ར་བ་ཚ་ན་ཨ་སྲི་ཏ་ཨ་སྲི་ཏི་གེ་ར། མ་ཏྲ་མུ་ད་མ་རྩ་པ་ཏེ། ཨཱ་ ཏུ་ར་ཨཱུ་ཏུ་ར། མ་མ་ཨཱ་ཡུ་སྦྱོ་དྲུ་ར་ཏི། ཕོ་ཧྲ་ཡ་ཕོ་ཧྲ་ཡ། པི་ཕོ་ཧྲ་ཡ་པི་ཕོ་ཧྲ་ ཡ། ག་ག་ན་སྦ་བྷ་ཝ། པི་ཤུ་དྡྷེ། ཡུ་ཀྲྀ་ཏ་པི་ཧྲ་ཡ་པ་རི་ཤུ་དྡྷེ། ས་ཏུ་སུ་རསྨྲི་ སཱ་ཙ་ དི་ཏེ། སཱ་ཏ་ཏུ་ཐྲ་ག་ཏུ་ཨ་བ་ལོ་ཀི་ནི། ཥཏ་པ་ར་མི་ཏ་པ་རི་པུ་ར་ཎི། སཱ་ཏ་ ཏུ་ཐྲ་ག་ཏུ་མ་ཏེ། ད་ཤ་བྷུ་མི་པྲ་ཏི་ཥྛི་ཏེ། སཱ་ཏ་ཏུ་ཐྲ་ག་ཏུ་ཧྲི་ད་ཡ། ཨ་སྲི་ ཥྛ་ན་ཨ་སྲི་ཥྛི་ཏེ། སུ་རེ་སུ་རེ། མ་ཏྲ་མུ་རེ། བཛྲ་ཀཱ་ཡ་སོ་ཧཏ་ན་པ་རི་ཤུ་དྡྷེ། སཱ་ཏ་ཀརྨ་ཨ་བ་ར་ཎ་བི་ཤུ་དྡྷེ། པྲ་ཏི་ནི་བཏྲ་ཡ་མ་མ་ཨཱུ་ཡུར། པི་ཤུ་དྡྷེ་ སཱ་ཏ་ ཐྲ་ག་ཏ། ས་མ་ཡ་ཨ་དྷིཥྛ་ན་ཨ་དྷིཥྛི་ཏེ། ཨོ་མུ་ནི་མུ་ནི་མ་ཧཱ་མུ་ནི། པི་མུ་ནི་པི་ མུ་ནི་མ་ཧཱ་པི་མུ་ནི། མ་ཏི་མ་ཏི་མ་ཧཱ་མ་ཏི། མ་མ་ཏི་སུ་མ་ཏི་ཏ་ཐྭ་ཏཱ། བྷུ་ ཏ་ཀོ་ཏི་པ་རི་ཤུ་དྡྷེ། པི་སྥུ་ཏ་བུ་དྡྷི་ཤུ་དྡྷེ། ཧེ་ཧེ་ཛ་ཡ་ཛ་ཡ། པི་ཛ་ཡ་པི་ཛ་ཡ། སྨ་ར་སྨ་ར། སྥ་ར་སྥ་ར། སྥཱ་ར་ཡ་སྥཱ་ར་ཡ། སཱ་ཏ་བུ་དྡྷ་ཨ་དྷིཥྛ་ན་ཨ་སྲི་ཥྛི་ཏེ། ཤུ་དྡྷེ་ཤུ་དྡྷེ། བུ་དྡྷེ་བུ་དྡྷེ། བ་ཛྲི་བཛྲི་མ་ཧཱ་བཛྲི། སུ་བཛྲི་བཛྲ་གརྦྷེ་ཛ་ཡ་གརྦྷེ། པི་ ཛ་ཡ་གརྦྷེ། བཛྲ་ཛྭ་ལ་གརྦྷེ། བཛྲོ་དྷྭ་ཝེ། བཛྲ་སོ་བྷ་ཝེ། བཛྲ་བཛྲི་ཎི། བཛྲ་ མ་བྷ་ཝ་ཏུ་མ་མ་ཤ་རི་རཾ། སཱ་ཏ་སཏྭ་ནཉྩ་ཀཱ་ཡ། པ་རི་ཤུ་དྡྷིརྦྷ་བ་ཏུ། མེ་ས་ ད་སཱ་ཏ་གཏི་པ་རི་ཤུ་དྡྷིཤྩ། སཱ་ཏ་ཏ་ཐྲ་ག་ཏུ་ཤྩ་ མཱ་ས་མ་ཨ་ཤྭ་ས་ཡ་ནྟུ། བུ་དྡྷ་བུ་དྡྷ། སི་དྡྷ་སི་དྡྷ། བོ་དྷ་ཡ་བོ་དྷ་ཡ། པི་བོ་དྷ་ཡ་པི་བོ་དྷ་ཡ། མོ་ཙ་ཡ་མོ་ཙ་ཡ། པི་མོ་ ཙ་ཡ་པི་མོ་ཙ་ཡ། ཤོ་དྷ་ཡ་ཤོ་དྷ་ཡ། པི་ཤོ་དྷ་ཡ་པི་ཤོ་དྷ་ཡ། ས་མཉྩནྟོ་ཙ་ ཡ་མོ་ཙ་ཡ། ས་མ་ཏ་རསྨི་པ་རི་ཤུ་དྡྷེ། སཱ་ཏ་ཏུ་ཐྲ་ག་ཏུ་ཧྲི་ད་ཡ། ཨ་དྷིཥྛ་ན་ཨ་ དྷིཥྛི་ཏེ། སུ་རེ་སུ་རེ་མ་ཏྲ་མུ་རེ། མ་ཏྲ་མུ་ཏྲ་མ་ཧཱ་པ་ཏེ་སྭ་ཧཱ།

The short mantra is this:

OM BHRUM SVAHA / OM AMRITA AYUR DA DE SVAHA

ༀ་བྷྲུྃ་སྭཱ་ཧཱ། ༀ་ཨ་སྲི་ཏ་ཨ་ཡུར་དེ་སྭཱ་ཧཱ།

At the conclusion, you recite:

OM AMITE / AMITODA BHAVE / AMITE VIKRANTE / AMITA
GATRE / AMITO GAMINI / AMITA AYURDADE / GAGANA
KIRTI KARE SARVA KLESHA KSHAYAM KARI YE SVAHA

ཨོཾ་ཨ་མི་ཏེ། ཨ་མི་ཏོ་ད་རྦ་བེ། ཨ་མི་ཏེ་བི་ཀྲན་ཏེ། ཨ་མི་ཏ་གཏྲེ། ཨ་མི་ཏོ་ག་
མི་ནི། ཨ་མི་ཏ་ཨྱུརྡ་དེ། ག་ག་ན་གིརྟི་ག་རེ་སརྦ་ཀྲེ་ཤ་ཀྱ་ཡོཾ་ག་རི་ཡེ་སྭཱ་ཧཱ།

Namgyalma is a deity for long life and purification. Both the long
Namgyalma mantra and the short one have skies of benefits. If you
recite the mantra daily, you will have a pure life at all times, you will
always meet buddhas and bodhisattvas in each life, and you will achieve
enlightenment.

Namgyalma's mantra is said to be so powerful that anybody who
hears it will never again be reborn in the lower realms. There is a story
from the time Guru Shakyamuni Buddha was on the earth concerning
a god called Paripu Denpa. As he was dying, Denpa saw that he was
about to be reborn as an animal—a dog or monkey or something. Very
worried, he asked King Indra for advice and Indra suggested that he
see the Buddha, which he did. The Buddha manifested as the deity
Namgyalma and gave him the mantra. Denpa recited it six times daily,
and in seven days completely changed his karma so that he did not have
to be reborn as an animal.

Even if you are in danger of dying because the karma that determines
your lifespan is running out, if you wash your body, wear clean clothes,
and, abiding in the eight Mahayana precepts, recite the Namgyalma
mantra one thousand times, you can increase your lifespan, purify your
obscurations, and free yourself from disease.

By reciting this mantra twenty-one times and blowing on mustard
seeds, when you throw them onto the bones of a being, even one who
has created many heavy negative karmas, they will immediately be liberated from the lower realms and reborn in a higher realm.

When I give refuge and lay vows, I often give the students a card with
the Namgyalma mantra on it as well a blessing string and a picture of

the bodhisattva Kshitigarbha.[138] These things are incredible because just having them constantly purifies negative karma.

Putting the Namgyalma mantra up somewhere in your home brings it protection and makes it a holy place. Then, whatever sentient beings are inside—dogs, cats, mosquitoes—always have their negative karma purified and they obtain a higher rebirth. If even the shadow of the house touches any being, like an insect or a person, their negative karma is purified, and they obtain a higher rebirth. If the Namgyalma mantra is on top of a mountain, the whole mountain becomes holy and the negative karma of any being who climbs or touches the mountain is purified and they obtain a higher rebirth. And it is vital to have it in your car.

When Lama Yeshe[139] and I were visiting my root guru, His Holiness Trijang Rinpoche, in Mundgod in India,[140] Rinpoche chatted with us while maintaining his meditation practice at the same time. Afterward, he explained he was doing the Namgyalma mantra for all the people who had sent him offerings. The purpose was twofold. Because the people who sent the offerings had delusions, the offerings were polluted and the mantra purified that pollution, but it also purified the negative karma of the people and helped them have a long life. That is how powerful the Namgyalma mantra is.

The Stainless Pinnacle Deity Mantra
The Stainless Pinnacle Deity mantra is this:

OM NAMAS TRAIYA DHVIKANAM / SARVA TATHAGATA HRI-DAYA GARBHE JVALA JVALA / DHARMA DHATU GARBHE / SAMBHARA MAMA AYUH SAMSHODHAYA / MAMA SARVA PAPAM / SARVA TATHAGATA SAMANTOSHNISHA VIMALE VISHUDDHE HUM HUM HUM HUM / AM VAM SAM JA SVAHA

ཨོཾ་ན་མ་ཏྲི་ཡ་དྷྭི་ཀ་ནཱཾ། སརྦ་ཏ་ཐཱ་ག་ཏ་ཧྲི་ད་ཡ་གརྦྷེ་ཛྭ་ལ་ཛྭ་ལ། ཆཀྲ་ཧྲི་ད་ཀྲཱི། མེ་ཧྲ་ར་མ་མ་ཨཱ་ཡུཿམེ་ཤོ་དྷ་ཡ། མ་མ་སརྦ་པཱ་པཾ། སརྦ་ཏ་ཐཱ་ག་ཏ་ས་མནྟོཥྞི་ཥ་བི་མ་ལེ་བི་ཤུ་དྡྷེ། ཧཱུྃ་ཧཱུྃ་ཧཱུྃ་ཧཱུྃ། ཨཾ་བཾ་སཾ་ཛ་སྭཱ་ཧཱ།

THE FIVE GREAT MANTRAS   167

The Stainless Pinnacle Deity mantra is one of the four dharmakaya relic mantras. Hearing or seeing the Stainless Pinnacle Deity mantra liberates from all negative karmas and defilements and the fears of the lower realms. Like fire that turns hay to fine ash, which is then swept away by the wind, similarly, all negative karmas are consumed and swept away completely. The mantra is also compared to a flash flood that sweeps away all the garbage lying on the ground, or to a goldsmith's fire that softens the hard metal and makes it pure and workable. This relates to how reciting or seeing this mantra purifies you and makes your body malleable, a suitable vessel for helping others. When the sun rises, its beams cover the whole world, beautifying it. In the same way, this mantra beautifies anyone who keeps it on them.

Merely by remembering or reciting this mantra, your obstacles are pacified and you have long life. If you put this mantra inside a stupa, no matter what size, it helps prolong the life of somebody whose life is nearly finished. A text describing the benefits of the mantra says that when death comes, just as a snake changes its skin, your consciousness leaves your body and immediately goes to Amitabha's pure land. Then, you will never be reborn in the lower realms and never experience the feeling of death, which I think means suffering. Once you get to a pure land, you will never again hear the word "hell," let alone experience any suffering.

That is why I usually encourage people to build stupas that have mantras such as the Stainless Pinnacle Deity mantra inside. There are incalculable benefits for those involved with planning it, those who fundraise for it, those who actually build it, and so forth. It is a very skillful way to liberate sentient beings. Then for the hundreds or thousands of years that the stupa stands, whenever any being sees it, they collect merits greater than making offerings of divine clothes—where one ornament is of greater value than all the wealth of this world—and divine food to as many arhats liberated from samsara as there are grains of sand in the River Ganges. For animals that go near the stupa, for insects and birds that fly around it and land on it, the merit they collect is unbelievable and the negative karma they purify is incalculable. And that is the same for people who see it, remember it, talk about it, and so forth. The stupa is a protection, a blessing for the area, for the country, for humans and even nonhumans: spirits and nagas, and so forth.

The Wish-Granting Wheel Mantra

The Wish-Granting Wheel mantra is this:

OM PADMO USHNISHA VIMALE HUM PHAT

ཨོཾ་པ་རྫོ་ཨུཥྞི་ཥ་བི་མ་ལེ་ཧཱུྃ་ཕཊ།

This mantra also has unbelievable benefits. If you recite it seven times every day, you accumulate merit equivalent to that of making offerings to buddhas equal in number to the grains of sand in the River Ganges. In your next life, you will be reborn in a pure realm and will be able to achieve great concentration.

It not only purifies and heals you, but, if you recite it and then blow on the clothes you wear, it purifies and heals any other sentient being who touches them. If the clothes are made of an animal product, such as leather, silk, or fur, it purifies the negative karma of the animal that died in making them and helps them be reborn in an upper realm.

Recalling this mantra just once has the power to purify even the five immediate negativities. It prevents rebirth in inexhaustible hot hell, the heaviest of all the hells. For many eons you will not have to be reborn in this state of unbearable suffering. It enables you to remember past lives and see future lives. It helps you achieve the complete qualities of a buddha.

If you recite this mantra, blow upon sand, and sprinkle that sand onto a dead body, even if the dead person had broken vows and was reborn in a lower realm, you can change their life and they will be reborn in a higher realm.

If you recite it and blow on burning incense or on perfume, it purifies all sentient beings who smell it, even curing them of contagious diseases. It is said in the Kangyur that anybody who passes underneath the Wish-Granting Wheel mantra has a thousand eons' negative karma purified. That is why I encourage students to put this mantra and the other powerful mantras above a door in their house. It is also good to have it in the car so that insects that touch the car are purified. If the car gets rained on, the rainwater becomes like holy water after touching the Wish-Granting Wheel mantra.

CONCLUSION: THE BENEFITS OF RECITING MANTRAS ARE UNCOUNTABLE

No matter which mantra we recite, OM MANI PADME HUM, the Medicine Buddha's mantra, the names of the Thirty-Five Buddhas, or whatever, our mind is transformed and protected by the power of that mantra. Because each mantra contains the enlightened being's name, each links us directly to the dharmakaya, the omniscient mind of all the buddhas. Knowing how powerful mantra recitation is, our devotion to the Buddha, Dharma, and Sangha, and to our own guru, becomes stronger and stronger, and that transforms our mind, protecting us from suffering.

When our mind is about to slip into negativity, reciting a mantra protects us, keeping it virtuous. Reciting a mantra can also destroy the negative karmic imprints that are on our mindstream that will otherwise manifest as suffering when the conditions arise. Every mantra does this, not just the great purification mantras like Vajrasattva. Because of that purification, we are spared all sorts of suffering, such as sickness, relationship problems, and so forth, as well as being saved from an unfortunate rebirth. A mantra is like a flame that can burn up all our negative karma.

How effective our mantra recitation is depends on our motivation. Because of the power of the mantra itself, we can gain some benefit even if we do it with a selfish motivation. For instance, reciting a White Tara mantra to be saved from sickness or untimely death without any altruistic intention will definitely help, but it is not Dharma. For a mantra recitation to be Dharma, we must have the motivation of attaining a fortunate rebirth, achieving liberation from samsara, or—the very best motivation—attaining enlightenment in order to benefit all sentient beings. Reciting a mantra such as OM MANI PADME HUM even once with a bodhichitta motivation has the power to totally transform our mind. It is like reciting one hundred thousand mantras with a lesser motivation.

The reason we are alive, the reason we have this precious human body, is to benefit other sentient beings. Therefore, it is vital that we bring this motivation into everything we do, and that includes practicing a tantric deity and reciting a mantra. Every action—eating, walking, sleeping, working—should be purely to benefit others, so of course our Dharma practice should be to benefit others. This should be our attitude for life. When we do everything with this motivation, everything becomes the cause of enlightenment.

When we understand the benefits of reciting mantras and know how powerful they are, reciting a mantra comes as easily as breathing. It is a joy to do. Then, with every mantra we recite, our mind is profoundly transformed. The drops of water that comprise all the oceans can be counted, the atoms of the earth can be counted, each snowflake in a countryside covered in snow can be counted, but we can never finish counting the benefits of mantras; they are infinite.

APPENDIX 1:
PREPARING FOR PRACTICE[141]

CREATING A SACRED SPACE

It is very helpful for your practice to have a special area of your home dedicated for your daily practice, whether it is a separate meditation room or a part of another room kept for that purpose. You can make your meditation space simple or ornate, but I strongly recommend making it as beautiful as you can, with an altar with offering bowls and an image of the Buddha. Of course, it is even better to have ten images and better still to have ten thousand!

If you have an altar in your home and you offer incense and lights to the statues on that altar with the mind of bodhichitta, the effect is so powerful. You can also do this with a "mental altar" just by visualizing the Buddha, but a physical altar can become the focus of your meditations. Once your altar is set up, every time you see the altar you see the Buddha. This is not some projection from your own side. The Buddha *is* there. To think this is just in your imagination disturbs your practice. Whether you have a statue or not, there is no place where the omniscient mind doesn't reside, and so when you make offerings to the altar, you are not making offerings to a small bronze statue but to the actual Buddha.

Westerners seem to lead incredibly busy lives. Students are always telling me that they have no time to meditate. But they certainly have time to buy food and make lots and lots of cups of tea. In all that running here and there, you can easily sacrifice just a few minutes filling a few water bowls instead of (or as well as) filling the kettle. It's not difficult, it doesn't take much time, and it creates incredible merit.

The main items to include in your meditation room or space should be an altar, your meditation seat, and perhaps a text table and a bookshelf to hold your Dharma books. The altar is where you place the holy objects, pictures, and texts that inspire you. It should be used only as an altar and not double as a coffee table or desk, and it should be kept in a clean, respectful place. The objects should be placed higher than the level of your head as you sit facing your altar.

Before setting up your altar for the first time, clean the space well and burn incense to purify the place. After initially setting up your altar, always keep the area clean. Sweep and dust every day before making offerings.

The Tibetan Buddhist altar contains a statue or photo of Buddha Shakyamuni and other deities you feel a connection with. These symbolize the enlightened holy body. Photographs of your spiritual teachers may be included here as well. Traditionally, statues of the Buddha and other deities are placed at the center of the altar, with pictures of teachers placed to either side of the deities. The statues need to be filled with certain mantras and incense and blessed.[142]

If you like, you may wrap each statue in a *khatak*—the silk scarf Tibetan Buddhists traditionally use for greeting and offering. You can do that by wrapping the scarf beautifully around the statue's base and part of the statue itself.

If you have sacred paintings of deities (*thangkas*), these can be hung on the wall above the altar or on either side of it. Often, a *khatak* is draped over the top of the *thangka*, or alternatively, wrapped around the decorative ends of the thangka at the bottom.

To the left of the Buddha as you face the altar, place a Dharma text. This symbolizes the enlightened holy speech. The text does not need to be written in Tibetan or Sanskrit; it can be in any language. If you use a cloth to wrap the texts it should be new and clean, or at least it should not have been used for anything in the past except wrapping texts.

To the right of the Buddha as you face the altar, place a stupa. The stupa symbolizes the enlightened mind of the Buddha. It doesn't have to be expensive—a simple plaster stupa or even a photograph of one is acceptable. If you have a real stupa, you might also like to wrap it in a *khatak*.

So, the order should be, from left to right (as you are facing the altar): text, Buddha, and stupa, with the offering bowls in front.

Your Daily Routine

Before you start your main meditation practice, such as a daily deity practice, there are certain preliminary practices that should be done:

- cleaning the room
- setting up the altar
- doing three prostrations
- sitting in a proper meditation posture
- doing some form of calming meditation such as watching the breath
- reciting the preliminary prayers, such as refuge, bodhichitta, the seven-limb prayer, and so forth[143]

The purpose of doing actions such as cleaning the room, making offerings, and prostrating to the enlightened beings is to purify your negativities. The power of these actions comes not only from the action itself but from the power born out of the limitless wisdom and compassion of the Buddha. As you make offerings or prostrate, if you are aware of the great qualities of the Buddha, this increases your devotion to him and therefore the effectiveness of the action. Making offerings and prostrating are not ritualistic customs without meaning or benefit. If you do them with full awareness, they can bring about the most profound purification. Even if you don't have so much as a stick of incense, just visualizing a buddha image and mentally offering it creates unbelievable merit.

Cleaning the Room and Setting Up the Altar

Even if the altar and meditation room are not particularly dirty, you should still clean them. You should think that this is Guru Shakyamuni Buddha's room, not yours. It's not like you are cleaning the room to impress a friend who is coming over; this is out of great respect for the Buddha. This is his mandala, his palace, and cleaning it is offering service to him, rather than becoming a service to your negative mind. You should therefore check your motivation carefully as you are cleaning the room.

After that, make offerings to the Buddha, Dharma, and Sangha on the altar. They should be clean, new, and honestly obtained. Offer only fresh food and flowers, never anything spoiled or dirty. Fill bowls or vases high with offerings to create the cause for abundance; never offer a bowl that isn't filled to the top. It is better to offer a small bowl heaped high with offerings than a large bowl that looks partly empty.

To make the offerings, you need to offer something, and the simplest, easiest, and cheapest thing is water—and, unlike a nice piece of chocolate, there is little likelihood of your becoming attached to it—and so you should have water bowls placed in front of the image. The traditional number of bowls in Tibetan Buddhism is seven or eight. The eighth bowl symbolizes music, so if you recite aloud, some traditions leave this out. If you don't have room, then one or two is also okay. A hundred thousand is better of course.

These are the offerings placed in the bowls at the front of the altar, from your left to right:

- *argham*: water for drinking
- *padyam*: water for cleaning the feet
- *pushpe*: flowers
- *dhupe*: incense
- *aloke*: light
- *ghande*: perfume
- *naividya*: food
- *shapta*: music

During the time of the Buddha, when someone important visited, these were offered as a sign of hospitality, and so this is according to Indian custom. If you can imagine a king coming to your home in ancient times, on a hot, dusty day, you would first offer him water to drink to quench his thirst and then water to wash the dust off his feet. The other offerings are to delight his senses. You would offer flowers, perhaps as a garland to place around his neck. There would be incense burning in the room and lights, such as candles, making the room visually beautiful. You would offer him perfume, perhaps a scented cloth to wipe his face, and food. Finally, while the king is eating, there would be beautiful music playing, an offering for the ear. If you think about the preparations you make for receiving a good friend in your house here in the twenty-first century, it is not that different.

Another way of laying out the offerings is with actual substances instead of water. So there would be incense, a candle, food, and flowers. This makes a very attractive offering.

It is good to make the offerings in the morning as you start your day, and to take them down in the evening, dispensing the blessed water respectfully, by pouring it over the flowers in your garden, for instance.

You are making an offering to a holy being, so it's important not only to be mindful and respectful, but also to make the offerings and the action of offering as beneficial as possible. Don't be lazy or sloppy, and make sure everything is very clean—make sure the bowls are clean and the water is clean.

The bowls don't have to be big, but they shouldn't be tiny, like a child's plaything. They can be very simple; they can be glass or porcelain or even clay, but they should be as beautiful as possible. Crystal or gold bowls make the altar look so much nicer and the mind feels so much happier than if cheap, ugly ones are used.

If possible, use saffron water in the bowls. To do this, boil a pot of hot water and then put a small amount of saffron in the water. Cover the pot with a towel and let it sit until it is a deep yellow or orange color. Then place the water in a clean, covered container and refrigerate it. Each day, a small amount of this saffron water can be added to the water in the pitcher used to fill the bowls. The color of the saffron water in your bowls can vary—some teachers suggest it should be the color of a fine champagne, while others like the water to be a more vibrant yellow.

The bowls will be upside down from when you emptied them the previous day, so, traditionally, you "seed" the bowls. This means holding each bowl upside down and filling it with incense smoke to purify it, while saying OM AH HUM. An empty vessel should never be placed right side up on an altar, as this empty offering creates the cause to not receive the bounty of the Dharma. Then, with a pitcher of water, pour water into the first bowl until it is full. Then pour most (but not all) of the water from the first bowl into the second bowl and place the first bowl onto your altar, toward the left-hand side. Pour most of the water from the second bowl into the third, and place the second bowl onto the altar, just to the right of the first bowl. Continue in this way until all seven or eight bowls are on the altar in a straight line, each with some water in the bottom of it.

Make sure the bowls have been placed in a straight line, close together but not touching. Traditionally, the distance between bowls is about the width of a grain of wheat. The symbolism in this is that if the bowls are too far apart, you can create the karma to be separated from your guru; if they are too close together, you can create the karma to have a dull mind, without sharp intelligence.

Now, use your pitcher of water and, while reciting OM AH HUM, fill each bowl. The reason for saying OM AH HUM is to protect yourself from interference from spirits who can steal the essence of the offerings. For instance, it is said that if you don't say these three sacred syllables as you are offering light, it can be the cause to become very dull and distracted. So, you should always remember to say this. Even when you turn on a light in a room, especially one with holy objects in it, this is very good to do.

Pour the water like the shape of a wheat grain—in a thin stream at first, then gradually more, tapering off at the end. Try to pour the water neatly, without making noise. The water should fill the bowl to just about the size of a wheat grain from the top, so that the bowls are full but not too full. If your bowls are not full enough, your wisdom will be incomplete; if they are overfull, you create the cause for your wisdom to be incomplete or for it to be unstable. In addition, you might want to cover your mouth with a *khatak* or face mask, as it is important not to breathe on the offerings while making them.

As I have said, instead of water, you can offer flowers, incense, light, and food in their respective places in the lineup of water bowls. For instance, for the nonwater offerings, you can place some rice in the bowl and the offering on top of that—a small flower, a stick of incense, a tealight, a piece of fruit, and so forth. You can have water in the perfume bowl and add some fragrance you really like. For the music offering, you can have a bell or even a recording of beautiful music. For the nonwater offerings, you don't have to turn the bowls over when clearing away the offerings at the end of the day.

Whether you use just water or different substances depends on your resources and what suits you. Whatever you use, when you make the offering mentally, you transform it into divine nectar for the Buddha; it is no longer a bowl of water or an apple. The important thing is to feel very happy you are offering these substances and to make the offerings as beautiful as you can.

There are two ways of making offerings, actually transformed offerings and mentally transformed offerings. Physically, what you have in the bowls are just mundane substances—water, rice, incense, and so forth—but by saying the mantra OM AH HUM and visualizing the offerings as divine offerings, you transform them into what you are actually offering the Buddha. (There are also methods of increasing the offerings, using other mantras, which you can find in many sadhanas and pujas.)

You can even make offerings without anything physical there at all, merely by visualizing offerings. The main part of the offering doesn't take place on the altar but in your mind. You could have all the riches in the world in the room with that Buddha image, but that doesn't mean you are making vast offerings to the Buddha. The idea is to mentally create the most wonderful things and then freely offer them all up to the Buddha, without a shred of attachment from your side. In fact, offering is a direct antidote to miserliness.

And just as you can make the offerings as extensive as possible, dependent on your ability to visualize, you can make the field to which you are offering as extensive as possible. I have talked of offering to Guru Shakyamuni Buddha, but Tibetan Buddhism describes extensive merit fields—fields that allow you to create merit—with the Buddha or Lama Tsongkhapa at the center and all the buddhas, bodhisattvas, and lineage lamas surrounding.

When you make the offering, besides saying the mantra, it is very good to dedicate to not only the Buddha but to all sentient beings, that they might quickly attain enlightenment. Then even if it is the simplest of actions, just pouring a little water in a bowl, it covers all sentient beings; you have done a service for an infinite number of beings and so the benefits are infinite. It is so easy that way. For instance, as you light a candle for the light offering you can think, "By making this light offering, may the ignorance of all sentient beings be burned and destroyed and may the transcendental wisdom light shine forever in their minds." Think that all their dualistic thinking is consumed in the flames of the wisdom realizing emptiness. This sort of offering is very effective. And, of course, if your offering is imbued with the mind of enlightenment, bodhichitta, then it becomes so powerful.

Prostrations

A simple action like making a water bowl offering can have such vast results, and it's the same with prostrations. Many people new to Buddhism seem reluctant to prostrate, thinking prostrations are somehow both alien and hard work (even though the same people often spend so much time and money—and sweat—at the gym). When they are told about the Thirty-Five Buddhas practice, they put it off and put it off. If they could really see how prostrating to the Thirty-Five Buddhas can completely transform their minds, there would be nothing else they would want to do.

Doing prostrations correctly brings so many benefits. As you go down onto the floor, you have to prostrate to the Buddha, Dharma, and Sangha, otherwise it just becomes exercise. When you prostrate, you are wiping off the garbage, the obscurations, the negative karma collected through actions of your body, speech, and mind from beginningless rebirths. I don't know what the English word "prostration" means, but the Tibetan *chagtsel* has this meaning.

By purifying the negative karma collected with your body, speech, and mind, prostrations create the cause to achieve the vajra holy body, vajra holy speech, and vajra holy mind of the Buddha. A prostration is the particular remedy to a particular delusion in the same way that specific medicines are used for particular illnesses. Pride is a huge hindrance to developing on the path, and prostration is a very strong antidote to pride. Even if you don't do a full-length or a five-limb (half) prostration, when you recite the seven-limb prayer, with the line to do with prostrating, you must put your palms together in the prostration mudra. To not do so would be such a waste.

The prostration mudra is a very simple action that can take less than a second, but it is incredibly powerful. Each aspect of the mudra has significance. You place your hands at your chest, palms together and fingers straight and facing upward, much like a Christian prayer mudra. The thumbs are slightly tucked in.

This is also called the "lotus bud" mudra because it looks like the bud of a lotus plant, and it has great significance. Keeping the two thumbs inside signifies offering a jewel, rather than prostrating with empty hands with the palms flat, which is regarded as the non-Buddhist prostration method. The hollow between the palms signifies the dharmakaya and the two thumbs inside that hollow signify the rupakaya, the dharmakaya and rupakaya being the two buddha bodies that result from completing the two paths of wisdom and method.

The full-length prostration is according to the tradition of Naropa. It is good to begin with this mantra:

OM NAMO MANJUSHRIYE NAMO SUSHRIYE NAMO UTAMASHRIYE SVAHA

His Holiness Serkong Rinpoche explained the meaning of the mantra to me, but I didn't write it down immediately so I have forgotten. (I think it is quite uncommon for someone to know the meaning of these mantras.) It is said in the teachings that if you recite this mantra three times you not only receive the same merit as listening, reflecting, and meditating on the Tripitaka, the three baskets of teachings, but also, when you do three full-length prostrations with this mantra each day, you receive the benefit of being able to achieve the path of seeing—the wisdom directly perceiving emptiness—in this life, and you will not be afflicted by disease, spirits, or human beings. One of the main advantages of doing prostrations with this mantra is that it increases the benefits of each prostration one thousand-fold.

Furthermore, if you recite the following buddhas' names seven times at the beginning of doing prostrations, it increases the benefits of the prostrations ten million times.

CHOM DÄN DÄ DE ZHIN SHEG PA DRA CHOM PA YANG DAG PAR DZOG PÄI SANG GYÄ RINCHHEN GYÄLTSHÄN LA CHHAG TSHÄL LO

OM NAMO BHAGAVATE RATNA KETU RAJAYA / TATHAGA-TAYA / ARHATE SAMYAK SAMBUDDHAYA / TADYATHA / OM RATNE RATNE MAHA RATNE RATNA BIJA YE SVAHA

When you prostrate, keep your feet together, not separated, but also not like an army exercise. With your hands in the prostration mudra, first place them on your crown, which causes you to create the merit to achieve a crown pinnacle, one of a buddha's thirty-two holy signs and eighty holy exemplifications. Then, touch them to the forehead, which, according to Kyabje Pabongka Rinpoche, purifies the negative karmas collected with the body from beginningless rebirths. It creates the cause to achieve the holy sign of the clockwise curled hair at the center of a buddha's eyebrows, for which unbelievable merit is needed. It also creates the cause to achieve the vajra holy body. Then, touch your folded hands to the throat, which purifies the negative karmas collected from speech from beginningless rebirths and creates the cause to achieve the vajra holy speech. Then, touch them to the heart, which purifies the negative karmas collected with the mind from beginningless rebirths and creates the cause to achieve the vajra holy mind.

When you go down, either with a full or half prostration, you must touch the ground with your forehead, otherwise it doesn't become a complete prostration. But then, you should get up quickly, signifying a quick release from samsara. To lie there without immediately getting up creates the karma to be reborn as a worm or snake—a creature who slides along the ground!

You should also be careful to hold your hands in the correct fashion when you are on the ground, with the fingers straight out. If you splay them you create the karma to be reborn as a duck or a creature with webbed feet, and if you bunch them up you create the karma to be reborn as a horse or a creature with hooves. Doing prostrations correctly brings the most amazing benefits, but because you are prostrating to the Buddha, Dharma, and Sangha, a sloppy prostration can bring great suffering results.

With the full-length prostration, you then lie flat on the floor, stretching your arms in front of you and touching your head to the floor. The more you spread your body, the more atoms touch the ground. It is said in the *Lankavatara Sutra* that when you do a full-length prostration, with your hands fully extended, you create the merit to be born a wheel-turning king a thousand times for each atom of the floor your body covers, and that is not just the atoms on the surface, but from the surface right down to the center of the earth. It is unimaginable.

A five-limb or half prostration is when you simply go down on your knees and touch your head to the floor.

You can increase the power of your prostration in many ways. Firstly, if prostrating to one buddha creates vast merit, then prostrating to countless buddhas creates even more, and so, if you can, it is good to visualize the merit field as not just Guru Shakyamuni Buddha but as a whole field of buddhas, bodhisattvas, and gurus, such as you see in the illustrations of the Guru Puja merit field.

Also, rather than prostrating alone, one body making offerings to the buddhas, you can visualize countless other sentient beings surrounding you, in all directions, covering the entire planet. Then, however many bodies you can visualize prostrating with you, you collect that much merit. If you visualize a hundred thousand beings prostrating with you, you collect the merit of a hundred thousand prostrations with just one movement. This is the most extensive way to collect merit when you prostrate, which is reflected in the verse from *The King of Prayers*:

> With the energy of aspiration for the bodhisattva way,
> with a sense of deep respect,
> and with as many bodies as atoms of the world,
> to all you buddhas visualized as real, I bow down.[144]

The Posture

Then, having cleaned the room; made offerings to the Buddha, Dharma, and Sangha on your altar; and prostrated, you sit down in a proper meditation posture. The texts say this should be Vairochana's seven-point meditation posture:

- legs in vajra (full lotus) position or crossed
- hands in meditation mudra
- back straight
- head tilted forward
- eyes slightly open, gaze directed downward
- jaw relaxed, tongue against palate
- shoulders level and relaxed

The full vajra position is where your legs are crossed with each foot, sole upward, placed on the opposite thigh. This is difficult for many Westerners, so a half vajra (with just one foot on the thigh) or with the legs just crossed is also acceptable. It's good to have a cushion that raises your buttocks slightly. This will enable you to easily keep your back straight for an extended period. If sitting on the floor is too uncomfortable, you can also sit on a chair.

The meditation mudra is holding your hands on your lap, just below the navel, palms upward with the right hand on top of the left and thumbs touching, forming a triangle. Arms and shoulders should be relaxed, and you should hold your arms out slightly from your body to allow the circulation of air.

Your back should be straight but relaxed. It helps to imagine your spine as a pile of coins rising straight up. Your gaze should be slightly down to prevent mental wandering (if the gaze is too high) or drowsiness (if it is too low). Your eyes should be half open. This is often difficult for new meditators, so having them closed is acceptable. However, this can lead to drowsiness, just as having them fully open can lead to distractions. Your jaw should be relaxed, with your tongue lightly touching the roof of your mouth, just behind the teeth. Your teeth should be slightly apart and your lips lightly together.

When you are sitting comfortably, you can do some form of calming meditation, such as watching the breath, and then begin reciting the preliminary prayers.

APPENDIX 2: PRELIMINARY PRAYERS AND DEDICATIONS[145]

Preliminary Prayers

Taking Refuge and Generating Bodhichitta

I go for refuge until I am enlightened
to the Buddha, the Dharma, and the Supreme Assembly.
By my practice of giving and other perfections,
may I become a buddha to benefit all sentient beings. *(3x)*

The Four Immeasurable Thoughts

May all sentient beings have happiness and the causes of
happiness.
May all sentient beings be free from suffering and the causes of
suffering.
May all sentient beings be inseparable from the happiness that is
free from suffering.
May all sentient beings abide in equanimity, free from attachment for friends and hatred for enemies.

Seven-Limb Prayer

Reverently, I prostrate with my body, speech, and mind;
I present clouds of every type of offering, actual and imagined;
I declare all my negative actions accumulated since beginningless
time

and rejoice in the merit of all holy and ordinary beings.
Please, remain until the end of cyclic existence
and turn the wheel of Dharma for living beings.
I dedicate my own merits and those of all others to the great
   enlightenment.

Short Mandala Offering

This ground, anointed with perfume, strewn with flowers,
adorned with Mount Meru, four continents, the sun, and the
   moon:
I imagine this as a buddha field and offer it.
May all living beings enjoy this pure land!

IDAM GURU RATNA MANDALAKAM NIRYATAYAMI

DEDICATION PRAYERS

Due to the merits of these virtuous actions,
may I quickly attain the state of a Guru-Buddha
and lead all living beings, without exception,
into that enlightened state.

May the supreme jewel bodhichitta
that has not arisen, arise and grow;
and may that which has arisen not diminish
but increase more and more.

You may include many other dedication prayers, especially prayers for
the long life of your gurus, such as His Holiness the Dalai Lama.

APPENDIX 3: MEDITATION ON THE SEVEN WISDOMS[146]

THIS PRACTICE OF ATTAINING the seven wisdoms is a part of the *Lama Tsongkhapa Daily Guru Yoga Meditation.*

VISUALIZATION FOR CLEANSING AWAY IMPURITIES

Visualize Lama Tsongkhapa, who is Manjushri; Gyaltsap Jé, who is Chenrezig; and Khedrup Jé, who is Vajrapani, in the space in front of you, and then focus on Lama Tsongkhapa in particular. For this to become a guru yoga practice, it is important to maintain the awareness that your root guru is inseparable from Lama Tsongkhapa, who in essence is the three deities: Manjushri, the embodiment of all the buddhas' wisdom; Chenrezig, the embodiment of all the buddhas' compassion; and Vajrapani, the embodiment of all the buddhas' power.

By the force of my having fervently requested in this way,
from the hearts of the three—the perfect, pure Father and
    Sons[147]—
hollow beams of white light are emitted
and, combining into one, enter my crown.
White nectar, the color of milk,
flows from the opening of the tube of white light,
cleansing away all my sicknesses, harm from spirits, negative
    karmas,
obscurations, and their imprints without exception.
My body becomes as pure and clear as crystal.

FIVE-LINE PRAYER TO LAMA TSONGKHAPA (MIGTSEMA)

Mig me tse wäi ter chhen chän rä zig
Chenrezig[148] great treasure of nonobjectifying compassion;
dri me khyen päi wang po jam päi yang
Manjushri, master of stainless wisdom;
dü pung ma lü jom dzä sang wäi dag
Lord of Secrets, destroyer of the entire host of maras;
gang chän khä pä tsug gyän tsong kha pa
Tsongkhapa, crown jewel of the sages of the Land of Snow;
lo zang drag pä zhab la söl wa deb
Losang Dragpa, at your feet I make requests.

VISUALIZATIONS FOR ACHIEVING THE SEVEN WISDOMS

Continue reciting the five-line *migtsema* while doing the following visualizations for achieving the seven wisdoms. For the last three wisdoms, spend more time on the particular wisdom that you wish to achieve.

1. Great Wisdom

Please bless me to achieve great wisdom,
which is unimpeded in discerning the meanings of the infinite
scriptures.

Once again, great wisdom flows forth
in the form of orange nectar, whereby my body is filled.
Light radiates from the atoms of the nectar,   ·
which are clarified in the form of perfect, pure Manjushris.

The great wisdom of the victorious ones of the ten directions and
their sons

absorbs into me in the form of bodies of the deity, whereby my
body is filled.

2. Clear Wisdom

Please bless me to achieve clear wisdom,
which clarifies the detailed, subtle, and difficult vital points
without mixing them up.

Once again, clear wisdom flows forth
in the form of orange nectar, whereby my body is filled.
Light radiates from the atoms of the nectar,
which are clarified in the form of AH RA PA CHA NA DHI.

The clear wisdom of the victorious ones of the ten directions and
their sons
absorbs into me in the form of the mantras, whereby my body is
filled.

3. Quick Wisdom

Please bless me to achieve quick wisdom,
which quickly cuts through nonunderstanding, misunderstand-
ing, and doubt.

Once again, quick wisdom flows forth
in the form of orange nectar, whereby my body is filled.
Light radiates from the atoms of the nectar,
which are clarified in the form of orange DHI syllables.

The quick wisdom of the victorious ones of the ten directions
and their sons

absorbs into me in the form of the seed syllables, whereby my
body is filled.

4. Profound Wisdom

Please bless me to achieve profound wisdom,
which is unfathomable in discerning the meanings of the
scriptures.

Once again, profound wisdom flows forth
in the form of orange nectar, whereby my body is filled.
Light radiates from the atoms of the nectar,
which are clarified in the form of texts and swords.

The profound wisdom of the victorious ones of the ten directions
and their sons
absorbs into me in the form of the hand implements, whereby
my body is filled.

5. Wisdom of Explaining

Please bless me to achieve the wisdom of explaining,
which gives supreme ascertainment regarding all words and their
meanings.

Once again, the wisdom of explaining flows forth
in the form of orange nectar, whereby my body is filled.
Light radiates from the atoms of the nectar,
which are clarified in the form of the texts that are explained.

The wisdom of explaining of the victorious ones of the ten directions and their sons
absorbs into me in the form of the texts, whereby my body is
filled.

6. Wisdom of Debating

Please bless me to achieve the wisdom of debating,
which thoroughly deprives malicious debaters of their
self-confidence.

Once again, the wisdom of debating flows forth
in the form of orange nectar, whereby my body is filled.
Light radiates from the atoms of the nectar,
which are clarified in the form of wheels of swords.

The wisdom of debating of the victorious ones of the ten directions and their sons
absorbs into me in the form of the wheels, whereby my body is
filled.

7. Wisdom of Composing

Please bless me to achieve the wisdom of composing,
which gives rise to a joyous, clear understanding of the excellent
words and their meanings.

Once again, the wisdom of composing flows forth
in the form of orange nectar, whereby my body is filled.
Light radiates from the atoms of the nectar,
which are clarified in the form of texts and wheels.

The wisdom of composing of the victorious ones of the ten directions and their sons
absorbs into me in the form of the texts and wheels, whereby my
body is filled.

REQUEST

May my wisdoms of listening, reflecting, and meditating
   increase.
May my wisdoms of explaining, debating, and composing
   develop.
May I be granted the supreme and common realizations.
Please bless me to quickly become like you. *(3x)*

May my transcendental wisdom of simultaneously-born great
   bliss arise.
May my stains of mistakenly grasping things as real be purified.
May my net of doubts that is only mind be cut.
Please bless me to quickly become like you. *(3x)*

The special benefit of meditating on these seven wisdoms within the
Lama Tsongkhapa Guru Yoga is that you quickly develop your wisdom.
Practicing for even a month, you can see the development. Whatever
you do—listening, reflecting, meditating, or whatever—becomes effective, subduing your mind and eliminating the obstacles to practicing
the Dharma.

Furthermore, when you die you will be able to be born in Tushita
pure land, the pure land of Lama Tsongkhapa and Maitreya Buddha.
And, even more special than that, in future lives you will be able to meet
Lama Tsongkhapa's teachings. They say that meeting Lama Tsongkhapa's teachings is much rarer than being born in Amitabha's pure land,
because his teachings are the unification of sutra and tantra. That means
you will have the opportunity to practice tantra.

APPENDIX 4: A SHORT GREEN TARA SADHANA[149]

A Glance Meditation on the Graduated Path

Refuge

> I take refuge in the holy guru, essence of all buddhas, original grantor of all holy teachings and lord of all supreme beings.

Prayer for Success in Dharma Practice

> Please, Guru-Buddhas, bestow on me the ability to unify my mind with the Dharma and be successful in practicing the Dharma in order to achieve the graduated path. May no hindrances occur while achieving this path.

Prayer of the Practitioner of Lower Capability

> Please bless me to realize that I have received a perfect human rebirth, which is highly meaningful, for many reasons difficult to obtain, but perishable, transient, and fragile, decaying in the shortest moment because of its changeable nature. Thus, my death is definite, but its actual time is most indefinite, and after death I am far more likely to be reborn in the lower suffering realms, having created infinitely more negative than positive karma in this life and all previous lives.

Please bless me to comprehend how incredibly unendurable is the suffering of the lower realms, that I might take refuge in Buddha, Dharma, and Sangha with all my heart, and realize the evolution of karma in all its profundity, that I might perform only virtuous actions and abandon all negative creations.

Prayer of the Practitioner of Middling Capability

By practicing in this way I will be reborn in the upper realms but will still have to experience unlimited samsaric suffering because of uncontrolled delusion and karma.

Please bless me to realize fully the evolution of samsara, from uncontrolled rebirth to death to rebirth, and to follow day and night the three higher trainings of the path: higher conduct, higher concentration, and higher wisdom, which are the main methods to release me from samsara.

The Prayer of the Practitioner of the Higher Capability
The Sutra Path

But as each sentient being has been my mother and as most of them are in extreme suffering, please bless me to bring success to all by renouncing the perfect happiness of self and practicing the bodhisattva's deeds of the six perfections with a bodhisattva's mind of bodhichitta, on the basis of the equanimity meditation. Thus shall I have no sorrow in experiencing the samsaric suffering of all other sentient beings for no matter how long, having trained my mind in the general path.

The Vajrayana Path

Please bless me to follow the quick Vajrayana teachings, by feeling sentient beings' suffering, very unimaginably unbearable for even the shortest moment, as my own, and to achieve the attainment of Shakyamuni Buddha immediately, at this very moment, by keeping my ordinations and the instructions of the guru with the best and highest care in life for the sole purpose of enlightening all sentient beings.

VISUALIZATION

Above the crown of my head I visualize a lotus and a moon disk. Upon these is the great treasury of compassion, Arya Tara, mother of all enlightened beings, who is oneness with my kind root guru. My guru is seated in the full lotus position within a transparent bubble of rainbow-colored light, is pink in complexion, and wears saffron robes and a pandit's hat. His right hand is at his heart in the gesture of teaching the Dharma and holds a vajra and the stem of a white lotus that blooms beside his right ear. His left hand rests on his hip; it holds a bell and the stem of another white lotus that blooms beside his left ear.

At my guru's heart is Arya Tara in female aspect, green in color and seated in the dancing posture within a rainbow bubble. Her left leg is bent up, and her right leg is outstretched. Her left hand is at her heart in the mudra symbolizing the Triple Gem and holding the stem of a blue utpala flower. Her right hand extended over her right knee is in the mudra of granting sublime realizations. She is beautifully adorned with jeweled ornaments and scarves and at her three places (crown, throat, and heart) are syllables OM ༀ, AH ཨཱཿ, HUM ཧཱུྃ. At her heart is a lotus and moon seat on which stands a radiant green syllable TAM ཏཱྃ. Rays of green light radiate in all directions from the TAM and invoke all the enlightened beings of the ten directions. They are all absorbed into Arya Tara and become one.

Make a heartfelt prayer:

Please remain above my head until I receive enlightenment.

REFUGE AND BODHICHITTA

I go for refuge until I am enlightened
to the Buddha, the Dharma, and the Supreme Assembly.
By my merit from giving and other perfections,
may I become a buddha in order to benefit all sentient beings.
(3x)

SEVEN-LIMB PRAYER

Reverently, I prostrate with my body, speech, and mind;
I present clouds of every type of offering, actual and
    imagined;
I declare all my negative actions accumulated since beginningless
    time
and rejoice in the merit of all holy and ordinary beings.
Please, remain until the end of cyclic existence
and turn the wheel of Dharma for living beings.
I dedicate my own merits and those of all others to the great
    enlightenment.

MANDALA OFFERINGS (OUTER AND INNER)

This ground, anointed with perfume, strewn with flowers,
adorned with Mount Meru, four continents, the sun, and the
    moon:
I imagine this as a buddha-field and offer it.
May all living beings enjoy this pure land!

The objects of my attachment, aversion, and ignorance—
friends, enemies, and strangers—and my body, wealth, and
   enjoyments:
without any sense of loss I offer this collection.
Please accept it with pleasure and
bless me with freedom from the three poisons.

IDAM GURU RATNA MANDALAKAM NIRYATAYAMI

PURIFICATION

Request:

Please bless me to purify all obscurations of my body, so that
it will become one in essence with Guru Tara's holy vajra
body.

Visualize:
White light emanates from the OM at Arya Tara's brow and curves in an
arc to enter my brow. My body is purified completely of all obscurations
and becomes one in essence with Guru Tara's holy vajra body.

Request:

Please bless me to purify all obscurations of my speech so
that it will become one in essence with Guru Tara's holy vajra
speech.

Visualize:
Red light emanates from the AH at Arya Tara's throat and curves in an
arc to enter my throat. My speech is purified completely of all obscurations and becomes one in essence with Guru Tara's holy vajra speech.

Request:

> Please bless me to purify all obscurations of my mind so that it will become one in essence with Guru Tara's holy vajra mind.

Visualize:

Blue light emanates from the HUM at Arya Tara's heart and curves in an arc to enter my heart. My mind is purified of all obscurations and becomes one in essence with Guru Tara's holy vajra mind.

Request:

> Please bless me to purify all delusions and subtle obscurations to omniscience so that my body, speech, and mind will become one with Guru Tara's holy body, holy speech, and holy mind.

Visualize:

Now the three-colored beams emanate simultaneously from the OM, AH, and HUM syllables, curving in an arc and entering my three places, completely purifying all my delusions and subtle obscurations to omniscience. My body, speech, and mind become one in essence with Guru Tara's holy body, holy speech, and holy mind.

My root guru dissolves into Arya Tara who melts into green light, which flows into me. Instantly, my wrong conception that I and all other phenomena are self-existent, together with my dualistic mind and its views, disappear, becoming completely empty—not even a trace of them remains.

I concentrate one-pointedly in this empty state, with the wisdom that is indistinguishably one with Guru Tara's blissful omniscient mind.

Then, out of that emptiness, my wisdom manifests instantly as Arya Tara's holy body seated upon a lotus and moon cushion. At my heart is another lotus and moon, upon which in the center stands the syllable TAM surrounded in a clockwise direction by the syllables of the mantra: OM TARE TUTTARE TURE SVAHA. The TAM and the mantra are manifestations of Guru Tara's holy mind, with which my mind is totally united.

Green light radiates from all the letters. Spreading in every direction, it purifies the negative karmas, gross delusions, and subtle obscurations to omniscience of all sentient beings, who become Tara.

Again light radiates, bearing manifold offerings to the six transcendental senses of all the buddhas and sentient beings who have become Tara.

The enlightened beings are extremely pleased, and shower down the superlative qualities of Buddha Tara's holy body, holy speech, and holy mind—omniscient wisdom, supreme power, and infinite compassion, in the form of a great shower of light rays. As I recite the mantra, I absorb and am blessed by this rain.

OM TARE TUTTARE TURE SVAHA

DEDICATION

May I quickly become Guru Arya Tara and lead each and every sentient being into her enlightened state because of these merits.

May the supreme jewel bodhichitta that has not arisen, arise and grow; and may that which has arisen not diminish, but increase more and more.

APPENDIX 5: HEALING BUDDHA[150]

A PRACTICE FOR THE PREVENTION AND HEALING OF DISEASE
by Padmasambhava

THE ACTUAL PRACTICE

Motivation

The purpose of my life is to free all living beings from all of their problems and from the causes of these problems, which are in their minds; also to bring them peace and happiness, especially the peerless happiness of full enlightenment, which they need. In order to accomplish this, I need a perfect, pure, healthy mind and body. For this reason, in order to benefit all living beings equaling the extent of space, I am going to do this healing meditation.

Meditation

At dawn or at another time, visualize your ordinary body. In the center of your chest is your heart, upside down, pointing upward. Inside your heart is an eight-petaled white lotus. In the center of this is a moon disk, and on that is Medicine Buddha.

His holy body, clear and in the nature of deep blue light, is in the aspect of supreme transformation. He is holding an arura plant in his right hand and a begging bowl in his left. In front of Medicine Buddha is the white medicinal goddess Actualized Wisdom; to his right, the yellow medicinal goddess Simultaneous Wealth; behind him, the red forest goddess Neck of Peacock; to his left, the green tree goddess Having

Radiance. Each of these goddesses is in the nature of blissful radiant light and has one face and two arms. In her right hand, each goddess holds an arura plant, and in her left, a vase adorned with various ornaments. Each is seated cross-legged (not in the full vajra position) in an attitude of respecting Healing Buddha.

Visualization and Mantra Recitation

From the five deities in your heart, light beams are emitted in their respective colors. Your whole heart and body are filled with these blissful light beams, which completely purify all disease, harm from spirits, negative actions, and their imprints.

From all the pores of your body, five-colored light beams are emitted. Also, nectar flows down from the begging bowl and the vases held in the left hands of the five heart deities, completely filling your heart and body. Make a strong determination that all diseases have been completely pacified forever, that you can no longer experience any disease.

While one-pointedly concentrating on this visualization, recite the short or long mantra of Medicine Buddha seven, twenty-one, 108, or more times.

If you are ill with a contagious or other disease, after reciting the mantra, put some saliva on your left palm and rub it with the tip of your right ring finger. Then place the tip of the right ring finger at the base of the right and left nostrils, where there is a nerve called the All-Doing King Nerve. Then apply the saliva wherever there is disease.

Short Medicine Buddha Mantra

TADYATHA / OM BHAISHAJYE BHAISHAJYE MAHA BHAISHA-
JYE [BHAISHAJYE] / RAJA SAMUDGATE SVAHA

ཏད་ཡ། ཨོཾ་བྷཻ་ཥ་ཛྱེ་བྷཻ་ཥ་ཛྱེ་མ་ཧཱ་བྷཻ་ཥ་ཛྱེ་ [བྷཻ་ཥ་ཛྱེ་]། ར་ཛ་ས་མུ་དྒ་ཏེ་སྭཱ་ཧཱ།

Common pronunciation:

Ta ya ta / om bekanzay bekanzay maha bekanzay [bekanzay] / radza samudgatay soha

Long Medicine Buddha Mantra

OM NAMO BHAGAVATE BHAISHAJYE / GURU BAIDURYA / PRABHA RAJAYA / TATHAGATAYA / ARHATE SAMYAKSAM BUDDHAYA / TADYATHA / OM BHAISHAJYE BHAISHAJYE MAHA BHAISHAJYE [BHAISHAJYE] / RAJA SAMUDGATE SVAHA

ཨོཾ་ན་མོ་བྷ་ག་ཝ་ཏེ་བྷཻ་ཥ་ཛྱེ། གུ་རུ་བཻཌུཪྻ། པྲ་བྷ་རཱ་ཛཱ་ཡ། ཏ་ཐཱ་ག་ཏཱ་ཡ། ཨརྷ་ཏེ་སམྱཀྶཾ་བུ་དྡྷ་ཡ། ཏ་དྱ་ཐཱ། ཨོཾ་བྷཻ་ཥ་ཛྱེ་བྷཻ་ཥ་ཛྱེ་མ་ཧཱ་བྷཻ་ཥ་ཛྱེ་[བྷཻ་ཥ་ཛྱེ]། རཱ་ཛཱ་ས་མུ་དྒ་ཏེ་སྭཱ་ཧཱ།

Common pronunciation:

Om namo bagawatay bekanzay guru baidurya / praba radza ya / tatagataya / arhatay samyaksam buddhaya / ta ya ta / om bekanzay bekanzay maha bekanzay [bekanzay] / radza samudgatay soha

(The bracketed BHAISHAJYE is optional.)

Then make this request:

You, the destroyer, the qualified one gone beyond (Medicine Buddha) and the four medicinal goddesses, please help me to avoid experiencing the various diseases and to pacify immediately those that I am already experiencing.

After doing this, recite the mantras of the Sanskrit vowels and consonants as much as possible, and also the Heart of Dependent Arising mantra:

Sanskrit vowels

OM A AA I II U UU RI RII LI LII E AI O AU AM AH SVAHA

ༀ་ཨ་ཨཱ་ཨི་ཨཱི་ཨུ་ཨཱུ་རྀ་རཱྀ་ལྀ་ལཱྀ་ཨེ་ཨཻ་ཨོ་ཨཽ་ཨཾ་ཨཿསྭཱ་ཧཱ།

Sanskrit consonants

OM KA KHA GA GHA NGA / CHA CHHA JA JHA NYA / TA THA
DA DHA NA / TA THA DA DHA NA / PA PHA BA BHA MA / YA
RA LA VA / SHA SHA SA HA KSHA SVAHA

ༀ་ཀ་ཁ་ག་གྷ་ང་ ཙ་ཚ་ཛ་ཛྷ་ཉ། ཊ་ཋ་ཌ་ཌྷ་ཎ། ཏ་ཐ་ད་དྷ་ན། པ་ཕ་བ་བྷ་ མ། ཡ་ར་ལ་ཝ། ཤ་ཥ་ས་ཧ་ཀྵ་སྭཱ་ཧཱ།

The Heart of Dependent Arising Mantra:

OM YE DHARMA HETU PRABHAVA HETUN TESHAN
TATHAGATO HYAVADAT TESHAÑ CHA YO NIRODHA EVAM
VADI MAHA SHRAMANA YE SVAHA *(3x)*

ༀ་ཡེ་དྷརྨ་ཧེ་ཏུ་པྲ་བྷ་ཝ་ཧེ་ཏུཾ་ཏེ་ཥཱན་ཏ་ཐཱ་ག་ཏོ་ཧྱ་བ་ད་ཏ་ཏེ་ཥཉྩ་ཡོ་ནི་རོ་དྷ་ ཨེ་ཝཾ་བཱ་དཱི་མ་ཧཱ་ཤྲ་མ་ཎ་ཡེ་སྭཱ་ཧཱ།

This practice protects you from diseases not yet experienced and from those already being experienced. It is the terma (treasure) advice instruction of the Lotus Arisen One (Padmasambhava).

Dedication

Due to all my past, present, and future positive actions, which bring the result of happiness, may the ultimate good heart that cherishes and cares for all living beings, who are the source of all my and others' happiness in the past, present, and future, be generated in my mind and the minds of others. May that which has already arisen in my and others' minds increase.

Due to all my positive actions in the past, present, and future as well as those of all holy beings, who have the purest attitude, may all father and mother living beings have happiness, and may I cause this by myself alone. May the realms of the unfortunate beings (hell, hungry ghost, and animal) be emptied forever.

Wherever there are holy beings who dedicate their lives to bringing happiness to others, may all their prayers succeed immediately, and may I cause this by myself alone.

Due to my positive actions of the past, present, and future and those done by these holy beings, may I achieve the peerless happiness of full enlightenment—the state of mind that is free of all mistakes and possesses all positive qualities—and lead everyone to this state.

APPENDIX 6: MORE POWERFUL MANTRAS

THERE ARE GROUPS of mantras that I have been recommending for many years because of their great power. They are specifically those mantras than can benefit beings who are dying or dead and the four dharmakaya relic mantras.[151]

THE POWERFUL MANTRAS FOR BENEFITING BEINGS AT DEATH[152]

1. The Chenrezig Mantras
The short mantra:

OM MANI PADME HUM

ཨོཾ་མ་ཎི་པ་དྨེ་ཧཱུྃ།

The long mantra:

NAMO RATNA TRA YA YA / NAMA ARYA JNANA SAGARA / VAIROCHANA BYUHA RAJAYA / TATHAGATAYA / ARHATE / SAMYAKSAM BUDDHAYA/ NAMA SARVA TATHAGATE BHYA / ARHATE BHYA / SAMYAKSAM BUDDHE BHYA / NAMA ARYA AVALOKITESHVARAYA / BODHISATTVAYA / MAHA SATTVAYA / MAHA KARUNI KAYA / TADYATHA / OM DHARA DHARA / DHIRI DHIRI / DHURU DHURU / ITTE VATTE / CHALE CHALE / PRACHALE PRACHALE / KUSUME KUSUME VARE / ILI MILI / CHITI JALA APANAYE SVAHA

ན་མོ་རཏྣ་ཏྲ་ཡཱ་ཡ། ན་མཿཨཱ་ཪྻ་རྫྙཱ་ན་སཱ་ག་ར། བེ་རོ་ཙ་ན་བྱུ་ཧ་ཪཱ་ཛཱ་ཡ། ཏ་ཐཱ་ག་ཏཱ་ཡ། ཨརྷ་ཏེ། སམྱཀྶཾ་བུ་དྡྷཱ་ཡ། ན་མཿསརྦ་ཏ་ཐཱ་ག་ཏེ་བྷྱཿ ཨརྷ་ཏེ་བྷྱཿ སམྱཀྶཾ་བུ་དྡྷེ་བྷྱཿ ན་མཿཨཱ་ཪྻ་ཨ་ཝ་ལོ་ཀི་ཏེ་ཤྭ་རཱ་ཡ། བོ་དྷི་སཏྭཱ་ཡ། མཧཱ་སཏྭཱ་ཡ། མ་ཧཱ་ཀཱ་རུ་ཎི་ཀཱ་ཡ། ཏདྱ་ཐཱ། ཨོཾ་ཧ་ར་ཧ་ར། ཧྲི་རི་ཧྲི་རི། ཧྲུ་རུ་ཧྲུ་རུ། ཨི་ཊྛི་ལཊྛི། ཙ་ལེ་ཙ་ལེ། པྲ་ཙ་ལེ་པྲ་ཙ་ལེ། ཀུ་སུ་མེ་ཀུ་སུ་མེ་ཝ་རེ། ཨི་ལི་མི་ལི། ཙི་ཏི་ཛྭ་ལ་མ་པ་ན་ཡེ་སྭཱ་ཧཱ།

2. The Short Medicine Buddha Mantra:

TADYATHA / OM BHAISHAJYE BHAISHAJYE MAHA BHAISHA-
JYE [BHAISHAJYE] / RAJA SAMUDGATE SVAHA

ཏདྱ་ཐཱ། ཨོཾ་བྷཻ་ཥ་ཛྱེ་བྷཻ་ཥ་ཛྱེ་མ་ཧཱ་བྷཻ་ཥ་ཛྱེ་[བྷཻ་ཥ་ཛྱེ་]རཱ་ཛ་ས་མུ་ཏྒ་ཏེ་སྭཱ་ཧཱ།

Note: The bracketed BHAISHAJYE is optional.

3. The Wish-Granting Wheel Mantra:

OM PADMO USHNISHA VIMALE HUM PHAT

ཨོཾ་པ་དྨོ་ཨུཥྞི་ཥ་བི་མ་ལེ་ཧཱུྃ་ཕཊ།

4. The Mitrukpa Mantra:

NAMO RATNA TRAYAYA / OM KAMKANI KAMKANI
ROCHANI ROCHANI TROTANI TROTANI TRASANI TRASANI
PRATIHANA PRATIHANA SARVA KARMA PARAM PARA NI
ME SARVA SATTVA NANCHA SVAHA

ན་མོ་རཏྣ་ཏྲ་ཡཱ་ཡ། ཨོཾ་ཀཾ་ག་ཎི་ཀཾ་ག་ཎི། རོ་ཙ་ནི་རོ་ཙ་ནི། ཏྲོ་ཊ་ནི་ཏྲོ་ཊ་ནི། ཏྲཱ་ས་ནི་ཏྲཱ་ས་ནི། པྲ་ཏི་ཧ་ན་པྲ་ཏི་ཧ་ན། སརྦ་ཀརྨ་པ་རཾ་པ་རཱ་ཎི་མེ་སརྦ་ སཏྭ་ནཉྩ་སྭཱ་ཧཱ།

5. The Namgyalma Mantras

The long mantra:

OM NAMO BHAGAVATE SARVA TRAILOKYA PRATIVISH-
ISHTAYA / BUDDHAYA TE NAMA / TADYATHA / OM BHRUM
BHRUM BHRUM SHODHAYA SHODHAYA / VISHODHAYA
VISHODHAYA / ASAMA SAMANTA AVABHASA SPHARANA
GATI GAGANA SVABHAVA VISHUDDHE / ABHISHINCHANTU
MAM / SARVA TATHAGATA SUGATA VARA VACHANA
AMRITA ABHISHEKARA / MAHAMUDRA MANTRA PADAI /
AHARA AHARA / MAMA AYUS SAMDHARANI / SHODHAYA
SHODHAYA / VISHODHAYA VISHODHAYA / GAGANA
SVABHAVA VISHUDDHE / USHNISHA VIJAYA PARISHUD-
DHE / SAHASRA RASMI SANCHO DITE / SARVA TATHAGATA
AVALOKINI / SHAT PARAMITA PARIPURANI / SARVA
TATHAGATA MATE / DASHA BHUMI PRATISHTHITE / SARVA
TATHAGATA HRIDAYA / ADHISHTHANA ADHISHTHITE /
MUDRE MUDRE MAHA MUDRE / VAJRA KAYA SAMHATANA
PARISHUDDHE / SARVA KARMA AVARANA VISHUDDHE
/ PRATINI VARTAYA MAMA AYUR / VISHUDDHE SARVA
TATHAGATA / SAMAYA ADHISHTHANA ADHISHTHITE
/ OM MUNI MUNI MAHA MUNI / VIMUNI VIMUNI MAHA
VIMUNI / MATI MATI MAHA MATI / MAMATI SUMATI
TATHATA / BHUTA KOTI PARISHUDDHE / VISPHUTA BUD-
DHE SHUDDHE / HE HE JAYA JAYA / VIJAYA VIJAYA / SMR-
ARA SMRARA / SPHARA SPHARA / SPHARAYA SPHARAYA
/ SARVA BUDDHA ADHISHTHANA ADHISHTHITE / SHUD-
DHE SHUDDHE / BUDDHE BUDDHE / VAJRE VAJRE MAHA

VAJRE / SUVAJRE VAJRA GARBHE JAYA GARBHE / VIJAYA
GARBHE / VAJRA JVALA GARBHE / VAJROD BHAVE / VAJRA
SAMBHAVE / VAJRE VAJRINI / VAJRAMA BHAVATU MAMA
SHARIRAM / SARVA SATTVA NANCHA KAYA PARISHUDDHIR
BHAVATU / ME SADA SARVA GATI PARISHUDDHISHCHA
/ SARVA TATHAGATASHCHA / MAM SAMASHVAS YANTU
/ BUDDHYA BUDDHYA / SIDDHYA SIDDHYA / BODHAYA
BODHAYA / VIBODHAYA VIBODHAYA / MOCHAYA MOCHAYA
/ VIMOCHAYA VIMOCHAYA / SHODHAYA SHODHAYA /
VISHODHAYA VISHODHAYA / SAMANTANA MOCHAYA
MOCHAYA / SAMANTA RASMI PARISHUDDHE / SARVA
TATHAGATA HRIDAYA / ADHISHTHANA ADHISHTHITE /
MUDRE MUDRE MAHA MUDRE / MAHAMUDRA MANTRA
PADAI SVAHA

ཨོཾ་ན་མོ་ཧྲ་ག་ཕ་ཊེ་སརྦ་ཊེ་ལོ་ཀྱ་སྱ་ཊེ་བི་ཧིཉྩ་ཡ། བུཧྲ་ཡ་ཊེ་ན་མཿ ཏུཧྲ་ས།
ཨོཾ་ཧྲུཧྲུཧྲུཾ། ཧོ་ཧྲ་ཡ་ཨོ་ཧྲ་ཡ། བི་ཧོ་ཧྲ་ཡ་བི་ཧོ་ཧྲ་ཡ། ཨ་ས་མ་ས་མཽྣ་ཨ་བ་
ཧྲ་ས་སྤ་ར་ཙ་ག་ཊི་ག་ག་ན་སྭ་བྷཱ་བ་བི་ཤུཧྲེ། ཨཱྦྱི་ཧྲིཙྪུ་ཏུ་མོ། སརྦ་ཏ་ཐཱ་ག་
ཏུ་སུ་ག་ཏ་བ་ར་བ་ཙ་ན་ཨ་མྲི་ཊ་ཨ་བྷི་ཥེ་ཀེ་ར། མཧཱ་མུ་ཧྲ་མ཈ྩ་པ་ཧེ། ཨུ་
ཊ་ར་ཨུ་ཊ་ར། མ་མ་ཨུ་ཡུ་སཾ་ཧྲ་ར་ཧི། ཧོ་ཧྲ་ཡ་ཧོ་ཧྲ་ཡ། བི་ཧོ་ཧྲ་ཡ་བི་ཧོ་ཧྲ་
ཡ། ག་ག་ན་སྭ་བྷཱ་ཝ། བི་ཤུཧྲེ། ཨུཥྞི་ཥ་བི་ཛ་ཡ་པ་རི་ཤུཧྲེ། ས་ཧ་སྲ་རཤྨི་
སཾཙྩོ་ཊེ། སརྦ་ཏ་ཐཱ་ག་ཏུ་ཨ་བ་ལོ་ཀཱི་ནི། ཥཊ་པ་ར་མི་ཏ་པ་རི་པུ་ར་ཎི།
སརྦ་ཏ་ཐཱ་ག་ཏུ་ཨ་ཏེ། ཧྲ་ཐ་ཝྀ་ཥྱ་ཏེ་ཥྛི་ཏེ། སརྦ་ཏ་ཐཱ་ག་ཏུ་ཧྲི་ཏ་ཡ།
ཨ་ཧྲི་ཥྛ་ན་ཨ་ཧྲི་ཥྛི་ཏེ། མུ་ཧྲེ་མུ་ཧྲེ། མ་ཧཱ་མུ་ཧྲེ། བཛྲ་ཀཱ་ཡ་སཾ་ཏ་ཏ་ན་པ་རི་
ཤུཧྲེ། སརྦ་ཀརྨ་ཨ་བ་ར་ཎ་བི་ཤུཧྲེ། པྲ་ཊེ་ནི་བཏྟ་ཡ་མ་མ་ཨཱ་ཡུཿ་བི་ཤུཧྲེ།
སརྦ་ཏ་ཐཱ་ག་ཏྲ། ས་མ་ཡ་ཨཱཧྲིཥྛ་ན་ཨཱཧྲིཥྛི་ཏེ། ཨོཾ་མུ་ནི་མུ་ནི་མ་ཧཱ་མུ་ནི། བི་
མུ་ནི་བི་མུ་ནི་མ་ཧཱ་བི་མུ་ནི། མ་ཏེ་མ་ཏེ་མ་ཧཱ་མ་ཏེ། མ་མ་ཏེ་སུ་མ་ཏེ་ཏ་
ཐཱ་ཏ། བྷུ་ཏ་ཀོ་ཏི་པ་རི་ཤུཧྲེ། བི་སྥུ་ཊ་བུཧྲེ་ཤུཧྲེ། ཧེ་ཧེ་ཛ་ཡ་ཛ་ཡ། བི་ཛ་ཡ་
བི་ཛ་ཡ། སྨ་ར་སྨ་ར། སྥ་ར་སྥ་ར། སྥཱ་ར་ཡ་སྥཱ་ར་ཡ། སརྦ་བུཧྲ་ཨ་ཧྲིཥྛ་ན་ཨ་
ཧྲིཥྛི་ཏེ། ཤུཧྲེ་ཤུཧྲེ། བུཧྲེ་བུཧྲེ། བཛྲེ་བཛྲེ་མ་ཧཱ་བཛྲེ། སུ་བཛྲེ་བཛྲ་གརྦྷེ་ཛ་ཡ་

གཉྫེ། བི་ཏ་ཡ་གཉྫེ། བཛྲ་དྷ་ལ་གཉྫེ། བཙོ་རྙ་ལེ། བཛྲ་སོ་རྙ་ལེ། བཛེ་བཛི་ནི། བཛྲ་མ་རྙ་ལྤུ་ཏུ་མ་མ་ཕ་རི་རཾ། སརྦ་བདྡ་བཚུ་ཀུ་ཡ། པ་རི་ཤུ་དྡྷ་རྙ་པ་ཏུ། མེ་ས་དུ་སརྦ་གཏེ་པ་རི་ཤུ་དྡྷ་སརྦ་ཏ་ཐཱ་ག་ཏུ་ཙྪ་མོ་ས་མ་ཤྭ་ས་ཡཀྲུ་འཇྲ་འཇྲ། སི་ཛྲ་སི་ཛྲ། བོ་རྙ་ཡ་བོ་རྙ་ཡ། བི་བོ་རྙ་ཡ་བི་བོ་རྙ་ཡ། མོ་ཙ་ཡ་མོ་ཙ་ཡ། བི་མོ་ཙ་ཡ་བི་མོ་ཙ་ཡ། ཤོ་རྙ་ཡ་ཤོ་རྙ་ཡ། བི་ཤོ་རྙ་ཡ་བི་ཤོ་རྙ་ཡ། ས་མཎྚན་མོ་ཙ་ཡ་མོ་ཙ་ཡ། ས་མཎྟ་རྨྨི་པ་རི་ཤུ་དྡྷེ། སརྦ་ཏ་ཐཱ་ག་ཏུ་ཧྲི་ད་ཡ། ཨ་དྷིཥྛཱ་ན་ཨ་དྷིཥྛིཏེ། སུ་རེ་སུ་རེ་མཎྜ་སུ་རེ། མཎྜ་མུཎྜ་མཉྫ་པདེ་སྭ་ཧཱ།

The short mantra:

[TADYATHA] OM BHRUM SVAHA / OM AMRITA AYUR DADE
SVAHA

[དྱ་ཐཱ།] ཨོཾ་བྷྲུ་སྭ་ཧཱ། ཨོཾ་ཨ་མྲྀཏ་ཨ་ཡུརྡ་དེ་སྭ་ཧཱ།

At the conclusion, recite:

OM AMITE / AMITODA BHAVE / AMITE VIKRANTE / AMITA
GATRE / AMITO GAMINI / AMITA AYURDADE / GAGANA
KIRTI KARE SARVA KLESHA KSHAYAM KARI YE SVAHA

ཨོཾ་ཨ་མི་ཏེ། ཨ་མི་ཏོ་ད་བྷ་བེ། ཨ་མི་ཏེ་བིཀྲན་ཏེ། ཨ་མི་ཏ་གཏྲེ། ཨ་མི་ཏོ་ག་མི་ནི། ཨ་མི་ཏ་ཡུརྡ་དེ། ག་ག་ན་གིརྟི་ག་རེ་སརྦ་ཀླེ་ཤཿཀྵ་ཡཾ་ག་རི་ཡེ་སྭ་ཧཱ།

6. *The Padmasambhava Mantra:*

OM AH HUM VAJRA GURU PADMA SIDDHI HUM

ཨོཾ་ཨཱཿཧཱུྃ་བཛྲ་གུ་རུ་པདྨ་སིདྡྷི་ཧཱུྃ།

7. *The Kunrik Mantra:*

OM NAMO BHAGAVATE / SARVA DURGATE PARI SHODHANI
RAJAYA / TATHAGATAYA / ARHATE SAMYAKSAM BUD-
DHAYA / TADYATHA / OM SHODHANI / SHODHANI / SARVA
PAPAM BISHODHANI / SHUDHE BISHUDHE / SARVA KARMA
AVARANA BISHODHANI SVAHA

ཨོཾ་ན་མོ་བྷ་ག་ཝ་ཏེ། སརྦ་དུརྒ་ཏེ་པ་རི་ཤོ་དྷ་ནི་ར་ཛ་ཡ། ཏ་ཐཱ་ག་ཏཱ་ཡ།
ཨརྷ་ཏེ་སམྱཀྶཾ་བུ་དྡྷཱ་ཡ། ཏ་དྱ་ཐཱ། ཨོཾ་ཤོ་དྷ་ནི། ཤོ་དྷ་ནི། སརྦ་པཱ་པ་བི་ཤོ་དྷ་ནི།
ཤུ་དྡྷེ་བི་ཤུ་དྡྷེ། སརྦ་ཀརྨ་ཨཱ་ཝ་ར་ཎ་བི་ཤུ་དྡྷེ་སྭཱ་ཧཱ།

8. *The Milarepa Mantra:*

OM AH GURU HASA VAJRA SARVA SIDDHI PHALA HUM

ཨོཾ་ཨཱཿགུ་རུ་ཧ་ས་བཛྲ་སརྦ་སིདྡྷི་ཕ་ལ་ཧཱུྃ།

9. *The Zung of the Exalted Completely Pure Stainless Light (1):*

NAMA SAPTANAM / SAMYAKSAM BUDDHA KOTINÄN PARI-
SHUDDHE MA NA SI / ABHYA CHITA PATISHTHA TUNÄN /
NAMO BHAGAVATE / AMRITA AH YU SHASYA / TATHAGATA
SYA / OM SARVA TATHAGATA SHUDDHI / AH YUR
BISHODHANI / SAMHARA SAMHARA / SARVA TATHAGATA
BIRYA BA LE NA PRATI SAMHARA AYU SARA SARA / SARVA
TATHAGATA SAMAYA/ BODHI BODHI/ BUDDHA BUDDHYA
/ BODHAYA / BODHAYA / MAMA SARVA PAPAM AVARANA
BISHUDHE / BIGATA MALAM / CHHARA SU BUDDHYA BUD-
DHE HURU HURU SVAHA

ན་མཿསཔྟཱ་ནཱཾ། སམྱཀྶཾ་བུ་དྡྷ་ཀོ་ཊི་ནཱན་པ་རི་ཤུ་དྡྷེ་མ་ན་སི། ཨ་བྷྱ་ཙི་ཏ་པ་ཏི་

ཏུ་ནྲན། ནཐོ་ཊྚ་ག་བ་ཏེ། ཨ་སྨྲི་ཏུ་ཡྩུ་ཡུ་ཊ་སྒྱ། ཏ་ཧྲ་ག་ཏ་སྒྱ། ཨོཾ་སཏ་ཏུ་
སྲ་ག་ཏ་ཡྲྀ། ཡྩུ་ཡུར་བི་ཕོ་ཊྚ་ནི། སོ་ཏུ་ར་སོ་ཏུ་ར། སརྟ་ཏུ་སྲ་ག་ཏུ་བྲྀཉ་བ
ཨེ་ནུ་པ་ཏི་སོ་ཏུ་ར་ཡྩུ་ཡུ་སྲ་ར་སྲྲ་ར། སརྟ་ཏུ་སྲ་ག་ཏུ་ས་མ་ཡ། པོ་ཊྚི་པོ་ཊྚི།
བྲྀཉ་བྲྀཉ། པོ་ཊྚ་ཡ་པོ་ཊྚ་ཡ། མ་མ་སརྟ་པུ་པོ་ཡྩུ་བ་ར་ཅ་བི་ཡྲྀཉི། པི་ག་ཏུ་མ
ལི། ཚར་སུ་བྲྀཉ་བྲྀཉི་ཏུ་ར་ཏུ་ར་སྭྲ་ཧྲ།

10. *The Zung of the Exalted Completely Pure Stainless Light (2):*

NAMA NAWA NAWA TINAM / TATHAGATA GAM GANAM
DIWA LUKA NAM / KOTI NIYUTA SHATA SAHASRANAN / OM
BO BO RI / TSARI NI TSARI / MORI GORI TSALA WARI SVAHA

ན་མཿན་བ་ན་བ་ཏི་ནཾ། ཏ་སྲ་ག་ཏ་གཾ་གྲ་ནཾ་ནྲི་ནུ་ལུ་ཀ་ནཾ། གོ་ཏི་ནི་ཡུ་ཏ་ས
ཏ་ས་ཏུ་སྲྲྀ། ཨོཾ་པོ་པོ་རི། ཚ་རི་ཉི་ཚ་རི། མོ་རི་གོ་ལི་ཚ་ལ་བྲ་རི་སྭྲ་ཧྲ།

11. *The Maitreya Buddha mantras*

The mantra of Maitreya Buddha's promise:

NAMO RATNA TRAYAYA / NAMO BHAGAVATE SHAKYAMU-
NIYE / TATHAGATAYA / ARHATE SAMYAKSAM BUDDHAYA
/ TADYATHA / OM AJITE AJITE APARAJITE / AJITANCHAYA
HA RA HA RA MAITRI AVALOKITE KARA KARA MAHA
SAMAYA SIDDHI BHARA BHARA MAHA BODHI MANDA BIJA
SMARA SMARA AHSMA KAM SAMAYA BODHI BODHI MAHA
BODHI SVAHA

ན་མོ་རྩྣ་ཏྲ་ཡུ་ཡ། ན་མོ་ཊྚ་ག་བ་ཏེ། ཤྲྀཀྱུ་མུ་ན་ཡེ། ཏ་ཐྲ་ག་ཏ་ཡ། ཨརྷ་ཏེ
སརྐྱུ་བྲྀ་ཡ། ཏ་དྱ་ཐྲ། ཨོཾ་ཨ་ཛྀ་ཏེ། ཨ་ཛྀ་ཏེ། ཨ་པ་ར་ཛྀ་ཏེ། ཨ་ཛྀ་ཏ་ཉྩ་ཡ།
ཧ་ར་ཧ་ར། མེ་ཏྲི་ཨ་བ་ལོ་གི་ཏེ། ག་ར་ག་ར། མ་ཧྲ་ས་མ་ཡ་སིཉི། བྷ་ར་བྷ

ར། མཏུ་བོ་རྗེ་མརྟྲ་དྲི་ཧོ། སྨ་ར་སྨ་ར། ཨསྨ་ཀཾ་ས་མ་ཡ། བོ་རྗེ་བོ་རྗེ། མཏུ་བོ
རྗེ་སྭཱ་ཧཱ།

The heart mantra:

OM MOHI MOHI MAHA MOHI SVAHA

ཨོ་མོ་ཧི་མོ་ཧི་མཏུ་མོ་ཧི་སྭཱ་ཧཱ།

The close heart mantra:

OM MUNI MUNI SMARA SVAHA

ཨོ་མུ་ནི་མུ་ནི་སྨ་ར་སྭཱ་ཧཱ།

12. *The Buddha Rinchen Tsugtorchen Name Prayer:*

De zhin sheg pa rin chhen tsug tor chän la chhag tshäl lo
To Tathagata Precious Ushnisha, I prostrate.

13. *The Lotus Pinnacle of Amoghapasha:*

OM PADMO USHNISHA VIMALE HUM PHAT

ཨོ་པ་དྨོ་ཨུཥྚི་ཪ་བི་མ་ལེ་ཧཱུྃ་ཕཊ།

14. *The Celestial Mansion Extremely Secret Sublime Success:*

OM VIPULA GARBHE / MANI PRABHE / TATHAGATA NIRDE-
SHANE / MANI MANI / SUPRABHE / VIMALE / SAGARA GAM-

BHIRE / HUM HUM / JVALA JVALA / BUDDHA VILOKITE /
GUHYA ADHISHTHITA /GARBHE SVAHA

ཨོཾ་བི་དུ་ལ་ག་ཏྲེ། མ་ཚི་པུ་ཏྲེ། ཏ་བྲ་ག་ཏ་ནི་ར་དེ་ན་ནེ། མ་ཚི་མ་ཏི། སུ་པུ་
ཏྲེ། བི་མ་ལེ། ས་ག་ར་ག་ཏྲི་ནེ། ཧྰུཾ་ཧྰུཾ། དྲུ་ལ་དྲུ་ལ། བུཊྚ་བི་ལོ་ཀི་ཏེ། གུ་ཧྱ་
ཨརྡྷི་ཐི་ཏེ། གརྦྷེ་སྭཱ་ཧཱ།

15. *The mantra from the Sutra of Great Liberation:*

NAMO BUDDHAYA / NAMO DHARMAYA / NAMAH SANG-
HAYA / ADANTI DHARAṆI / TADYATHA / AKASHANI VAVINI
/ SARVA DHARMA NI VANI / ISHAMANA / VIPASHANA /
VIMALA SUPARI / DHARMA NI KHANA / VARUNI CHAYA
TAMALE / CHALE / HULU HULU / SHIVITE / MANTRA MAN-
TRA SVAHA

ན་མོ་བུཊྚ་ཡ། ན་མོ་དྷརྨ་ཡ། ན་མཿསཾ་གྷ་ཡ། ཨ་དན་ཏི་དྷཱ་ར་ཎི། ཏ་དྱ་ཐཱ། ཨཱ་
ཀཱ་ཤ་ནི་བྷཱ་བི་ནི། སརྦ་དྷརྨ་ནི་བ་ནི། ཡི་ཤ་མ་ན། བི་པ་ཤ་ན། བི་མ་ལ་སུ་པ་
རི། དྷརྨ་ནི་ཁ་ན། བ་རུ་ཎི་ཚ་ཡ་ཏ་མ་ལེ། ཚ་ལེ། ཧུ་ལུ་ཧུ་ལུ། ཤི་བི་ཏེ། མནྟྲ་
མནྟྲ་མནྟྲཿསྭཱ་ཧཱ།

THE FOUR DHARMAKAYA RELIC MANTRAS[153]

There are four dharmakaya relic mantras:

  1. The Stainless Pinnacle Deity Mantra
  2. The Secret Relic Mantra
  3. The Zung of the Exalted Completely Pure Stainless Light
  4. The Hundred Thousand Ornaments of Enlightenment Mantra

These four mantras are the relics of the dharmakaya, the relics of the

Buddha. Other relics that we normally see, such as robes or parts of the Buddha's holy body, are secondary relics. These are the highest relics. After I learned about the unbelievable benefits of each of these mantras, I had them written down and we printed many copies. These are normally what we should put inside stupas, statues, and so on.

By putting these mantras inside a stupa, even a bell that is offered to the stupa brings unimaginable benefit. For example, the negative karma of all sentient beings who hear the sound of that bell is purified; they are liberated from the lower realms and receive a good rebirth. In that way, it makes it so easy for sentient beings to purify negative karma and reach enlightenment.

Even while building a stupa, people's minds are transformed. Students tell me how their hearts become softer, and they can definitely see some purification. To put just one brick or stone in a stupa being built becomes the cause for enlightenment. And when the stupa is finished, especially if it contains these four very powerful mantras, it blesses the whole environment around it; it protects it and helps all beings: humans, animals, even spirits and nagas.

You don't have to be Buddhist to benefit from a stupa. I remember the builders who built the Kadampa stupa at Institut Vajrayogini in France were Christians, a very special group whose service to their church was to build and restore holy objects.

There was also a stupa built in Iceland. A student at Tushita, Dharamsala, asked me what she should do after the meditation course, so I suggested building a stupa, which she did back at home in Iceland.[154] Most of the people who helped her build it were non-Buddhists. I went there to bless it. When the sun is shining there, the area of the stupa is so pleasant, close to the main road and overlooking the city. But when I was there, the weather was very bad: windy, foggy, snowing! I ended up having to do half the ceremony in the car, which was being rocked by the wind. I have no idea how they managed to build the stupa in such a place. After it was consecrated, it was offered to the government, so the mayor came to give a speech—even in all that foggy weather. Now, the stupa is easily seen from the road and many people stop to look at it. It is of great benefit to Iceland.

The benefits of circumambulating and so forth are extensively explained in sutras such as *Arya Compassionate Eye Looking One* and *Compassionate White Lotus*.

1. The Stainless Pinnacle Deity Mantra

As we have seen, the heart mantra of Stainless Pinnacle Deity (*Tsugtor Drime*) is this:

OM NAMAS TRAIYA DHVIKANAM / SARVA TATHAGATA HRI-
DAYA GARBHE JVALA JVALA / DHARMA DHATU GARBHE /
SAMBHARA MAMA AYUH SAMSHODHAYA / MAMA SARVA
PAPAM / SARVA TATHAGATA SAMANTOSHNISHA VIMALE
VISHUDDHE HUM HUM HUM HUM / AM VAM SAM JA SVAHA

ཨོཾ་ན་མ་སྟྲཻ་ཡ་དྷྭི་ཀཱ་ནཱྃ། སརྦ་ཏ་ཐཱ་ག་ཏ་ཧྲྀ་ད་ཡ་གརྦྷེ་ཛྭ་ལ་ཛྭ་ལ། དྷརྨ་དྷཱ་
ཏུ་གརྦྷེ། སཾབྷ་ར་མ་མ་ཨཱ་ཡུཿསཾ་ཤོ་དྷ་ཡ། མ་མ་སརྦ་པཱ་པཾ། སརྦ་ཏ་ཐཱ་ག་ཏ་
ས་མནྟོཥྞི་ཥ་བི་མ་ལེ་བི་ཤུདྡྷེ། ཧཱུྃ་ཧཱུྃ་ཧཱུྃ་ཧཱུྃ། ཨཱྃ་བཾ་སཾ་ཛ་སྭཱ་ཧཱ།

As explained by the Buddha in the Kangyur, there are skies of benefits for making even just one prostration, circumambulation, or offering to a holy object containing the Stainless Pinnacle Deity mantra:

- It completely purifies the karmic obstacles of the five immediate negativities.
- You will be completely liberated from the hell, hungry ghost, and animal realms, and from the evil-gone realm of the yama world.[155]
- You will have a long life.
- Like a snake changing its skin, when leaving the body, you will have the fortune to go to the blissful realm (that is, a pure land).
- You will never be stained by the smell of the womb.
- All your wishes will be completely and exactly fulfilled.
- If you put this mantra inside a stupa, you will never be reborn

in the lower realms and will have a pure life until you achieve enlightenment.

- You will have good rebirths up until enlightenment is achieved.

This is most amazing. We have so many human problems that are unbearable, so how could we bear the sufferings of the lower realms, such as being born as an insect, much less being born a hell being or a hungry ghost? When we human beings have problems, we can communicate and try many ways to resolve the problems, but animals and hungry ghosts cannot do this, and their suffering is so much greater. And if their problems are unimaginably terrible, there is no question that the sufferings of the hell beings are so much worse. Therefore it is incredibly precious that just by putting this mantra inside a stupa, we can be freed forever from these sufferings, be ensured pure lives, and have higher rebirths until enlightenment is achieved.

2. The Secret Relic Mantra

The Secret Relic (Sangwa Rigsel) Mantra is this:

NAMO STRAIYA DHIKANAM / SARVA TATHAGATA NAM / OM BHU PI BHA BAN BA RE BA CHE TAU / CHU LU CHU LU / DHA RA DHA RA / SARVA TATHAGATA / DHATU DHA RE / PADMA GARBHE / JAYA BARE / ACHALE / SAMRA TATHAGATA / DHARMACHAKRA / PRAVARTANA / VAJRA BODHI / MANDA ALAMKARA / ALAMKRITE / SARVA TATHAGATA / ADHISHTHITE / BODHAYA BODHAYA / BODHANI BODHANI / BUDDHYA BUDDHYA / SAMBODHANI SAMBODHAYA / CHALA CHALA / CHALANTU SARVA ABARANANI / SARVA PAPAM VIGATE / HURU HURU / SARVA SHOKA VIGATE / SARVA TATHAGATA HRIDAYA / VAJRINI / SAMBHAVA SAM-BHAVA / SARVA TATHAGATA GUHYE / DHARANI MUDRE / BUDDHE / SUBUDDHE / SARVA TATHAGATA ADHISHTHITE / DHATU GARBHE SVAHA / SAMAYA ADHISHTHITE SVAHA / SARVA TATHAGATA HRIDAYA / DHATU MUDRE SVAHA

/ SUPRATISHTHITA STUPE TATHAGATA ADHISHTHITE
/ HUM HUM SVAHA / OM SARVA TATHAGATA USHNISHA
DHATU MUDRANI SARVA TATHAGATA DHARMA DHATU
VIBHUSHITE ADHISHTHITE HURU HURU HUM HUM SVAHA

ན་མ་སྟྲེ་ཡ་རྫེ་ཀུ་རྣཱ། སཏ་ཏ་སྲ་ག་ཏ་རྣཱ། ཨོཾ་རྱ་ཡི་རྩ་ནྲུན་བ་རེ་བ་ཚོ་ལཱ། ཧུ་

ཀུ་ཚུ་ཀྱུ། རྲ་ར་རྲ་ར། སཏ་ཏ་སྲ་ག་ཏ། རྫུ་ཏུ་རྫུ་རེ། པརྫ་ག་ཏྲེ། ཧ་ཡ་བ་རེ།

ཨ་ཚ་ལེ། སླུ་ར་ཏ་སྲ་ག་ཏ། རྱ་ཚཱག། སུ་བཏ་ན། བཛྲ་པོ་རྫེ། མ་ཙ་ཨ་ལོ་

ཀུ་ར། ཨ་ལོ་ཀཱི་ཏེ། སཏ་ཏ་སྲ་ག་ཏ། ཨ་རྫི་རྫི་ཏེ། པོ་རྲ་ཡ་པོ་རྲ་ཡ། པོ་རྲ་རྣི་པོ་

རྲ་རྣི། བུརྲ་ཡ་བུརྲ་ཡ། སོ་པོ་རྲ་རྣི་སོ་པོ་རྲ་ཡ། ཚ་ལ་ཚ་ལ། ཚ་ལོ་ཏུ་སཏ་ཨཱ

བ་ར་ཊ་ན། སཏ་སུ་པོ་བི་ག་ཏེ། ཧུ་ར་ཧུ་ར། སཏ་ཚོ་ག་བི་ག་ཏེ། སཏ་ཏ་སྲ

ག་ཏུ་ཙི་ད་ཡ། བཛྲ་རྙི། སོ་སྲ་བ་སོ་སྲ་བ། སཏ་ཏ་སྲ་ག་ཏུ་གུ་ཊྱེ། རྲ་ར་ཅི་སུ

རེ། བུརྫེ། སུ་བུརྫེ། སཏ་ཏ་སྲ་ག་ཏུ་ཨ་རྫི་རྫི་ཏེ། རྫུ་ཏུ་ག་རྫེ་སྭ་རྡ། ས་མ་ཡ་ཨ

རྫི་རྫི་ཏེ་སྭ་རྡ། སཏ་ཏ་སྲ་ག་ཏུ་ཙི་ད་ཡ། རྫུ་ཏུ་སུ་རེ་སྲ་རྡ། སུ་པ་ཏི་རྫི་ཏ་སྟུ་པེ

ཏ་སྲ་ག་ཏུ་ཨ་རྫི་རྫི་ཏེ། རྣུ་རྣུ་སྭ་རྡ། ཨོཾ་སཏ་ཏ་སྲ་ག་ཏུ་ཨུཥྐི་ཞ་རྡུ་ཏུ་སུ་རྡ་རི

སཏ་ཏ་སྲ་ག་ཏུ་རྱ་རྫུ་ཏུ་བི་རྦུ་ཥི་ཏ་ཨ་རྫི་རྫི་ཏེ་ཧུ་ར་ཧུ་ར་རྦུ་རྦུ་སྭ་རྡ།

The heart mantra is this:

OM SARVA TATHAGATA USHNISHA DHATU MUDRANI SARVA
TATHAGATA DHARMA DHATU VIBHUSHITE ADHISHTHITE
HURU HURU HUM HUM SVAHA

ཨོཾ་སཏ་ཏ་སྲ་ག་ཏ་ཨུཥྐི་ཞ་རྡུ་ཏུ་སུ་རྡ་རི་ཞ་སཏ་ཏ་སྲ་ག་ཏུ་རྱ་རྫུ་ཏུ་བི་རྦུ་ཥི

ཏེ་ཨ་རྫི་རྫི་ཏེ་ཧུ་ར་ཧུ་ར་རྦུ་རྦུ་སྭ་རྡ།

As explained by the Buddha in the Kangyur, if you have this mantra
inside a holy object, then all the buddhas will abide in that holy object.
Therefore, there are skies of benefits for making even just one prostration, circumambulation, or offering to a holy object containing the
Secret Relic Mantra:

- You purify the negative karma of the ten nonvirtuous actions as well as the five immediate negativities and so forth, and will be completely liberated from the eight hot hells.
- You will never turn back from peerless enlightenment. (That is, your life will always be directed toward enlightenment. This is irreversible; you will never go in the opposite direction.)
- You will always attain higher rebirth.
- By printing the Secret Relic Mantra just once, you collect the same amount of merit as making offerings to one hundred thousand times ten million times one hundred billion buddhas. This was told to Vajrapani.
- You create the same merit as having made offerings to as many buddhas as there are in ninety-nine sesame seed pods and you are always guided by that many buddhas.

This is just a tiny drop from the unimaginable benefits of this mantra.

3. The Zung of the Completely Pure Stainless Light
There are many Zung of the Exalted Completely Pure Stainless Light (Özer Drime) mantras, and they are all contained within the Four Dharmakaya Relic Mantras.[156] Some of them are this:

NAMAH SAPTANAM / SAMYAKSAM BUDDHA KOTINÄN PARISHUDDHE MA NA SI / ABHYA CHITA PATISHTHA TUNÄN / NAMO BHAGAVATE / AMRITA AH YU SHASYA / TATHAGATA SYA / OM SARVA TATHAGATA SHUDDHI / AH YUR BISHODHANI / SAMHARA SAMHARA / SARVA TATHAGATA BIRYA BA LE NA PRATI SAMHARA AYU SARA SARA / SARVA TATHAGATA SAMAYA/ BODHI BODHI/ BUDDHA BUDDHYA / BODHAYA / BODHAYA / MAMA SARVA PAPAM AVARANA BISHUDHE / BIGATA MALAM / CHHARA SU BUDDHYA BUDDHE HURU HURU SVAHA

NAMAH NAWA NAWA TINAM / TATHAGATA GAM GANAM

DIWA LUKA NAM / KOTI NIYUTA SHATA SAHASRANAN / OM
BO BO RI / TSARI NI TSARI / MORI GORI TSALA WARI SVAHA

ན་མཿསརྦ་ནོ། སཔྱོ་བཛྲ་གོ་ཊི་ནན་པ་རི་ཕཛྲེ་མ་ན་སི། ཨ་བྷུ་ཙི་ཏ་པ་ཏྲྀ་
ཧུ་ནྣ། ན་མོ་ཧྲ་ག་བ་ཏེ། ཨ་སྨི་ཏ་ཨྱུ་ལུ་ཏ་སྱ། ཏ་ཐཱ་ག་ཏ་སྱ། ཨོཾ་སརྦ་ཏ་ཧྲ་
ག་ཏ་ཕུཛྲེ། ཨྱུ་ཡུར་བི་ཤོ་ཏྲ་ནི། སོ་ཏ་ར་སོ་ཏ་ར། སརྦ་ཏ་ཧྲ་ག་ཏ་ཕྲིཏ་བ་ལེ་
ན་པྲ་ཏི་སོ་ཏ་ར་ཨྱུ་ཡུ་སྨྲ་ར་སྨྲ་ར། སརྦ་ཏ་ཧྲ་ག་ཏ་ས་མ་ཡ། བོ་ཊི་བོ་ཊི།
བུཛྲ་བུཛྲི། བོ་ཊ་ཡ་བོ་ཊ་ཡ། མ་མ་སརྦ་དུ་པོ་ཨྱུ་བ་ར་ཧ་བི་ཕཛྲེ། བི་ག་ཏ་མ་
ལེ། ཚ་ར་སུ་བུཛྲ་བཛྲེ་ཧུ་ཏུ་ཏུ་ཏུ་སྭཱ་ཧཱ།

ན་མཿན་བ་ན་བ་ཏི་ནོ། ཏ་ཧྲ་ག་ཏ་གོ་གྲ་ནོ་ཏི་བུ་ལུ་ཀུ་ནོ། གོ་ཊི་ནི་ཡུ་ཏ་ཤ་
ཏ་ས་ཧ་སྲཧཱི། ཨོཾ་བོ་བོ་རི། ཙ་རི་ཙི་ཙ་རི། མོ་རི་གོ་ལི་ཚ་ལ་ནུ་རི་སྭཱ་ཧཱ།

The heart mantra is this:

OM SARVA TATHAGATA MALA VISHODHANI RUDDHA / VOLA
PRATI SAMKARA / TATHAGATA / DHATU DHARE / SAM-
DHARA SAMDHARA / SARVA TATHAGATA ADHISHTHANA
ADHISHTHITE SVAHA

ཨོཾ་སརྦ་ཏ་ཧྲ་ག་ཏ་མ་ལ་བི་ཤོད་ནི་རུ་ཊྚ། བ་ལེ་པྲ་ཏི་སཾ་སྐྲ་ར། ཏ་ཧྲ་ག་ཏ་
ཧྲ་ཏུ་ཧྲ་རེ། ཧྲ་ར་ཧྲ་ར། སོ་ཧྲ་ར་སོ་ཧྲ་ར། སརྦ་ཏ་ཧྲ་ག་ཏ་ཨ་ཏྲི་ཥྛ་ན་ཨ་ཏྲི་
ཥྛི་ཏེ་སྭཱ་ཧཱ།

As explained by the Buddha in the Kangyur, there are skies of benefit
in making even just one prostration, circumambulation, or offering to a
holy object containing the Zung of the Completely Pure Stainless Light:

> If you offer even a bell to a stupa containing this mantra,
> all the sentient beings in that area, animals or humans, by
> hearing the sound of that bell will be completely purified of
> the five immediate negativities.[157]

Normally, committing the five immediate negativities is the cause to be reborn in the lowest hot hell, which is the most extreme suffering there is, but having this mantra inside a stupa purifies that. This shows how unbelievably powerful this mantra is. Since even hearing the sound of a bell offered to such a stupa has incredible power to purify, there is no question that any insect or other being who sees or touches the stupa is purified of negative karma. The mantra is so powerful that even just *thinking* about the stupa purifies the five immediate negativities. That is amazing! It is like a small flame that eventually grows into a fire that burns many thousands of miles of forest or entire cities.

If water, rain, or dust just touches the stupa, it is so blessed that it purifies all the negative karmas of the insects on the ground who come into contact with it. And the wind that touches such a stupa purifies the negative karmas of people or animals that it contacts, ensuring a good rebirth. Even the shadow of the stupa does this.

Everything that touches the land the stupa is on becomes meaningful, including the rain that touches the stupa and then flows to the ground and touches worms. The worms' negative karma is purified, and they will receive a higher rebirth.

4. The Hundred Thousand Ornaments of Enlightenment Mantra

The mantra of the Hundred Thousand Ornaments of Enlightenment (Jangchub Gyänbum) is this:

OM NAMO BHAGAVATE PI PU LA BADANA KANCHA NOTA
KASHIPTA / PRABHA SAKETU MURDHANE / TATHAGATAYA
/ ARHATE / SAMYAKSAM BUDDHAYA / NAMO BHAGAVATE
SHAKYA MUNAYE / TATHAGATAYA / ARHATE / SAMYAK-
SAM BUDDHAYA / TADYATHA / BODHI BODHI / BODHANI
BODHANI / SARVA TATHAGATA GOCHARI / DHARA DHARA
/ HARA HARA / PRAHARA PRAHARA / MAHA BODHI CHITTA
DHARE / CHULU CHULU / SHA TA RASMI SANCHODITE /
SARVA TATHAGATA VISHIKTE / GUNI GUNAVATE / SARVA
BUDDHA GUNA VABHASE / MILI MILI / GAGANA TALE /

SARVA TATHAGATA ADHISHTHITE / NABHA STALE / SHAME
SHAME / PRASHAME PRASHAME / SARVA TATHAGATA
SARVA PAPAM PRASHAMANE / SARVA PAPAM VISHODHANE
/ HULU HULU / MAHA BODHI MARGA SAMPRATISHTHITE
/ SARVA TATHAGATA SUPRATESHTHITE SHUDDHE SVAHA
/ OM SARVA TATHAGA GATA BYA AVALOKITE / JAYA JAYA
SVAHA / OM HULU HULU / JAYA MUKHE SVAHA / OM VAJRA
AYUSHE SVAHA

ཨོཾ་ན་མོ་བྷ་ག་བ་ཏེ་པི་སུ་ལ་བ་ད་ན་ཀུ་ཀྲུ་ནོ་ད་རྒྲི་ན༔ ཏ་ཐཱ་ག་ཏ་ཡ༔ ཨ་རྷ་ཏེ༔ ས་མྱཀྶཾ་བུ་དྷཱ་ཡ༔ ན་མོ་བྷ་ག་བ་ཏེ་ཤྲཱ་ཀྱ་མུ་ན་
ཡེ༔ ཏ་ཐཱ་ག་ཏ་ཡ༔ ཨ་རྷ་ཏེ༔ ས་མྱཀྶཾ་བུ་དྷཱ་ཡ༔ ཏདྱ་ཐཱ༔ པོ་དྷི་པོ་དྷི༔ པོ་དྷ་ནི་
སརྦ་ཏ་ཐཱ་ག་ཏ་གོ་ཙ་ནི༔ དྷ་ར་དྷ་ར༔ ཧ་ར་ཧ་ར༔ པྲ་ཧ་ར་པྲ་ཧ་ར༔
མ་ཧཱ་པོ་དྷི་ཙི་ཏྟ་དྷཱ་རེ༔ ཙུ་ལུ་ཙུ་ལུ༔ ཤ་ཏ་ར་ཤྨི་ས་ཚོདྀ་ཏེ༔ སརྦ་ཏ་ཐཱ་ག་ཏ་
པི་ཥི་ཀྟེ༔ གུ་ཎི་གུ་ན་པ་ཏེ༔ སརྦ་བུདྡྷ་གུ་ཎ་བ་དྷ་སེ༔ མི་ལི་མི་ལི༔ ག་ག་ན་ཏ་
ལེ༔ སརྦ་ཏ་ཐཱ་ག་ཏ་དྷི་ཥི་ཋི་ཏེ༔ ན་བྷ་ཧྥ་ལེ༔ ཤ་མེ་ཤ་མེ༔ པྲ་ཤ་མེ་པྲ་ཤ་མེ༔ སརྦ་
ཏ་ཐཱ་ག་ཏ་སརྦ་པཱ་པཾ་པྲ་ཤ་མ་ནེ༔ སརྦ་པཱ་པཾ་པི་ཤོདྷ་ནེ༔ ཧུ་ལུ་ཧུ་ལུ༔ མ་ཧཱ་
པོ་དྷི་མ་རྒ་སཾ་པྲ་ཏི་ཥྛི་ཏེ༔ སརྦ་ཏ་ཐཱ་ག་ཏ་སུ་པྲ་ཏིཥྛི་ཏེ་ཤུ་དྡྷེ་སྭཱ་ཧཱ༔ ཨོཾ་སརྦ་
ཏ་ཐཱ་ག་ཏ་བྱ་བ་ལོ་ཀི་ཏེ་སྭཱ་ཧཱ༔ ཛ་ཡ་ཛ་ཡ་སྭཱ་ཧཱ༔ ཨོཾ་ཧུ་ལུ་ཧུ་ལུ༔ ཛ་ཡ་མུ་ཁེ་སྭཱ་
ཧཱ༔ ཨོཾ་བཛྲ་ཨཱ་ཡུ་ཥེ་སྭཱ་ཧཱ༔

It has both heart mantra and nearing heart mantra. The heart mantra
is this:

OM SARVA TATHAGATA VYAVALOKITE SVAHA / JAYA JAYA
SVAHA / OM HULU HULU / JAYA MUSHE SVAHA

ཨོཾ་སརྦ་ཏ་ཐཱ་ག་ཏ་བྱ་བ་ལོ་ཀི་ཏེ་སྭཱ་ཧཱ༔ ཛ་ཡ་ཛ་ཡ་སྭཱ་ཧཱ༔ ཨོཾ་ཧུ་ལུ་ཧུ་ལུ༔ ཛ་
ཡ་མུ་ཁེ་སྭཱ་ཧཱ༔

The close heart mantra is this:

OM VAJRA AYUSHE SVAHA

ༀ་བཛྲ་ཨཱ་ཡུ་ཥེ་སྭཱ་ཧཱ།

As explained by the Buddha in the Kangyur, there are skies of benefits
for making even just one prostration, circumambulation, or offering to
a holy object containing the Hundred Thousand Ornaments of Enlightenment Mantra. When you do, you are not only making offerings to
the stupa but also to all the Three Rare Sublime Ones that exist in the
ten directions, in every universe.

By putting even just one mantra inside a stupa, it brings the same
merit as having built one hundred thousand stupas—whether the stupa
is gigantic like Bodhgaya or just the size of a finger. By dedicating this
merit for the happiness of all sentient beings up to full enlightenment,
both you and they receive unbelievable benefits.

A wonderful practice is to chant the name of somebody who has died
at the exact moment you put this mantra inside a stupa. Then you make
offerings to the stupa—either actual offerings or visualized offerings,
as in the seven-limb prayer. If you visualize offerings, you can include
all the flowers inside and outside, all the food offerings, all the water
offerings, all the light offerings, everything! You can use all the offerings
at my houses in California and Washington, as well as all the offerings
at all the FPMT centers.

The Buddha said to Ananda,

> I explained this sutra for those beings who have very little
> merit and no devotion, for those who are overcome by doubt
> and cannot believe in the Dharma. For those sentient beings,
> I explained the Hundred Thousand Ornaments of Enlight-
> enment mantra.

That means the Buddha explained this mantra for us. The Buddha also
told Ananda,

In future times, if ordained ones don't read this sutra that contains the benefits of this mantra and don't make offering to this mantra, which makes it so unbelievably easy to purify the negative karma that are the cause to be reborn in the lower realms and to accumulate the merit to achieve enlightenment and then offer extensive benefit to sentient beings, those ordained ones will suffer in the same way as householders. But if they listen to this teaching and then make even one stupa with this mantra inside, they make offering to all the eighty-four thousand teachings of the Buddha.

This means that this mantra is an antidote to the eighty-four thousand delusions, and you create inconceivable heaps of merit through reciting it. When you put these four dharmakaya relic mantras inside a stupa, even mentioning the name of a person or animal that has died and praying for them brings them a good rebirth, such as birth in a pure land. That person will definitely be liberated from the lower realms. Placing the mantras inside a holy object such as a stupa, saying the seven-limb practice, and making dedications for that person or animal is a very powerful method for healing.

Holy objects such as these liberate sentient beings continuously, twenty-four hours a day, every day. They purify the causes of the lower realms and bring sentient beings to the higher realms where they can meet the Dharma and then reach liberation and enlightenment.

As soon as stupas and statues of the Buddha are made, they have the power to cause sentient beings to do actions such as circumambulating, prostrating, offering, and so forth, which then become virtuous actions creating the cause of enlightenment, even if they are done with the eight worldly dharmas and nonvirtuous thoughts. So even though you might not have any realizations such as bodhichitta or emptiness, the holy objects you make still have the power to liberate sentient beings from the oceans of samsaric suffering, to actualize all the realizations of the path, and then to achieve enlightenment.

A Commentary on "Blessing the Speech According to the Instructions of Great Yogi Khyungpo"

Why and When to Do the Practice Blessing the Speech

According to the Instructions of Great Yogi Khyungpo,[159] this is a method to make the speech perfect. According to my root guru, Kyabje Trijang Rinpoche, this practice of blessing the speech multiplies the recitation of mantra ten million times. I received the oral transmission of this practice from Kyabje Kirti Tsenshab Rinpoche. You should do the blessing of the speech and recite the daily mantras first thing in the morning before you begin to speak, even while you are still in bed.

Visualizing Yourself as the Deity

Purify the truly existent I in emptiness. Then your wisdom realizing emptiness, which is nondual with great bliss, manifests as a deity.

I clarify myself as the deity.

To do this practice, you need to transform yourself into the form of a deity. You don't just change a truly existent human body into a truly existent deity body; it is not like that. First you purify the truly existent I in emptiness by looking at the real I as empty, as it is empty. Then, your wisdom of realizing emptiness, which is nondual with great bliss, manifests as a deity. Usually you arise as the main deity with whom you have a karmic connection and by means of which you will achieve enlightenment most quickly. However, if you are doing a deity retreat, you can arise as that deity. You are only allowed to clarify yourself as a deity after having received a great initiation of a lower tantra or highest yoga tantra deity. If you haven't received a great initiation, you can visualize yourself as Guru Shakyamuni Buddha. My guru Kyabje Denma Locho Rinpoche said that this is an exception based on the Buddha being the founder of the present Buddhadharma. However, for Medicine Buddha, Chenrezig, and all other deities, you must have received the initiation of the deity in order to visualize yourself as that deity. If you haven't received a great initiation, it might also be okay to do the blessing of the speech with your ordinary body, but I haven't actually heard that.

Visualizing the Seed Syllable and Mantra Garlands

On my tongue, a syllable ĀḤ transforms into a moon. On top of it appears a white syllable OṂ encircled by the white Sanskrit vowels standing clockwise, the red Sanskrit consonants standing counterclockwise, and the blue Dependent Related Heart Mantra standing clockwise.

On your tongue, in the center, visualize a white syllable ĀḤ. The ĀḤ transforms into a white moon disk, transparent like a magnifying glass and of the nature of light. In the center of the moon disk is a white OṂ, standing upright and facing forward. Standing clockwise around the OṂ are the white Sanskrit vowels, called ALI in Sanskrit—OṂ A Ā I Ī U Ū ṚI ṜI ḶI ḸI E Ē O Ō ANG AH SVĀHĀ. Standing counterclockwise around the vowels are the red Sanskrit consonants, called *kali* in Sanskrit—OṂ KA KHA GA GHA ṄGA / TSA TSHA DZA GYA ÑA / ṬA ṬHA ḌA ḌHA ṆA / TA THA DA DHA NA / PA PHA BA BHA MA / YA RA LA WA / ŚHA KA SA HA KYA SVĀHĀ. Standing clockwise around the consonants is the blue Dependent Related Heart Mantra—OṂ YE DHARMĀ HETU PRABHAWĀ HETUN TEKĀN TATHĀGATO HYAVADÄ / TEKĀÑ TSA YO NIRODHA EWAM VĀDĪ MAHĀ ŚHRAMAṆAYE SVĀHĀ. All the letters of the mantras are standing upright and are radiant, like neon signs on hotels and restaurants at night. The three OṂ's that begin the three mantras are in front of the syllable OM that is in the center of the moon disk. The mantra garlands do not circle the OM in the sense of turning or spinning around it.

Visualizing Hooking Back the Power and Blessings of Speech

> Light beams radiate from the syllable OM and the mantra garlands, hooking back the blessings and power of the speech of those beyond and not beyond the world in the form of the three mantras, the seven sublime precious objects of a king's reign, the eight auspicious signs, [and the eight auspicious substances].[160]

Those who are beyond the world are the buddhas, arya bodhisattvas abiding on the three pure bhumis, and arhats. Those who are not beyond the world are the yogis who are accomplishing the path and the sages who have actualized words of truth. Due to the power of abiding in silence and living in the morality of abstaining from negative karmas of speech, the words of these sages have much power and so whatever they pray for is successful.

All their blessings and power of speech are hooked back in the form of the three mantras, the seven precious objects of a king's reign, the eight auspicious signs, and the eight auspicious substances, filling the whole sky. They absorb into the mantras on the moon disk on your tongue, like rain falling on the ocean.

Visualize that light beams are emitted from the syllable OM and the three mantra garlands on your tongue. They hook back the blessings and power of speech of those who are beyond the world and those who are not beyond the world.

"Those who are beyond the world" does not mean those who are distant from the world, but those who are beyond samsara; that is, beyond aggregates caused by karma and delusions. They are the buddhas, arya bodhisattvas abiding on the three pure bhumis, and arhats—those who have achieved liberation from samsara through developing their minds in renunciation and the wisdom realizing emptiness.

First, visualize that beams are emitted from the syllable OM and the three mantra garlands on your tongue and hook back all the blessings and power of their holy speech in the form of the three mantras—the vowels, consonants, and Dependent Related Heart Mantra, which absorb into the mantras on your tongue. Then, beams are emitted and hook back all the blessings and power of their holy speech in the form of the seven precious objects of a king's reign, the eight auspicious signs, and the eight auspicious substances. These fill the sky in different layers, like the layers of clouds you see when you travel by plane. Visualize that many sets of the seven precious objects of a king's reign absorb into the mantras on your tongue, like snowfall or rainfall. Then visualize that many sets of the eight auspicious signs absorb into the mantras on your tongue, like snowfall or rainfall. Then visualize that many sets of the eight auspicious substances absorb into the mantras on your tongue, like snowfall or rainfall.

Those who are not beyond the world are samsaric beings—those whose aggregates are caused by karma and delusion. They include some yogis. Yogis can be of different levels—those who have achieved high realizations of secret mantra and are beyond samsara and those who are still samsaric beings. The beings who are not beyond the world also include sages who have actualized words of truth. Due to living their whole life in silence and practicing the morality of abandoning negative karmas of speech by abstaining from telling lies, gossiping, and so forth, their words have power and so their prayers are quickly actualized.

Visualize that the blessings and power of the speech of these yogis and sages are hooked back in the form of the three mantras, the seven precious objects of a king's reign, the eight auspicious signs, and the eight auspicious substances. These are not material things; they are of the nature of light. They absorb into the mantras on the moon disk on your tongue, like rain falling on the ocean.

Visualizing the Purification of Negative Karmas and Obscurations

I have added a visualization here that is not mentioned in the actual practice. As you recite the vowels three times, visualize that from each syllable of the white vowels, white nectar beams are emitted. They totally illuminate and fill the inside of your whole body from your feet up to your head, like a glass filled with milk. All your negative karmas and obscurations collected with the body from beginningless rebirths are completely purified.

As you recite the consonants three times, visualize that from each syllable of the red consonants, red nectar beams are emitted and completely fill your whole body. All your negative karmas and obscurations collected with the speech from beginningless rebirths are completely purified.

As you recite the Dependent Related Heart Mantra three times, visualize that from each syllable of the blue mantra, blue nectar beams are emitted and completely fill your whole body. All your negative karmas and obscurations collected with the mind from beginningless rebirths are completely purified.

Reciting the Mantras

Mantras for Blessing the Speech

> Concentrate on the visualization and recite the mantras beginning from the inner circle.

Recite the mantras one by one, three times each, beginning with the vowels, the inner circle; then the consonants; and then the Dependent Related Heart Mantra, the outer circle.

When you recite mantras, you have to recite them very clearly and slowly. For example, when you recite the vowels, say OM A Ā (pause), I Ī (pause), U Ū (pause), RI ṚI (pause), and so forth.

When Kyabje Choden Rinpoche gave a commentary on Secret Vajrapani at Vajrapani Institute, he talked about how important it is to recite mantras correctly. Rinpoche used this example of the Sanskrit vowels to show how they should be recited very clearly and very precisely, with the sounds of all the syllables pronounced correctly.

There are different techniques for reciting these mantras, but according to the great yogi Drubchen Khyungpo, all three mantras—the vowels, consonants, and Dependent Related Heart Mantra—have OM at the beginning and SVĀHĀ at the end.

Sanskrit Vowels (*Ali*)

As you recite the vowels, white nectar beams flow down from the mantra and fill your whole body. All negative karmas collected with your body from beginningless rebirths are completely purified.

OM A Ā I Ī U Ū ṚI ṜI ḶI ḸI E Ē O Ō ANG AH SVĀHĀ *(3x)*

ཨོཾ་ཨ་ཨཱ་ཨི་ཨཱི་ཨུ་ཨཱུ་རྀ་རཱྀ་ལྀ་ལཱྀ་ཨེ་ཨཻ་ཨོ་ཨཽ་ཨཾ་ཨཿ་སྭཱ་ཧཱ།

Sanskrit Consonants (*Kali*)

As you recite the consonants, red nectar beams flow down from the mantra and fill your whole body. All negative karmas collected with your speech from beginningless rebirths are completely purified.

OM KA KHA GA GHA ṄGA / TSA TSHA DZA GYA ÑA / ṬA ṬHA ḌA ḌHA ṆA / TA THA DA DHA NA / PA PHA BA BHA MA / YA RA LA WA / ŚHA KA SA HA KYA SVĀHĀ *(3x)*

ཨོཾ་ཀ་ཁ་ག་གྷ་ང་ཙ་ཚ་ཛ་ཇ་ཉ་ཊ་ཋ་ཌ་ཌྷ་ཎ་ཏ་ཐ་ད་དྷ་ན་པ་ཕ་བ་བྷ་མ་ཡ་ར་ལ་ཝ་ཤ་ཀ་ས་ཧ་ཀྵ་སྭཱ་ཧཱ།

The second set of consonants should be pronounced *tsa tsha dza gya ña*, not *cha chha ja gya ña*,[161] as that is how the ancient pandits wrote them in Tibetan. If you pronounce these letters as *cha chha ja gya ña*, it means that they made a mistake. Since those pandits had a purpose in writing them like this in Tibetan, I think it is better to recite them the Tibetan way. Without the diacritic marks these two sets of Sanskrit letters—*ṭa ṭha ḍa ḍha ṇa* and *ta tha da dha na*—look exactly the same, which would mean that you would say the same thing twice. But in Sanskrit and Tibetan they are totally different letters because the letters in the first set are reversed. Then, there is *śha ṣha sa ha kṣha*, but Tibetans normally say *śha ka sa ha kya*.

Dependent Related Heart Mantra

> As you recite the mantra, blue nectar beams flow down from the mantra and fill your whole body. All negative karmas collected with your mind from beginningless rebirths are completely purified.

OM YE DHARMĀ HETU PRABHAVĀ HETUN TESHÄN TATHĀGATO HYAVADÄT / TESHÄÑ CHA YO NIRODHA EVAM VĀDĪ MAHĀ ŚHRAMAṆA YE SVĀHĀ *(3x)*

ཨོཾ་ཡེ་དྷརྨ་ཧེ་ཏུ་པྲ་བྷ་བ་ཧེ་ཏུ་ནྟེ་ཥཱནྟ་ཐཱ་ག་ཏོ་ཧྱ་བ་དཏ་ཏེ་ཥཱ་ཉྩ་ཡོ་ནི་རོ་དྷ་ཨེ་ཝཾ་བཱ་དི་མ་ཧཱ་ཤྲ་མ་ཎ་ཡེ་སྭཱ་ཧཱ།

Although there is no break in the Tibetan writing, you have to pause between *yo* and *ni*. This is because if you recite *yo* and *ni* together as *yoni*, the mantra would have the very strange meaning of "May the female sex organ be destroyed." But if you pause after YO and then recite NIRODHA EWAM VĀDĪ MAHĀ ŚHRAMAṆAYE SVĀHĀ, it doesn't mean that. This way of reciting the mantra is explained and emphasized in the texts. Reciting this mantra stops all inauspicious things, gathers all good things, and fulfills all wishes.

Absorption of the Mantras

> The Dependent Related Heart Mantra absorbs into the consonants, the consonants into the vowels, the vowels into the syllable OM, and the OM into the moon cushion. That transforms into a syllable ĀḤ. The ĀḤ melts into pink nectar and absorbs into my tongue, which becomes of the nature of a vajra.

Your tongue becomes very heavy and strong, as if difficult to move, and as indestructible as a vajra. Generate very strong faith that all the blessings and power of the speech of all the buddhas, bodhisattvas, arhats, yogis, and sages have entered your speech and made it perfect. Think: "My speech has become perfect."

When you have finished reciting the three mantras, visualize that the outer mantras gradually absorb into the inner ones. First visualize that the Dependent Related Heart Mantra absorbs into the consonants. Then the consonants absorb into the vowels. Then the vowels absorb into the syllable OM in the center of the moon disk. The OM absorbs into the moon disk. The moon disk transforms into a syllable ĀḤ, which is what it originally came from. Here you should visualize a Tibetan letter ĀḤ like this, ཨཱཿ, with a small *a*, ཨ, and the two dots, ཿ. The ཨཱཿ melts into pink nectar, which absorbs into your tongue. Your tongue becomes the nature of a vajra, indestructible. Eating black foods can no longer destroy the power of your speech. Think that your tongue becomes solid, like iron or a rock, as well as very strong and very heavy, almost as if you cannot move it. Generate very strong faith that the blessings and power of speech of all the buddhas, bodhisattvas, arhats, yogis, and sages have entered your speech and made it perfect. Think: "My speech has become perfect."

The Benefits of Blessing the Speech

The benefits of blessing the speech are: (1) the power of your speech becomes perfect; (2) whatever you recite is multiplied ten million times; (3) the power of your speech is not taken away by eating wrong foods; and (4) gossiping becomes the recitation of mantra.

When you bless your speech, all the blessings and power of the holy speech of all the buddhas and other holy beings are received in your tongue, and you get an unbelievable number of benefits. I don't know how many millions and zillions of benefits are received! However, there are four particular benefits.

The first benefit of blessing the speech is that it makes the power of your speech perfect. Due to this, when you teach the Dharma, everyone listens to you and practices the Dharma. When you do counseling, everyone pays attention and follows your advice. When you give a lecture, even a political speech, all the people pay attention and listen to you. When you speak to an important person, they listen to you and help you. In short, when your speech has power, other people listen to you, pay attention to you, and keep your words in their hearts.

Therefore, you should bless your speech in the morning, not only for your recitation of mantras to have power, but even for your ordinary speech to have power. Whether it is to do your job, to request someone's help, or to explain something to someone, your speech needs power. If your speech doesn't have power, nothing will work.

The second benefit of blessing the speech is that any prayer or mantra you recite is multiplied ten million times. For example, if you recite a mantra such as OM MAṆI PADME HŪM or the Vajrasattva mantra one time, you get the benefit of having recited it ten million times. It is unbelievably powerful. However, other mantras and practices also do that.

The third benefit is a particular benefit of the practice of blessing the speech—it stops the power of your speech, including the power of your mantras, from being taken away or degenerated by eating black foods. According to the Kadampa text *Tenrim Chenmo*, eating garlic takes away the power of speech for seven days, onion for five days, and radish for nine days. There are different types of radish, but I think this is a particular radish that is large, round, and very strong; it makes the breath smell, produces a lot of gas, and pollutes the whole body. Eating nettles causes the power of your speech to be lost for half a year. When nettles are cooked well they are very delicious, but eating them has this shortcoming. Eating animal tongue, in particular sheep tongue, takes away the power of your speech for your whole life. Animals such as sheep are extremely ignorant, so when you eat their meat, in particular the lower parts of their bodies, the heart, and, worst of all, the tongue, due to a dependent arising it dulls your mind and causes your intelligence and wisdom to degenerate. Blessing your speech in the morning stops all the harm that comes from eating these wrong foods.

If you are very sensitive, you can feel the harmful effects of having eaten black foods. They make your mind unclear and can also make your body kind of tough and even cause it to change color. Because black foods destroy the power of your mind and body, in addition to the power of your speech, it is best to avoid eating them. However, it is different for a great yogi of secret mantra who has complete control over their mind and the winds that are the vehicle of the mind. Such a person can eat black foods, and even poisons that would normally kill an ordinary person, and not be harmed. Instead these foods only become a cause to increase their bliss and realizations.

The fourth benefit is also a particular benefit of the practice of blessing the speech—anything you say, even gossip, becomes the recitation of mantra. If you do the practice of blessing the speech in the morning, from then until sunrise the next morning, by the power of this practice all your gossip becomes the recitation of mantra. This probably means that whatever you say becomes virtue. There are also other specific benefits of blessing the speech. For example, Lama Atisha taught that when reciting a certain number of mantras, such as twenty-one or a hundred, if you engage in ordinary talk before you finish the recitation, your mantras are as if stabbed with a *phurba*¹⁶² and their power is taken away. If you do this blessing of the speech, that doesn't happen.

Dedication

> May my tongue sense base
> have all the courage of the ones gone to bliss.
> By the magnificence and power of my words,
> may all sentient beings be subdued.
> May all the meanings of whatever words I say be accomplished.

I added this dedication from a Nyingma prayer book containing a collection of daily practices. It is a very good and important dedication that summarizes the purpose of blessing the speech in three requests.

First dedicate for your tongue sense base, or sense power, to have the courage or power of the ones gone to bliss, the buddhas. Then dedicate for the magnificence and power of your words to subdue the minds of sentient beings, so that when you give teachings and when you talk to others, you will be able to bring inner peace to them by pacifying their delusions, selfish mind, and negative thoughts. Then, when you say, "May all the meanings of whatever words I say be accomplished," dedicate that whenever you teach the Dharma, or even when you explain something to someone, give someone advice, or ask someone to do something, you will be able to accomplish whatever you say because they will listen to you.

Nagarjuna's Heart Practice

Nagarjuna's heart practice is to recite these three mantras—the Sanskrit vowels, Sanskrit consonants, and Dependent Related Heart Mantra—three times each after doing any virtuous activity of body, speech, or mind. In particular, it is good to recite these mantras after reciting the mantras of a deity when doing a sadhana or during a session in retreat. By doing this, the purpose for which you recited those particular mantras will be accomplished. For example, you can recite mantras for pacification (to pacify sicknesses, harm from spirits, negative karmas, and defilements), for increase (to increase life, merits, wisdom, wealth, and realizations), for control (to have the necessary outer conditions, such as material things, for your practice of Dharma and your actions to benefit others to be successful), or for wrath (to gain control over evil beings so that they listen to you and stop engaging in heavy negative karma, so you can then bring them into the Dharma and to enlightenment).

A Commentary on "Daily Mantras" and "Mantras for Specific Occasions"

Daily Mantras

It is very good to recite these mantras first thing in the morning to make your life meaningful and to increase all the merits you collect during the day.

The Mantra to Bless the Mala

OṂ RUTSIRA MAṆI PRAVARTAYA HŪṂ *(7x)*

ཨོཾ་རུ་ཙི་ར་མ་ཎི་པྲ་བརྟ་ཡ་ཧཱུྃ།

Recite this mantra seven times and then blow on your mala. All the recitations you do of the secret mantras taught by the Tathagata are multiplied one hundred sextillion times (10^{23}). This is taught in *Unfathomable Mansion of Increasing Jewels*.

If you recite OṂ RUTSIRA MAṆI PRAVARTAYA HŪṂ seven times and then blow on your mala, the power of any mantra taught by the Buddha that you recite, such as OṂ MAṆI PADME HŪṂ or the Vajrasattva mantra, is increased ten million times one hundred billion times a hundred thousand. Although other mantras can be used to bless the mala in order to increase the power of mantra recitation, the benefits of this one are unbelievable.

This mantra was taught in the sutra *Unfathomable Mansion of Increasing Jewels*. The name of the sutra is mentioned here to show that this mantra came from the Buddha. The Buddha taught it so that sentient beings' merits could be increased. Due to the power of the Buddha's compassionate wish to bring sentient beings to enlightenment, reciting even one mantra can become very powerful.

I asked a Sanskrit expert how the Sanskrit syllable HŪṂ should be pronounced. He said that although it can be pronounced *hūm*, it is better to say *hūng*, as if it had the Tibetan letter *nga* at the end rather than the letter *ma*. However, I don't know what other people who know Sanskrit would say about that.

The Mantra to Multiply Virtue

OṂ SAMBHARA SAMBHARA BIMANA SARA MAHĀ DZAWA HŪṂ / OṂ SMARA SMARA BIMANA SKARA MAHĀ DZAWA HŪṂ *(7x)*

ཨོཾ་སམྦྷ་ར་སམྦྷ་ར་བི་མ་ན་ས་ར་མཧཱ་ཛྭ་བུ། ཨོཾ་སྨ་ར་སྨ་ར་བི་མ་ན་སྐ་ར་མཧཱ་ཛྭ་བུ།

If you recite this mantra seven times, any virtuous activity you do is multiplied by a hundred thousand. This is taught in the *Sutra of the Wheel of Complete Dedication*.

There are many different mantras to increase the merits that you collect during the day. If you recite this particular mantra seven times, any virtuous activity you do with your body, speech, or mind during the day will increase one hundred thousand times. The Buddha taught this mantra in the *Sutra of the Wheel of Complete Dedication*.

In your daily life, because you don't want suffering and want only happiness, you need to make the fewest mistakes—nonvirtues—possible and create the most merits—virtues—possible. This is because suffering comes from nonvirtue and happiness comes from virtue. Therefore, reciting this mantra is very important; it makes the way you live your life very wise.

The Zung of the Completely Pure Stainless Light

NAMAḤ NAWA NAWA TĪNÄN / TATHĀGATA GANG GĀNAṂ
DĪWĀ LUKĀ NÄN / KOṬI NIYUTA ŚHATA SAHASRĀṆÄN / OṂ
BO BO RI / TSARI ṆI TSARI / MORI GORI TSALA WĀRI SVĀHĀ
(21, 10, or a few times)

ན་མཿན་བ་ན་བ་ཏི་ནཱ། ཏ་ཐཱ་ག་ཏ་གཾ་གུ་ནཾ་དཱི་བྲ་ལུ་ཀུ་ནཱ། ཀོ་ཊི་ནི་ཡུ་ཏ་ཤ་
ཏ་ས་ཏ་སྲཱ། ཨོཾ་བོ་བོ་རི། ཙ་རི་ཎི་ཙ་རི། མོ་རི་གོ་རི་ཙ་ལ་བཱ་རི་སྭཱ་ཧཱ།

Talking to a person who has recited this mantra purifies even the five heavy negative karmas without break. Just hearing the voice of a person who has recited this mantra, being touched by their shadow, or touching their body purifies negative karmas collected in this and past lives. If you recite this mantra, you won't be harmed by poison, spirits, lightning, and so forth. All the buddhas will protect you, Chenrezig will look after you, and all the devas and those who are living in samaya will support you. You won't be harmed by black magic mantras, rituals, and substances. If this mantra is put inside a stupa, the negative karmas of anyone who sees the stupa, hears of it, touches it, or is touched by earth, dust, or wind that has touched it get purified. They won't be reborn in the lower realms and instead will be born as a happy transmigratory being.

This mantra, one of the dharmakaya relic mantras, is from the Kangyur, the Buddha's teachings. I received the oral transmission of all four mantras and their benefits from Kyabje Kyongla Rato Rinpoche in San Jose, California. It is good to recite the Zung of the Completely Pure Stainless Light after blessing your speech in the morning, before you begin to talk and engage in impure speech. You can recite it twenty-one times, ten times, or even just three, four, or five times.

The *Ritual for Blessing Stupas: Exalted Stainless Beam Totally Pure Light Mantra* says that if someone recites this mantra after blessing their speech in the morning, the five heavy negative karmas without break of anyone who talks to them get purified. What does "without break" mean? Without the break of another life. Because these negative karmas are very powerful, right after you die you are reborn in the lowest hell, the inexhaustible hell, where the suffering is the heaviest in samsara and experienced for the longest time—one intermediate eon. And if your karma to be there is not finished when this world ends, you will be reborn in that hell in another universe.

Also, after you have recited this mantra, there is unbelievable benefit for anyone who hears your voice, whose body is touched by your shadow, and who touches your body (for example, a person who shakes your hand or an insect that lands on your body). Not only are their negative karmas of this life purified, but also their negative karmas from past lives. Because even their very heavy negative karmas without break are purified, there is no doubt that their ten nonvirtuous actions are also purified. Therefore, whether you are doing counseling, teaching in a school, or just engaging in conversation, reciting this mantra becomes beneficial for others when they hear your voice. Even if someone is blind and cannot see you, you can speak to them so that they hear your voice and you can touch their body, hands, or face and bring them unimaginable benefit. You should remember this when you are talking to and touching others.

Also, due to reciting this mantra you will be protected by all the buddhas. You will be supported and helped by Chenrezig. All the devas and all those living in samaya will be happy with you. You won't be harmed by others' black magic mantras, rituals, and substances.

If this mantra is put inside a stupa, the negative karmas are purified of anyone who sees the stupa, hears about it, touches it (including the insects that land on it), or is touched by earth, dust, or wind that has touched the stupa, and they won't be reborn in the lower realms. Instead they will be reborn as happy transmigratory beings, as devas or human beings. In short, it will be impossible for those who are in the lower realms to be born back there again.

Guru Shakyamuni Buddha explained to Bodhisattva Great Sattva Eliminating All Obscurations, Lord of Secrets (Vajrapani), the Four Great Kings, and the gods, including Brahma, who is the lord of this unbearable suffering world; the devas of Brahma Type; and Maheshvara,

> Holy beings, I am handing you the essence of the king of secret mantras. You should always respect and offer service to it. Keep it and put it inside a jewel container. Then announce it in all places and unceasingly show it to sentient beings. If you make them see and hear it, their five negative karmas without break will be purified.[163]

Usually big statues and stupas have a life-tree inside them on which the four dharmakaya relic mantras are written in gold, but this mantra can be put in small statues and stupas instead of it. Even if there is just one Zung of the Completely Pure Stainless Light in a statue or stupa, there is unbelievable benefit—the negative karmas and obscurations of anyone who sees it get purified.

The Mantra of Great Wisdom Bimala Ushnisha

OṂ HRIYADHE SARVA TATHĀGATA HRIDAYA GARBHE / JVALA DHARMADHATU GARBHE / SANG HARANA ĀYUḤ SANGŚHODHAYA / PĀPAṂ SARVA TATHAGATA SAMENDRA UṢHṆĪKHA BIMALE BIŚHUDHE SVĀHĀ *(a few times)*

ཨོཾ་ཧྲི་ཡ་དྷེ་སརྦ་ཏ་ཐཱ་ག་ཏ་ཧྲི་ད་ཡ་གརྦྷེ། ཛྭ་ལ་དྷརྨ་དྷཱ་ཏུ་གརྦྷེ། སོ་ཧ་ར་ཎ་
ཨཱ་ཡུཿསཾ་ཤོ་དྷ་ཡ། པཱ་པཾ་སརྦ་ཏ་ཐཱ་ག་ཏ་ས་མཉྫུ་ཥྚི་ཀ་བི་མ་ལེ་བི་ཤུ་དྷེ་སྭཱ་ཧཱ།

This mantra has two major benefits. The first is that it purifies the five heavy negative karmas without break of anyone who hears it. The second is that because it is the most powerful mantra for consecration, it can be used to consecrate holy objects as well as rocks, trees, mountains, and so forth.

There are two versions of the Mantra of Great Wisdom Bimala Ushnisha.[164] One version begins with OM HRIYADHE and the other with OM TRAIYADHVE. The rest of the mantra is the same. I found the first version in a book written by a very great and learned lama in Tibet to educate young incarnate lamas. It explains to them how to do prayers and practices in order to help people, for example, how to do *powa*, transference of consciousness, for the dying, what prayers to do for the sick, and so forth. There must be a valid source for this version of the mantra, but so far I haven't been able to find it in the Kangyur, whereas the version that begins with OM TRAIYADHVE is found in the Kangyur. The benefits of reciting this mantra are mentioned in the book from Tibet. There it says,

> After you recite this mantra, if you make one stupa *tsatsa*, it becomes the same as having made ten million stupa tsatsas. Also after you have recited this mantra, if any of the four elements touches you, it becomes twice as powerful as a stupa, and anyone who sees or touches the element will be liberated, their five heavy negative karmas without break will be purified, they will be reborn in a high caste, have a long life and wealth, remember their past lives, be protected from all harm, and achieve enlightenment. This is taught by Drodren Gyalwa Cho.

If you recite this mantra and make a huge stupa, such as a billion-story stupa, or a small tsatsa stupa the size of a fingernail, you receive the same benefit, or the same amount of merit, as having made ten million huge or small stupas.

The merits you receive from making one stupa, which are inconceivable, are multiplied by ten million by reciting this mantra. Because it has this unbelievable benefit, it is important to recite this mantra before you begin the work of building a stupa, but you should also recite it every day during its construction. You can use it to bless the bricks, cement, and any other material that you are going to use. If you were to actually make ten million stupas, even small ones, can you imagine how many years it would take? If you were to build ten million big stupas the size of Lama Yeshe's stupa at Chenrezig Institute, can you imagine how many lifetimes it would take? But if you recite this mantra when you start to build a stupa, you get the same benefit as having built ten million stupas without needing to undergo all the hardship. The whole point is that the more merit you are able to collect, the more easily and quickly you will be able to achieve enlightenment, which means that you will be able to liberate sentient beings from the sufferings of samsara and bring them to enlightenment more quickly.

By reciting this mantra, if any element—earth, water, fire, or wind—touches your body, it gets blessed. It gains the power to liberate other sentient beings by purifying their negative karmas. For example, if you recite this mantra and then swim in water, the water becomes blessed and when it touches the numberless creatures living in it—from the largest whale down to the tiniest microscopic insect—and when it touches the human beings who are diving and playing in it, they are liberated from their negative karmas and the lower realms. It's the same for the rest of the elements; by your reciting this mantra and touching them, the elements gain the power, double that of a stupa, to purify other sentient beings.

This advice was taught by Drodren Gyalwa Cho, which might be the name of one of Buddha's past lives. However, the term *drodren* is confusing. *Dro* means "transmigratory being" and *dren* means "guide." I'm not sure whether Drodren Gyalwa Cho is the name of a buddha or if it is simply talking about the function of a buddha, which is to guide transmigratory beings to enlightenment.

This mantra can be recited a few times at the beginning of each day along with other morning prayers and mantras, as well as before making statues, stupas, or tsatsas. The people who, in particular, can use this mantra to benefit others are those who are seen by and who touch many people or animals, such as performers, models, public speakers, teachers, nurses, doctors, veterinarians, and so forth, as well as those who touch objects or elements that other sentient beings see or touch, such as cooks, bakers, potters, artists, painters, factory workers, dry cleaners, swimmers, and so forth.

There are also two major benefits of this mantra. The first is that reciting it purifies the five heavy negative karmas without break of anyone who hears it, whether they created these negative karmas in this life or in past lives. Because of this, I try to chant it, along with Maitreya Buddha's mantra, whenever I recite mantras for people and animals. Hearing Maitreya Buddha's mantra makes it impossible for that sentient being to be reborn in the lower realms. Also, if they do not become enlightened during Buddha Shakyamuni's time, when Maitreya Buddha descends they will be among his first disciples and will receive teachings from him and a prediction regarding their enlightenment.

The second benefit of this mantra is that it can be used for consecration. In the Kangyur, the Buddha said that among the many different prayers for consecration, this mantra is the most powerful. If you chant this mantra on a holy object, all the buddhas' wisdom absorbs into it. But even if you chant this mantra on a tree, rock, mountain, and so forth, all the buddhas' wisdom absorbs into it and then you and other sentient beings can circumambulate it. Because of this benefit, I often add this mantra to the usual short consecration ritual. Since this mantra is not common and most people don't know it, when I do consecration with others I usually end up being the only one saying the mantra!

Because all the buddhas' wisdom abides in any object on which this mantra is recited, I only recite it on holy objects, since they will be treated with respect. I don't recite it on malas that people give me to bless, because people treat them as ornaments and tend to leave them lying around anywhere. I just recite OM PADMO UṢHṆĪṢHA VIMALE HŪM PHAṬ a few times and then blow on the mala. If that mantra is recited on a mala, when the person touches and uses it, all their negative karmas, and especially their five heavy negative karmas without break, get purified.[165]

In short, because this is a very powerful mantra for consecration, you can use it even if you don't know any other prayers for consecration. Also, when you don't have much time, you can do a short consecration by reciting the mantra of Bimala Ushnisha three times. Then, say the two prayers: "Please, Bhagavan, the destroyer qualified gone beyond one, abide until this world ends," and "Please grant all sentient beings the common and sublime realizations." When there is time you can do a longer version. The most elaborate consecration ritual involves doing sessions for seven days with a lot of offerings and a fire puja at the end. There is another ritual that involves reciting the Yamantaka sadhana, which takes about two hours to do. Then there is a very short consecration that has seven outlines and includes offering a torma to the interferers and a bath offering. However, the mantra of Bimala Ushnisha is the most important one

The Holy Name Mantra That Fulfills Wishes

Recite the homage and mantra together for each recitation:

De zhin sheg pa sa dzin gyäl po la chhag tshäl lo
To Tathagata Earth-Holder King, I prostrate.

TAYATHĀ / OṂ DHARE DHARE / DHARAṆI BÄNDHE SVĀHĀ
(108x, 54x, or 21x)

ཏ་ཪྱ་ཐཱ། ༀ་དྷ་ཪེ་དྷ་ཪེ། དྷ་ཪ་ཎི་བནྡྷེ་སྭཱ་ཧཱ།

Whoever memorizes the name of this tathagata and the words of this mantra will have all their wishes fulfilled without exception.

This mantra is found in the Kangyur. You can recite the buddha's name, Sadzin Gyalpo (Earth-Holder King), and the mantra together for one mala, half a mala, or twenty-one times. Although there are other mantras to achieve success, those who are able to and would like to can recite this one. It is not difficult to recite and even if you recite it just a few times, it will be very helpful.

Mantras for Specific Occasions
Mantra to Increase the Power of Recitation

Recite this mantra before reading and reciting prayers, sutras, and so forth.

TAYATHĀ / OṂ DHARE DHARE BHENDHARE SVĀHĀ *(7x)*

ཏ་ད་ཐཱ། ཨོཾ་དྷ་རེ་དྷ་རེ་བྷེནྡྷ་རེ་སྭཱ་ཧཱ།

I received the oral transmission of this mantra from my guru Geshe Sengé, who was a disciple of Gonsar Rinpoche's previous incarnation in Mongolia. If you recite it seven times before you read a Dharma text, such as *Diamond Cutter Sutra*, *Golden Light Sutra*, and so forth, it is as if you read the text millions of times. When you read the text, you should think that you are teaching it to the six-realm sentient beings, who all hear it in their own language.

Mantra to Bless the Feet

Recite the mantra seven times and then spit on the soles of your feet. It is taught that any insects that die under your feet will be reborn as devas in the Realm of the Thirty-Three.

OṂ KHRETSA RAGHANA HŪṂ HRĪ SVĀHĀ *(7x)*

ཨོཾ་ཁྲེ་ཙ་རག་ན་ཧཱུྃ་ཧྲཱི་སྭཱ་ཧཱ།

This mantra can also be used to bless the wheels of vehicles and other things that can crush and kill sentient beings. It should be recited when the specific need arises, such as having to walk on ground where there are many insects or other small creatures and when driving a car, riding a bicycle, and so forth.

My Tibetan prayer book doesn't mention which text this mantra comes from. However, I found it in the *Manjushri Root Tantra*.

Some texts say to recite this mantra seven times, others say to recite it three times.[166] After reciting it, don't only blow on the soles of your feet, spit on them. Then, any insects that die under your feet that day will be reborn in the deva realm of the Thirty-Three.[167] Although the text says to spit on your feet, since you usually wear shoes, after reciting it seven or three times you should spit on the soles of your shoes because they are what actually kill the insects. If you generate faith and do this practice, it will be of great benefit to sentient beings.

I also suggest that before you drive somewhere you chant this mantra and then spit on the wheels of the car, which are what touch the ground. Or you can chant the mantra over some water, blow on it, and then sprinkle it on the wheels. Since there are definitely many insects on the roads, they will get killed when you drive a car, but if you do this at least they will get a higher rebirth. If you are working in a garden or building something, you can also recite this mantra and spit on the tools you are using. Don't only think to bless your feet or shoes—you can bless anything that could kill sentient beings.

In short, any time you find yourself in a place or situation where there is the danger of crushing and killing sentient beings, it is good to recite this mantra. Therefore, you should write it in a notebook and carry it with you all the time in case you need to recite it but can't remember it. Reciting it makes your life very fruitful and beneficial for other sentient beings. You should think from your heart that this mantra for blessing the feet and other things is important. It is one way to make your life meaningful. I want to emphasize this because otherwise, although this mantra is in your prayer book, you might never use it. Don't do that!

You must take advantage of this practice, since it is the Buddha's way of helping you by making it very easy for you to purify negative karmas, collect merits, gain realizations, and achieve enlightenment quickly. You must think about that and you must take each opportunity to use it. Don't just leave this mantra in your prayer book and then die without ever having taken advantage of it while you were alive!

GLOSSARY

....

absolute guru (*döndam lama*). The dharmakaya; the omniscient mind of a buddha, free from all gross and subtle delusions, compared to the conventional guru, the spiritual teacher.

aggregates (*skandha*). The psychophysical constituents that make up a sentient being: form, feeling, discrimination, compositional factors, and consciousness. Beings of the desire and form realms have all five, whereas beings in the formless realm no longer have the aggregate of form.

Akshobhya. See Mitrukpa

Amitabha (*Öpame*). One of the five buddha families or types (Dhyani Buddhas), red in color, representing the wisdom of discernment and the fully purified aggregate of discrimination. *See* five buddha types.

Amoghasiddhi (*Dönyo drubpa*). One of the five buddha families or types (Dhyani Buddhas), green in color, representing the all-accomplishing wisdom and the fully purified aggregate of compositional factors. *See* five buddha types.

anger. A disturbing thought that exaggerates the negative qualities of an object and wishes to harm it; one of the six root delusions.

arhat (*drachompa*). Literally, "foe destroyer." A person who has destroyed their inner enemy, the delusions, and attained liberation from cyclic existence.

arya (*phakpa*). Literally, "noble." One who has realized the wisdom of emptiness.

Atisha Dipamkara Shrijnana (982–1054). The renowned Indian master who went to Tibet in 1042 to help in the revival of Buddhism and established the Kadam tradition. His text *Lamp for the Path to Enlightenment* (*Bodhipathapradipa*) was the first lamrim text.

attachment. A disturbing thought that exaggerates the positive qualities of an object and wishes to possess it; one of the six root delusions.

Avalokiteshvara. See Chenrezig.

bhagavan (chom den dä). Epithet for a buddha; one who has destroyed *(chom)* all the defilements, possesses all qualities *(den)*, and has transcended the world *(dä).*

bodhichitta (jangchup sem). A principal consciousness that combines the two factors of wishing to free all beings from suffering and wishing to attain enlightenment in order to accomplish that.

bodhisattva (jangchup sempa). One who possesses bodhichitta.

bodhisattva vows. The vows taken when you enter the bodhisattva path.

buddha, a (sanggye). A fully enlightened being. One who has totally eliminated *(sang)* all obscurations veiling the mind and has fully developed *(gye)* all good qualities to perfection. *See also* enlightenment.

Buddha, the. The historical Buddha. *See* Shakyamuni Buddha.

Buddhadharma. The teachings of the Buddha. *See also* Dharma.

capable being (lower, middle, or *higher). See* graduated path of the three capable beings.

Chenrezig (Avalokiteshvara). Compassion Buddha. The meditational deity embodying the compassion of all the buddhas. The Dalai Lamas are said to be emanations of this deity.

compassion (karuna, nyingjé). The wish that others be free from suffering.

Compassion Buddha. See Chenrezig.

consort. See wisdom mother.

conventional truth (samvriti satya; kunzop denpa). As opposed to ultimate truth, which is the understanding of the ultimate nature of reality (emptiness), conventional truth is what is true to the valid conventional consciousness. It is also called concealer truth or all-obscuring truth because, although true on one level, it obscures the ultimate nature. Conventional and ultimate truth form the important subject in Buddhist philosophy called the two truths. *See also* ultimate truth.

cyclic existence. See samsara.

Dalai Lama (b. 1935). Gyalwa Tenzin Gyatso. Revered spiritual leader of the Tibetan people and tireless worker for world peace; winner of the Nobel Peace Prize in 1989; a guru of Lama Zopa Rinpoche.

deity (*ishtadevata, yidam*). An emanation of the enlightened mind used as the object of meditation in tantric practices.

delusion (*klesha, nyönmong*). An obscuration covering the essentially pure nature of the mind, causing suffering and dissatisfaction; the main delusion is ignorance, and all the others come from this. *See also* root delusions; three poisons.

demigod (*asura, lhamayin*). A being in the god realms who enjoys greater comfort and pleasure than human beings but who suffers from jealousy and quarreling. *See also* six realms; cyclic existence.

deva. *See* god.

Dharma (*chö*). The second refuge jewel. Literally, "that which holds or protects (from suffering)" and hence brings happiness and leads you toward liberation and enlightenment. In Buddhism, absolute Dharma is the realizations attained along the path to liberation and enlightenment, and conventional Dharma is seen as both the teachings of the Buddha and virtuous actions.

dharmakaya (*chöku*). The truth body of a buddha (the other "body" being the form body, or rupakaya); the blissful omniscient mind of a buddha, the result of the wisdom side of the path. It can be divided into the wisdom body (*jnanakaya; yeshe nyiku*) and the nature body (*svabhavikakaya; ngowo nyiku*). *See also* rupakaya.

disturbing thoughts. *See* delusion.

disturbing-thought obscurations (*kleshavarana; nyöndrip*). Also known as *gross obscurations*, these are the grosser of the two types of obscurations, the ones that block liberation. *See also* obscurations to knowledge; two obscurations.

eight fears. The eight internal and external dangers or fears that Tara saves us from. They are the fear of: fire and hatred; water and attachment; lions and pride; elephants and ignorance; hungry ghosts and doubt; imprisonment and miserliness; thieves and wrong views; and snakes and jealousy.

eight Mahayana precepts. One-day vows to abandon killing; stealing;

lying; sexual contact; taking intoxicants; sitting on high seats or beds; eating at an inappropriate time; and singing, dancing, and wearing perfumes and jewelry.

emptiness (*shunyata*; *tongpanyi*). The absence, or lack, of true existence. Ultimately every phenomenon is empty of existing truly or from its own side or independently.

enlightenment (*bodhi*; *jangchup*). Full awakening; buddhahood; omniscience. The ultimate goal of a Mahayana Buddhist, attained when all limitations have been removed from the mind and the positive potential has been completely and perfectly realized. It is a state characterized by infinite compassion, wisdom, and skill.

eon (*kalpa*). A world period, an inconceivably long period of time. The life span of the universe is divided into four great eons, which are themselves divided into twenty lesser eons.

equanimity. The absence of the usual discrimination of sentient beings into friend, enemy, or stranger, deriving from the realization that all sentient beings are equal in wanting happiness and not wanting suffering and that since beginningless time all beings have been all things to each other. An impartial mind that serves as the basis for the development of great love, great compassion, and bodhichitta.

five buddha types or families (*rik nga*). Also known as five Dhyani buddhas. Five buddhas that represent a different aspect of enlightenment, linked to a fully purified aggregate and a fully purified delusion. They are *Vairochana* (white, form aggregate, transforming ignorance into the mirror-like wisdom); *Ratnasambhava* (yellow, feeling aggregate, transforming miserliness or pride into the wisdom of equality); *Amitabha* (red, discrimination aggregate, transforming desire into the wisdom of discernment); *Amoghasiddhi* (green, compositional factors aggregate, transforming jealousy into the all-accomplishing wisdom); and *Akshobhya* (blue, consciousness aggregate, transforming anger into dharmadhatu wisdom).

five degenerations. The ways in which our world is degenerating: the degenerations of mind, lifespan, sentient beings, time, and view.

five immediate negativities (*pancanantarya*; *tsammä nga*). The five actions that are so heavy that they are the cause to be reborn in hell immediately after death. They are killing your father or mother, killing an arhat, maliciously drawing blood from a buddha, and creating a schism in the sangha.

five lay vows (*panchasila*; *ge nyen*). The precepts taken by lay Buddhist practitioners for life, to abstain from killing, stealing, lying, sexual misconduct, and taking intoxicants. *See also* pratimoksha vows.

five near immediate negativities (*anantarya sabhagah*; *nyeba tsammä nga*). Similar to the five immediate negativities in that they are the cause to be reborn in hell immediately after death, they are: killing a bodhisattva, killing an arya not yet an arhat, defiling your mother or a female arhat, stealing property from the sangha, and destroying a stupa.

five paths. The paths along which beings progress to liberation and enlightenment: the path of merit, the path of preparation, the path of seeing, the path of meditation, and the path of no more learning.

five powers. The five forces to be practiced both in this life and at the time of death: the power of motivation, the power of acquaintance, the power of the white seed (developing positive qualities), the power of destruction (of self-cherishing), and the power of prayer.

five transcendental wisdoms (*panchajnana*; *yeshe nga*). The wisdoms possessed by a buddha, they are the mirror-like wisdom, the wisdom of equality, the all-accomplishing wisdom, the wisdom of discernment or discriminating wisdom, and the dharmadhatu wisdom.

four dharmakaya relic mantras. Four mantras placed in holy objects such as stupas. Simply circumambulating an object containing these mantras purifies the karma to be reborn in the hot hells. They are the Stainless Pinnacle Deity Mantra (*Tsugtor Drime*), the Secret Relic Mantra (*Sangwa Rigsel*), the Zung of the Completely Pure Stainless Light (*Özer Drime*), and Hundred Thousand Ornaments of Enlightenment (*Jangchub Gyänbum*).

four immeasurables (*apramana*). Also known as the *four immeasurable thoughts* or the *four sublime attitudes* (*brahmavihara*), these are four states of mind or aspirations: loving-kindness (*maitri; jampa*), compassion (*karuna; nyingjé*), sympathetic joy (*mudita; gaba*), and equanimity (*upeksha; tang nyom*). They are usually expressed in this prayer, which also has longer variations: May all sentient beings have happiness and its causes, be free from suffering and its causes, be inseparable from sorrowless bliss, and abide in equanimity.

four noble truths. The subject of the Buddha's first turning of the wheel of Dharma: the truths of suffering, the origin of suffering, the cessation of suffering, and the path leading to the cessation of suffering as seen by an arya.

four opponent powers (*nyenpo tob zhi*). The four practices used to purify nonvirtuous imprints on the mindstream. They are: the *power of dependence*, taking refuge in the Three Rare Sublime Ones and generating bodhichitta; the *power of regret*, feeling deep regret for the negativity committed; the *power of restraint*, determining not to repeat that negativity; and the *power of remedy*, a practice such as Vajrasattva that effectively acts as an antidote to the negativity.

Geluk. One of the four main traditions of Tibetan Buddhism, it was founded by Lama Tsongkhapa in the early fifteenth century and has been propagated by such illustrious masters as the successive Dalai Lamas and Panchen Lamas.

Gen. Literally, "elder." A title of respect.

geshe. Literally, "a spiritual friend." The title conferred on those who have completed extensive studies and examinations at Geluk monastic universities.

god (*deva*). A being dwelling in a state with much comfort and pleasure in the god realms of the desire, form, or formless realms.

graduated path. See lamrim.

graduated path of the three capable beings. Also known as the *three scopes* or *three levels of practice,* the three levels of the lower, middle, and higher capable being, based on the motivations of trying to attain a better future rebirth, liberation, and enlightenment respectively.

See also higher capable being; middle capable being; lower capable being.

great compassion (*mahakaruna*; *nyingjé chenpo*). The compassion that includes not only the wish for all sentient beings to be free from suffering and its causes but the heartfelt determination to accomplish this on your own. *See also* immeasurable compassion.

Guide to the Bodhisattva's Way of Life (*Bodhicharyavatara*). The inspirational text written by the eight-century Indian master Shantideva.

guru (*lama*). A spiritual guide or teacher. One who shows a disciple the path to liberation and enlightenment. Literally, "heavy"—heavy with knowledge of the Dharma. In tantra, your teacher is seen as inseparable from the meditational deity and the Three Rare Sublime Ones.

guru devotion. The sutra or tantra practice of seeing the guru as a buddha, then devoting yourself to him or her with thought and action.

Guru Shakyamuni Buddha. The historical Buddha. Lama Zopa Rinpoche often adds "Guru" to remind us of the inseparability of the guru and the Buddha.

guru yoga. The fundamental tantric practice whereby your guru is seen as identical with the buddhas, your personal meditational deity, and the essential nature of your own mind.

happy transmigratory being. A samsaric being in the realms of gods (*devas* or *suras*), demigods (*asuras*), or humans (*manushyas*).

hell (*narak*). The samsaric realm with the greatest suffering. There are eight hot hells, eight cold hells, and four neighboring hells. *See also* six realms; cyclic existence.

heresy (*lokta*). Also called *mistaken wrong views*, one of the five afflicted views that are part of the root afflictions. A deluded intelligence that rejects the existence of something that exists, such as karma, reincarnation, the Three Rare Sublime Ones, and so forth, and ascribes existence to that which is nonexistent, such as inherent existence. It is also the holding of incorrect views about the guru.

higher capable being. The highest of the three levels of practice or scopes, it has the goal of full enlightenment. *See also* graduated path of the three capable beings; lower capable being; middle capable being.

highest yoga tantra (*anuttara yoga tantra*). The fourth and supreme division of tantric practice, sometimes called *maha-anuttara yoga tantra*. It consists of generation and completion stages. Through this practice you can attain full enlightenment within one lifetime. *See also* kriya tantra.

Hinayana. Literally, "Small, or Lesser, Vehicle." One of the two general divisions of Buddhism, the other being the Mahayana. His Holiness the Dalai Lama usually refers to this as the *Pali tradition* (with the Mahayana referred to as the *Sanskrit tradition*). It can also be called *Pratimokshayana* as compared to *Bodhisattvayana*. Hinayana practitioners' motivation for following the Dharma path is principally their intense wish for personal liberation from samsara. Two types of Hinayana practitioner are identified: hearers (*shravaka*) and solitary realizers (*pratyekabuddha*). *See also* Mahayana; individual liberation.

hungry ghost (*preta*). The hungry ghost realm is one of the three lower realms of cyclic existence, where the main suffering is hunger and thirst. *See also* six realms; cyclic existence.

ignorance (*avidya; marigpa*). Literally, "not seeing" that which exists or the way in which things exist. There are basically two kinds: ignorance of karma and ignorance of ultimate truth. The fundamental delusion from which all others spring. The first of the twelve links of dependent origination.

impermanence (*mitakpa*). The gross and subtle levels of the transience of phenomena, gross being the observable changes in things and events, and subtle being the moment-by-moment disintegration that happens the moment they come into existence.

impermanence and death. One of the initial practices of the graduated path of the lower capable being, showing how fragile this precious life is and how you must not waste a moment of it.

imprint (*bakcha*). The seed, or potential, left on the mind by positive or negative actions of body, speech, and mind.

individual liberation. The liberation achieved by the hearer (*shravaka*) or the solitary realizer (*pratyekabuddha*) within the Hinayana tradition, as compared with enlightenment achieved by a practitioner of the Mahayana tradition.

initiation. A transmission received from a tantric master allowing a disciple to engage in the practices of a particular meditational deity. It is also referred to as an *empowerment* and can be given as a full empowerment (*wang*) or a permission to practice (*jenang*).

intermediate state (*bardo*). The state between death and rebirth.

jangwa purifying puja. A powerful tantric practice done when somebody has just died to try to influence their next rebirth.

Kadampa geshe. A practitioner of Kadam lineage. Kadampa geshes are renowned for their practice of thought transformation.

Kangyur. Literally, "translation of the [Buddha's] word." The part of the Tibetan canon consisting of 108 volumes that contains the sutras and tantras. Commentaries on this from Indian and Tibetan masters are contained in the Tengyur, which consists of about 225 volumes (depending on the edition).

karma (*lé*). Action; the working of cause and effect, whereby positive (virtuous) actions produce happiness and negative (nonvirtuous) actions produce suffering.

Kirti Tsenshab Rinpoche (1926–2006). A highly attained and learned ascetic yogi who lived in Dharamsala, India, and who was one of Lama Zopa Rinpoche's gurus.

Kopan Monastery. The monastery near Boudhanath in the Kathmandu Valley, Nepal, founded by Lama Yeshe and Lama Zopa Rinpoche.

kriya tantra (*ja gyü; action tantra*). The first of the four classes of tantra, it emphasizes external activities, such as prayers, mudras, and so forth. *See also* highest yoga tantra.

Kunrik. A deity belonging to one of the lower tantras, known as the king of the deities purifying the lower realms. Somebody who has died who has a Kunrik practice or puja performed for them will be liberated from the lower realms, even if they have already been born there.

lama (guru). A spiritual guide or teacher; one who shows a disciple the path to liberation and enlightenment.

Lama Atisha. See Atisha Dipamkara Shrijnana.

Lama Tsongkhapa. See Tsongkhapa, Lama Jé Losang Drakpa.

lamrim. The graduated path. A presentation of Shakyamuni Buddha's teachings in a form suitable for the step-by-step training of a disciple. The lamrim was first formulated by the great Indian teacher Atisha when he came to Tibet in 1042. *See also* Atisha; three principal aspects of the path.

liberation (nirvana or moksha). The state of complete freedom from samsara; the goal of a practitioner seeking his or her own escape from suffering.

lineage lama. A spiritual teacher who is in the line of direct guru-disciple transmission of teachings, from Buddha to the teachers of the present day.

loving-kindness (maitri; yiong jampa). In the context of the seven points of cause and effect, the wish for all beings to have happiness and its causes, with the added dimension of *yiong* ("beautiful" or "affectionate"); often translated as "affectionate loving-kindness." Rinpoche suggests this is the "loving-kindness of seeing others in beauty."

lower capable being. The first of the three levels of practice or scopes, the lower capable being has the goal of a better future existence. *See also* graduated path of the three capable beings; higher capable being; middle capable being.

lower realms. The three realms of cyclic existence with the most suffering: the hell being (*naraka*), hungry ghost (*preta*), and animal (*tiryanc*) realms. *See also* six realms; cyclic existence.

Mahayana. Literally, "Great Vehicle." It is one of the two general divisions of Buddhism. Mahayana practitioners' motivation for following the Dharma path is principally their intense wish for all sentient beings to be liberated from samsara and to attain the full enlightenment of buddhahood in order to accomplish this. The Mahayana has two divisions, *Paramitayana* (*Sutrayana*) and *Vajrayana* (also known as *Tantrayana* or *Mantrayana*).

Maitreya (*Jampa*). After Shakyamuni Buddha, the next (fifth) of the thousand buddhas of this fortunate eon to descend to turn the wheel of Dharma. Presently residing in the pure land of Tushita (*Ganden*). Recipient of the method lineage of Shakyamuni Buddha's teachings, which, in a mystical transmission, he passed on to Asanga.

mala (*threngwa*). A rosary of beads for counting mantras.

mandala (*khyilkhor*). A circular diagram symbolic of the entire universe. The abode of a meditational deity.

Manjushri (*Jampalyang*). The buddha (or bodhisattva) of wisdom. Recipient of the wisdom lineage of Shakyamuni Buddha's teachings, which he passed on to Nagarjuna.

mantra (*ngag*). Literally, "mind protection." Mantras are Sanskrit syllables usually recited in conjunction with the practice of a particular meditational deity; they embody the qualities of the deity with which they are associated.

maras. The four external and internal hindrances or obstacles to our spiritual progress. They are the mara of the (contaminated) aggregates, the mara of delusions, the mara of the Lord of Death, and the mara of the deva's son (the demon of desire and temptation).

Medicine Buddha (*Buddha Bhaiṣajya-guru*; *Sangyé Menla*). A buddha who vowed as a bodhisattva to be able to completely free all sentient beings from their illnesses.

meditation (*gom*). Familiarization of the mind with a virtuous object. There are two types: single-pointed (*jok gom*), also called *stabilizing*, *placement*, or *fixed*; and analytic or insight meditation (*ché gom*).

merit. Positive imprints left on the mind by virtuous, or Dharma, actions. The principal cause of happiness. *See also* two merits.

method. All aspects of the path to enlightenment other than those related to emptiness, principally associated with the development of loving-kindness, compassion, and bodhichitta.

middle capable being. The second of the three levels of practice or scopes, the middle capable being has the goal of liberation from suffering.

See also graduated path of the three capable beings; higher capable being; lower capable being.

Mitrukpa (Akshobhya). One of the five buddha types or families, blue in color, representing the dharmadhatu wisdom and the fully purified aggregate of consciousness. *See* five buddha types.

Mount Meru. The mythical center of the universe in Buddhist cosmology.

mudra (chakgya). Literally, seal or token; a symbolic hand gesture, endowed with power not unlike a mantra.

nagas (klu). Snakelike beings of the animal realm who live in or near bodies of water; commonly associated with fertility of the land but can also function as protectors of religion.

Nalanda. A Mahayana Buddhist monastic university founded in the fifth century in North India, not far from Bodhgaya, which served as a major source of the Buddhist teachings that spread to Tibet.

Namgyalma (Ushnishavijaya). One of three long-life deities, with Amitayus and White Tara.

nonvirtue. Negative karma; that which results in suffering.

nirvana (nyang dä). Liberation; the state of complete freedom from samsara; the goal of the practitioner of the individual liberation path. "Lower nirvana" is used to refer to this state of self-liberation, while "higher nirvana" refers to the supreme attainment of the full enlightenment of buddhahood. "Natural nirvana" is the fundamentally pure nature of reality, where all things and events are devoid of any inherent existence.

nyungné. A two-day thousand-arm Chenrezig retreat that involves fasting, prostrations, and silence.

obscurations to knowledge (jneyavarana; shedrip). One of the two obscurations, these are the more subtle ones that block enlightenment; also known as *subtle obscurations, obscurations to enlightenment,* and *cognitive obscurations. See also* disturbing-thought obscurations; two obscurations.

OM MANI PADME HUM. The *mani*; the mantra of Chenrezig, buddha of compassion.

Pabongka Dechen Nyingpo (1871–1941). An influential and charismatic lama of the Geluk order, Pabongka Rinpoche was the root guru of His Holiness the Dalai Lama's senior and junior tutors. He also gave the teachings compiled in *Liberation in the Palm of Your Hand*.

Padmasambhava. The eighth-century Indian tantric master who played a key role in establishing Buddhism in Tibet; he is revered by all Tibetans but especially by followers of the Nyingma tradition, which he founded. Often known in Tibetan as Guru Rinpoche.

pandit. Scholar; learned person.

parinirvana. The final nirvana the Buddha attained when he passed away in Kushinagar.

perfect human rebirth. The rare human state, qualified by eight freedoms and ten richnesses, which is the ideal condition for practicing the Dharma and attaining enlightenment. The eight freedoms are being free from being born as a hell being, hungry ghost, animal, long-life god, or barbarian, or in a dark age when no buddha has descended, holding wrong views, and being born with mental or physical problems that preclude you from understanding the Dharma. The ten richnesses are being born as a human being, in a Dharma country, and with perfect mental and physical faculties; not having committed any of the five immediate negativities; having faith in the Buddha's teachings; being alive when a buddha has descended, the teachings have been revealed, the complete teachings still exist, and when there are still followers of the teachings; and having the necessary conditions to practice the Dharma, such as the kindness of others.

Perfection of Wisdom (Prajnaparamita). Sutras pertaining to the Buddha's second turning of the wheel of Dharma, in which the wisdom of emptiness and the path of the bodhisattva were set forth.

prajnaparamita. *See* Perfection of Wisdom.

pratimoksha vows. The various levels of individual liberation vows for lay and ordained, including the five lay vows, the novice vows, and full ordination taken by monks and nuns.

precepts. *See* vows.

preliminary practices (ngöndro). The practices that prepare the mind for successful tantric meditation by removing hindrances and accumulating merit. These practices are found in all schools of Tibetan Buddhism and are usually done 100,000 times each; the four main practices are recitation of the refuge formula, mandala offerings, prostrations, and Vajrasattva mantra recitation. The Geluk tradition adds five more: guru yoga, water bowl offerings, Damtsig Dorjé purifying meditation, making *tsatsas*, and the Dorjé Khadro burning offering practice. The term is also used to refer to the practices done on a daily basis before the main meditation session, such as cleaning the room, setting up the altar, doing a breathing meditation, and the preliminary prayers.

prostrations. Paying respect to the guru-deity with body, speech, and mind; one of the tantric preliminaries.

protector. A worldly or enlightened being who protects Buddhism and its practitioners.

puja. Literally, "offering"; a religious ceremony. The term is usually used to describe an offering ceremony such as the *Offering to the Spiritual Master* (*Guru Puja*).

pure land. A pure land of a buddha is a place where there is no suffering. In some but not all pure lands, after taking birth, the practitioner receives teachings directly from the buddha of that pure land, allowing them to actualize the rest of the path and then become enlightened.

purification. The elimination from the mind of negative imprints left by past nonvirtuous actions, which would otherwise ripen into suffering. The most effective methods of purification employ the four opponent powers, the powers of the dependence, regret, restraint, and the remedy.

Ratnasambhava (*Rinchen Jungné*). One of the five buddha types, yellow in color, representing the wisdom of equality and the purification of the feeling aggregate. *See* five buddha types.

realization. A valid mind that holds a stable, correct understanding of a Dharma subject, such as emptiness, that effects a deep change within the continuum of the person. The effortless experience resulting from study and meditation supported by guru devotion and ripened by purification and merit-building practices.

refuge. The door to the Dharma path. Having taken refuge from the heart, you become an inner being or Buddhist. There are three levels of refuge—Hinayana, Mahayana, and Vajrayana—and two or three causes necessary for taking refuge: *fearing* the sufferings of samsara in general and lower realms in particular; *faith* that Buddha, Dharma, and Sangha have the qualities and power to lead you to happiness, liberation, and enlightenment; and (for Mahayana refuge) *compassion* for all sentient beings.

renunciation. The state of mind of not having the slightest attraction to samsaric pleasures for even a second and having the strong wish for liberation. The first of the three principal aspects of the path to enlightenment. *See also* bodhichitta; emptiness.

rinpoche. Literally, "precious one." Epithet for an incarnate lama, that is, one who has intentionally taken rebirth in a human form to benefit sentient beings on the path to enlightenment.

root delusions. One of the six groups of mental factors, these are the deluded or nonvirtuous minds that subsequently lead to the secondary afflictions. There are six: desire, anger, pride, ignorance, afflicted doubt, and afflicted view. *See also* mental factors.

rupakaya (*zukku*). The form body of a fully enlightened being; the result of the complete and perfect accumulation of merit. It has two aspects: *sambhogakaya* (*longku*, enjoyment body), in which the enlightened mind appears to benefit highly realized bodhisattvas; and *nirmanakaya* (*tulku*, emanation body), in which the enlightened mind appears to benefit ordinary beings. *See also* dharmakaya.

sadhana. Method of accomplishment; the step-by-step instructions for practicing the meditations related to a particular meditational deity.

samsara (*khorwa*). Cyclic existence; the six realms of conditioned existence, three lower—hell being (*naraka*), hungry ghost (*preta*), and animal (*tiryanc*)—and three upper—human (*manushya*), demigod (*asura*), and god (*deva* or *sura*). The beginningless, recurring cycle of death and rebirth under the control of karma and delusion, fraught with suffering. Also refers to the contaminated aggregates of a sentient being.

sangha (gendun). Spiritual community; the third of the Three Rare Sublime Ones. In Tibetan *gendun* literally means "intending *(dun)* to virtue *(gen)*."

seed syllable (dru; yigé). In tantric visualizations, a Sanskrit syllable arising out of emptiness and out of which the meditational deity in turn arises. A single syllable representing a deity's entire mantra.

self-cherishing. The self-centered attitude of considering your own happiness to be more important than that of others.

sentient being. An unenlightened being; any being whose mind is not completely free from gross and subtle obscurations.

seven wisdoms. As explained in the Lama Tsongkhapa Daily Guru Yoga Meditation, these are the seven types of wisdom that need to be attained: great wisdom, clear wisdom, quick wisdom, profound wisdom, wisdom of explaining (the Dharma), wisdom of debating, and wisdom of composing.

Shakyamuni Buddha (563–483 BC). Fourth of the one thousand founding buddhas of this present world age. Born a prince of the Shakya clan in North India, he taught the sutra and tantra paths to liberation and enlightenment; founder of what came to be known as Buddhism. (From *buddha*, "fully awake.")

Shantideva (685–763). The Indian Buddhist philosopher and bodhisattva who wrote the quintessential Mahayana text, *A Guide to the Bodhisattva's Way of Life* (*Bodhicharayavatara*).

six perfections (paramita). The practices of a bodhisattva. On the basis of bodhichitta, a bodhisattva practices the six perfections: generosity, morality, patience, enthusiastic perseverance, concentration, and wisdom.

six realms. The general way that Buddhism divides the whole of cyclic existence, with three suffering realms (hell, hungry ghost, and animal) and three fortunate realms (human, demigod, and god). *See also* samsara.

six root delusions. See root delusions.

spirits. Beings not usually visible to ordinary people; they can belong to the hungry ghost or god realms, and they can be beneficent as well as harmful.

stupa. A dome-shaped structure, often containing Buddhist relics, that represents the enlightened mind; stupas range in size from huge to a few inches in height.

subtle obscurations. See obscurations to knowledge.

sutra. A discourse of the Buddha recognized as a canonical text.

tantra. The secret teachings of the Buddha; a scriptural text and the teachings and practices it contains. Also called *Vajrayana* or *Mantrayana.*

Tara (Drölma). A female meditational deity who embodies the enlightened activity of all the buddhas; often referred to as the mother of the buddhas of the past, present, and future. The *Praises to the Twenty-One Taras* prayer is the most popular prayer for lay and ordained Tibetans alike.

tathagata (dezhin shekpa). Epithet for a buddha; literally, "one who has gone to suchness."

ten nonvirtuous actions. General actions to be avoided so as not to create negative karma. Three of body (killing, stealing, and sexual misconduct); four of speech (lying, speaking harshly, slandering, and gossiping); and three of mind (covetousness, ill will, and wrong views).

Thirty-Five Buddhas. Also called *Thirty-Five Confession Buddhas.* Used in the practice of confessing and purifying negative karmas, the group of thirty-five buddhas visualized while reciting the *Sutra of the Three Heaps* and performing prostrations.

three poisons. Attachment, anger, and ignorance.

three principal aspects of the path. The three main divisions of the lamrim: renunciation, bodhichitta, and the right view (of emptiness).

Three Rare Sublime Ones (Triratna; Könchok Sum). Also called the *Three Jewels* or *Triple Gem*; the objects of Buddhist refuge: the Buddha, Dharma, and Sangha. Lama Zopa Rinpoche prefers "Three Rare Sublime Ones" as a more direct translation of *Könchok Sum.*

transmigratory beings. Sentient beings who pass from one realm to another, taking rebirth within cyclic existence.

Triple Gem. See Three Rare Sublime Ones

Tsongkhapa, Lama Jé (1357–1419). Founder of the Geluk tradition of Tibetan Buddhism and revitalizer of many sutra and tantra lineages as well as the monastic tradition in Tibet.

Tushita (Ganden). The Joyous Land. The pure land of the thousand buddhas of this eon, where the future buddha, Maitreya, and Lama Tsongkhapa reside.

two merits (sambharadvaya; tsok nyi). Also called the *two accumulations* or *two types of merit:* the merit of virtue (also called the *merit of fortune* or the *collection of merit*), which develops the method side of the path by practicing generosity and so forth; and the merit of (transcendental) wisdom (also called the *collection of wisdom*), which develops the wisdom side of the path by meditation on emptiness and so forth.

two obscurations (dvi-avarana; drip nyi). Deluded mental states that block the attainment of liberation and enlightenment. They are the grosser kind, called disturbing-thought obscurations or obscurations to liberation (*kleshavarana, nyöndrip*); and the subtle obscurations, the imprints left when those are purified, called obscurations to knowledge or obscurations to enlightenment (*jneyavarana, shedrip*).

two paths. The paths of method and wisdom.

two truths (satyadvaya; denpa nyi). The two ways of relating to phenomena: conventional or all-obscuring truth (*samvritisatya; kunzop denpa*), which is the truth to a worldly mind; and ultimate truth (*paramarthasatya; döndam denpa*), the truth to a mind engaged in ultimate analysis. *See also* conventional truth, ultimate truth.

ultimate truth (paramarthasatya, döndam denpa). One of the two truths, the other being conventional truth. It is the understanding of the ultimate nature of things and events, emptiness. *See also* conventional truth.

Vairochana (Nampar nangdze or *Namnang).* One of the five buddha types, white in color, representing mirror-like wisdom and the puri-fication of the form aggregate. *See* five buddha types.

vajra (dorjé). Literally, "adamantine"; the four- or five-spoke implement used in tantric practice.

Vajrapani (Chakna Dorjé). A male meditational deity embodying the power of all enlightened beings to accomplish their goals.

Vajrasattva (Dorjé Sempa). A male meditational deity symbolizing the inherent purity of all buddhas. A major tantric purification practice for removing obstacles created by negative karma and the breaking of vows.

Vajrayana. Another name for *tantra*; the Adamantine Vehicle; the sec-ond of the two Mahayana paths. It is also called *Tantrayana* or *Man-trayana*. This is the quickest vehicle of Buddhism, as it allows certain practitioners to attain enlightenment within a single lifetime.

virtue. Positive karma; that which results in happiness.

vows. Precepts taken on the basis of refuge at all levels of Buddhist practice. Pratimoksha precepts (vows of individual liberation) are the main vows in the Hinayana tradition and are taken by monks, nuns, and laypeople; they are the basis of all other vows. Bodhisattva and tantric vows are taken in the Mahayana tradition in association with a tantric initiation.

wisdom. Different levels of insight into the nature of reality. There are, for example, the three wisdoms of hearing, contemplation, and meditation. Ultimately, there is the wisdom of realizing emptiness, which frees beings from cyclic existence and eventually brings them to enlightenment. The complete and perfect accumulation of wis-dom results in the dharmakaya.

wisdom mother (sherabma). A tantric consort.

wish-granting jewel. Also called *wish-fulfilling jewel*. A jewel that brings its possessor everything that they desire.

yogi. A highly realized male meditator.

Zong Rinpoche (1905–1984). A powerful Gelukpa lama renowned for his wrathful aspect, who had impeccable knowledge of Tibetan Bud-dhist rituals, art, and science.

zung (*dharani*). Zungs resemble mantras, but are usually longer than a mantra, consisting of a homage or invocation of the deity, followed by a request to act.

NOTES
···

1. Dhammapada v.183. Taken from *Essential Buddhist Prayers, Volume 1*, FPMT 2008, 75–76.
2. Chenrezig is the Tibetan name for Avalokiteshvara, Compassion Buddha. Generally, in our tradition, we use the Sanskrit names for the deities, but because Chenrezig is such a beloved name for Tibetans, and the one that Rinpoche generally uses, we shall use it in this book.
3. Compare this with what Lama Yeshe said on the sound of a mantra: "It is a common misconception that reciting mantras is an external and unnatural mental exercise, rather than an internal and spontaneous occurrence. Reciting a mantra, however, does not mean the mere vocal repetition of speech syllables. Many meditators know from experience that the act of reciting mantras transcends external sounds and words. It is more like listening to a subtle inner sound that has always inhabited our nervous system. . . . The existence of inner sound cannot be denied. Our nervous system has its own specific inner sound. This is not something that Mahayanists have invented; it is an objective reality that exists within us. For example, the sound 'ah' exists within us from the moment of birth. All speech sounds are derived from 'ah.' Without 'ah' there could be no other sound. . . . Mantra is energy. It is always pure and cannot be contaminated by negative thought processes. As mantra is not gross energy, it cannot be corrupted the way sensory phenomena are corrupted by our own minds. One can easily discover the power of mantra for oneself by embarking upon a meditational retreat. Those endowed with skillful wisdom will naturally attain realizations through the power of mantra. Practitioners of mantra yoga will discover that their inner sound becomes completely one with the mantra itself. Then even their normal speech becomes mantra." (From a talk given at Kopan Monastery, 1975, published in Zopa and Yeshe 1979, 66.)
4. Shantideva 5.18, as translated by L. O. Gómez (forthcoming).
5. They are killing, stealing, sexual misconduct, lying, speaking harshly, slandering, gossiping, covetousness, ill will, and wrong views.
6. That all phenomena are impermanent is a key tenet of Buddhism, but here Rinpoche uses the term "impermanence and death" with reference to the aspect of Buddhist studies that explores just how fragile our life is—how it can end at any moment—and what can benefit us at such a time. This is one of the key subjects of the graduated path of the lower capable being.
7. For these mantras see appendix 7, Daily Mantras.
8. A deity (*ishtadevata*; *yidam*) refers to an emanation of the enlightened mind, and therefore is synonymous with "buddha." We generally refer to "deity" when we are talking about the meditational deity of a tantric practice.

9. The *lamrim* (Tib) is the common name within the Geluk tradition of Tibetan Buddhism for the graduated path to enlightenment, the step-by-step presentation of the Buddha's teachings allowing the practitioner to progress toward enlightenment. The other traditions have similar presentations.

10. The rare human state, qualified by eight freedoms and ten richnesses, which is the ideal condition for practicing the Dharma and attaining enlightenment. The eight freedoms are being free from being born as a hell being, hungry ghost, animal, long-life god, or barbarian, or in a dark age when no buddha has descended, holding wrong views, and being born with mental or physical problems that preclude you from understanding the Dharma. The ten richnesses are being born as a human being, in a Dharma country and with perfect mental and physical faculties, not having committed any of the five immediate negativities, having faith in the Buddha's teachings, being born when a buddha has descended, when the teachings have been revealed, when the complete teachings still exist, when there are still followers of the teachings, and having the necessary conditions to practice the Dharma, such as the kindness of others.

11. Here Rinpoche is differentiating between two levels of empowerment, a full empowerment or initiation (*wang*) and a permission to practice (*jenang*).

12. An oral transmission (*lung*) is a verbal transmission of a teaching, meditation practice, or mantra from guru to disciple, the guru having received the transmission in an unbroken lineage from the original source.

13. Nagarjuna 1998, 96, ch. 1, v. 20.

14. Quoted in Pabongka 1991, 125.

15. A realization, in the way the term is used in Tibetan Buddhism, is a valid mind that holds a stable, correct understanding of a Dharma subject, such as emptiness, so much so that it effects a deep change within the continuum of the person.

16. Mantras are often counted in malas (*threngwa*), rosaries of 108 beads; hence one mala is 108 mantras.

17. The four noble truths are the truth of suffering, the truth of the origin of suffering, the truth of the cessation of suffering, and the truth of the path that leads to the cessation of suffering. This is said to be the first turning of the Dharma wheel. In the second turning, at Vulture's Peak in Rajagriha (present day Rajgir), the Buddha taught the *prajnaparamita* sutras, the teachings on emptiness. In the third turning, the Buddha addressed buddha nature and the nature of the mind, allaying seeming contradictions between the teachings in the first two turnings of the Dharma wheel.

18. See also Zopa and McDonald 2010, 52; Pabongka 1991, 305; and a slightly different version of the quote in Walshe 1995, 270.

19. Padmasambhava, the eighth-century Indian tantric master mainly responsible for the establishment of Buddhism in Tibet, is revered by all Tibetans, especially the Nyingmapas. Atisha Dipamkara Shrijnana (982–1054) was the renowned Indian master who went to Tibet in 1042 to help in the revival of Buddhism. Lama Jé Tsongkhapa (1357–1419) was the founder of the Geluk tradition of Tibetan Buddhism and revitalizer of many sutra and tantra lineages and the monastic tradition in Tibet.

20. Lama Zopa often prefixes the Buddha's name with "Guru" to emphasize the inseparability of the guru and the Buddha, a key element in guru devotion.

21. The path of the individual practitioner, also known as Hinayana or Theravada, is the path taken by those wishing to attain liberation rather than enlightenment. The name is problematic. Generally the term Hinayana or Lesser Vehicle is more accurate but shunned (although this is the term that Rinpoche generally uses) because people feel it denigrates the path. However, Theravada, the "doctrine of the elders," a more commonly used term, is only one of the four root divisions of the Hinayana schools. It is widely practiced in Sri Lanka and most of Southeast Asia. His Holiness refers to the two vehicles as the Pali Canon Vehicle and the Sanskrit Canon Vehicle, referring to the languages the texts of the two vehicles were written in. Yangsi Rinpoche refers to them as the Pratimokshayana (literally, the "vehicle of individual liberation") and the Bodhisattvayana (the "vehicle of the bodhisattva"), referring to the two types of practitioners.

22. They are (1) descending from Tushita Heaven, (2) entering his mother's womb, (3) birth, (4) studying arts and handicrafts, (5) enjoying life in the palace, (6) renunciation, (7) undertaking ascetic practices, (8) going to Bodhgaya, (9) defeating the negative forces (Mara), (10) attaining enlightenment, (11) turning the wheel of Dharma, and (12) entering parinirvana (passing away).

23. A puja (*chöpa*), the Sanskrit term meaning offering or homage, differs from a deity practice in that it is in essence an offering to the deity or guru.

24. A mudra is a symbolic hand gesture, having power in the same way a mantra has power.

25. A buddha displays thirty-two major signs and eighty minor exemplifications. Not all texts agree entirely what they are, but the most commonly cited text listing them in Tibetan Buddhism seems to be Tsongkhapa's *Golden Rosary of Excellent Explanations* (*Legs bshad gser 'phreng*). See also Walshe 1995, 441–470, and Alexander Berzin's *The Thirty-Two Major Marks of a Buddha's Physical Body*: studybuddhism.com/en/advanced-studies/lam-rim/refuge/the-32-major-marks-of-a-buddha-s-physical-body. Accessed 03/20/2020.

26. Khunu Lama Rinpoche also said this of the mantra: "Guru Shakyamuni Buddha received enlightenment through reciting the mantra TADYATHA OM MUNE MUNE MAHA MUNEYE SVAHA. Therefore, you too should recite it continuously. Say it twenty-one times with the *tadyatha* at the beginning, then continue reciting without it, as many times as you can." Taken from *Teaching from Tibet*, ed. Ribush 2005, 212.

27. The bodies of a buddha are often enumerated as three: besides the dharmakaya, the rupakaya is divided into the sambhogakaya, or enjoyment body, and the nirmanakaya, or emanation body.

28. Geshe is the title conferred on those who have completed extensive studies and examinations at Geluk monastic universities on the five main topics: Abhidharma, Vinaya, Madhyamaka, Pramana, and Prajnaparamita.

29. This meditation has been adapted from the meditation given by Lama Zopa at Dorje Chang Institute, Auckland, July 1976, and included in Rinpoche's forthcoming LYWA book on refuge, as well the meditation © FPMT, Inc., 2008, 169–87.

The colophon states: "Compiled by the Venerable Lama Thubten Zopa Rinpoche, March 1992 in Taipei. Revised at Kopan Monastery, Kathmandu, Nepal, December 1995. Edited for publication at Wisdom Publications, Boston, July 1996. Lightly revised and reprinted by FPMT Education Department, February 2001. Reformatted and very lightly revised by Venerable Gyalten Mindrol, FPMT Education Department, December 2005. New absorption meditation given by Lama Zopa Rinpoche and lightly edited by Venerable Gyalten Mindrol, April 2008."

30. See appendix 2 for some standard preliminary and dedication prayers.

31. A mandala is a symbolic representation of the entire universe. It is usual in a daily sadhana to visualize this and offer it to all the buddhas and the sentient beings.

32. *Bhagavan* is an epithet for the Buddha, literally "One who has destroyed all defilements and possesses all qualities"; *tathagata*, another epithet, means "One who has gone to suchness"; *conqueror* refers to the Buddha having conquered all adversaries. See the section on the names of the buddhas in the Thirty-Five Buddhas for a full explanation of the meanings.

33. *Pema Chöling* in Tibetan.

34. *Gyälpo Zangpo Chok* in Tibetan. In Buddhist cosmology a wheel-turning king (*chakravartin*; *khorlo gyuwä gyelpo*) is a king who rules over all four continents with love and ethics, according to the Dharma. Ashoka is a prime example of this.

35. The Tibetan term is *dzü kye*, which means "entered and born." While sometimes translated as "miraculous birth," this term does not necessarily mean only that.

36. The six realms are the general way that Buddhism divides the whole of cyclic existence, with three suffering realms (hell, hungry ghost, and animal) and three fortunate realms (human, demigod, and god).

37. The three times are past, present, and future.

38. Mount Meru is the center of the universe in Buddhist cosmology.

39. For other versions, see Wangchen Rinpoche 1993, 8–9, and Bokar Rinpoche 2009, 28–33.

40. *Ser gyi mü kyü* in Tibetan.

41. *Mig me dzum* in Tibetan.

42. In this fortunate eon, it is said that a thousand buddhas will descend to benefit sentient beings, Shakyamuni Buddha being the fourth and the future buddha Maitreya the fifth.

43. The Tibetan is literally *chen* "eye," *re* "continually," *zik* "look." Compare this with the Sanskrit, *Avalokiteshvara*, which translates as the "lord who looks down on [the sorrows] of the world," and the Chinese Kuan Yin (pinyin *Guanshiyin*), which means "she who hears the sorrows of the world." In Japanese, the same characters are pronounced as Kannon.

44. Gomo Rinpoche (1921–85), an incarnation of Phadampa Sangye, a great Indian yogi who lived in Milarepa's time, was a lay lama and guru of both Lama Yeshe and Lama Zopa Rinpoche. He taught at many FPMT centers, especially in Italy before passing away in 1985. He reincarnated in Canada and is now a teacher and rap artist.

45. Quoted in Zopa 2017, 13–14.

46. Ganapati resembles but is distinct from Ganesh, the elephant-headed Hindu deity.

47. A two-day thousand-arm Chenrezig retreat that involves fasting, prostrations, and silence.

48. Kashyapa (*Sangye Ösung Barwé Gyalpo*) was the third of the thousand buddhas of this age, Shakyamuni being the fourth.

49. The four cardinal directions of north, south, east, and west, the four intermediate directions, and the nadir and zenith.

50. Slang for feces.

51. A dome-shaped structure, often containing Buddhist relics, that represents the enlightened mind. Stupas range in size from huge to a few inches in height.

52. Lukla is a small village in the Solu Khumbu region of Nepal, near Everest, which, because of its airport, is the favorite starting place for Everest treks. It is also the way to get to Namche Bazaar and Lawudo, near Rinpoche's birthplace, where there is an FPMT retreat center.

53. Nagas are snake-like beings that live near bodies of water. Some are very powerful.

54. Quoted in Zopa 2001, xviii–xix.

55. This practice is taken from the FPMT's *The Welfare of Living Beings That Pervades Space: The Meditation-Recitation of the Great Compassionate One.* © 2020 Foundation for the Preservation of the Mahayana Tradition, Inc. All rights reserved. The colophon states: "This meditation-recitation of the Great Compassionate One called *The Welfare of Living Beings That Pervades Space* is the blessed speech of the Mahasiddha Thangtong Gyalpo. The publisher's colophon: Translated by Ven. Steve Carlier, October 19, 2019 from *thang stong rgyal po, 'gro don mkha' khyab ma,* s.l.; s.n., s.d. Translation reviewed by Joona Repo, FPMT Translation Services, June 2020."

56. The three circles refers to the subject, object, and the action being engaged in.

57. Kirti Tsenshab Rinpoche (1926–2006) was born in Amdo, Tibet. He was a highly attained and learned yogi who lived in Dharamsala, India. Besides being one of Lama Zopa's teachers, he gave Kalachakra commentary to His Holiness the Dalai Lama. Rinpoche praised him as "a great Kadampa master, completely renounced."

58. Sakya Pandita (1182–1251) was a master of the Sakya tradition who spread Tibetan Buddhism in Mongolia and China.

59. See appendix 3 for a meditation on attaining the seven wisdoms.

60. There are four schools within Tibetan Buddhism: Sakya, Nyingma, Kagyü, and Geluk, Geluk being the most recent. Developing out of the Kadam tradition that was founded by Atisha and Dromtönpa, it was founded by Lama Tsongkhapa and his disciples in the early fifteenth century.

61. In tantric visualizations, a seed syllable (*dru*; *yigé*) is a Sanskrit syllable, usually the first syllable of the deity's name, which arises out of emptiness, and from which the deity arises. It resides at the heart of the deity or guru, depending on the practice. In the standard guru yoga practices, the guru is the nirmanakaya (emanation body), the deity is the sambhogakaya (enjoyment body), and the seed syllable is the dharmakaya (truth body).

62. Most buddha images are in a sambhogakaya aspect, with beautiful clothes and ornaments and holding ritual implements. Shakyamuni and Maitreya, as buddhas of this fortunate eon, are usually depicted in the nirmanakaya or emanation body

aspect, as monks in monk's robes, symbolizing this is the aspect that we deluded beings can see.

63. As the name implies, the Guru Puja is a puja or offering ceremony for the guru, in this case Lama Tsongkhapa. It is regularly performed on the tenth and twenty-fifth of the lunar calendar in Tibetan monasteries and Geluk Dharma centers.

64. Arya Asanga (c. 300–370) was the Indian master who received directly from Maitreya Buddha the extensive, or method, lineage of Shakyamuni Buddha's teachings. Said to have founded the Chittamatra school of Buddhist philosophy, he is one of six great Indian scholars known as the Six Ornaments. Aryadeva, also one of the Six Ornaments, was a third-century Indian Buddhist philosopher and the leading early proponent of Nagarjuna's Prasangika Madhyamaka philosophy, the most subtle of the various explanations of emptiness.

65. This short sadhana of Manjushri Arapatsana is taken from *Manjushri Arapatsana: Orange Manjushri According to the Sakya/Gelug Traditions*, © FPMT Inc., 2010. It was originally a kriya tantra sadhana and hence featured a self-generation visualization (seeing yourself as the deity). I have abbreviated it and adapted it slightly to a front-generation visualization for the purpose of this book. The colophon states: "It was compiled by Gelong Dharmabhadra by taking the best aspects of many other practices on Manjushri. Translated by Geshe Thubten Sherab, Taos, New Mexico, Sept 3, 2003. Scribed by Merry Colony. Edited and formatted by Ven. Constance Miller, FPMT Education Department, 30 September 2003."

66. See appendix 2 for some standard preliminary and dedication prayers.

67. As befits the most beloved deity in Tibetan Buddhism, there are many stories about the origin of Tara. Pabongka Rinpoche (and hence Lama Zopa) here seems to be following one of the most popular renditions, based on the work of Taranatha (1575–1634), a prolific scholar and Sanskrit translator. For a similar story see Bokar 1999, 19–21.

68. Some sources cite this as another name for Amoghasiddhi.

69. Rinpoche calls the eon "No Resistance" and the monk "Stainless," but I have used Willson's translation here as it seems closer to the Sanskrit and Tibetan.

70. For her story, see Mackenzie 1999.

71. A disciple of Gyalwa Ensapa and a guru of the first Panchen Lama, Losang Chökyi Gyaltsen.

72. Green Tara is often called Khadiravani Tara or Tara of the Acacia Grove, although this is not a term Lama Zopa has used.

73. The five transcendental wisdoms (*panchajnana*; *yeshe nga*), the five aspects of the primordial wisdom, correspond to the five buddha families (*panchakula*; *rik nga*). They are the mirror-like wisdom (white Vairochana); the *dharmadhatu* wisdom (blue Akshobhya); the wisdom of equality (yellow Ratnasambhava); the wisdom of discernment (red Amitabha); and the all-accomplishing wisdom (green Amoghasiddhi).

74. An utpala is a blue lotus, *Nymphaea caerulea*.

75. Chittamani Tara, the highest yoga tantra aspect of Tara, holds a blue utpala flower in both hands.

76. For the names in Sanskrit and Tibetan and illustrations of these eight Taras, see Bokar 1999, 157–160.

77. This is the Method of Performing Tara Purification Night.

78. Translated into a chantable form by Ven. Sangye Khadro for the FPMT education office.

79. The names, descriptions, Tibetan, and mantras are taken from *The Twenty-One Forms of Tara According the Tradition of Lord Atisha*, © Foundation for the Preservation of the Mahayana Tradition, Inc., 2020. I have merged what Rinpoche has said on each Tara with the text from the FPMT publication, which was compiled from oral commentaries by Ven. Kirti Tsenshab Rinpoche and Ven. Choden Rinpoche and Beyer's book *The Cult of Tara*, slightly edited and formatted by Kunga Dorje Gyalpo in November 2020.

80. Gandharvas (*driza*) are gods of the desire realm, of the lowest order, often depicted as horse-headed and as skilled musicians whose music can disturb a meditator. Yakshas (*nöjin*) are spirits, usually described in Tibetan Buddhism as flesh-eating cannibals, but which can been benevolent or malevolent in other forms of Buddhism.

81. In his commentary on the Twenty-One Taras, Lama Lhundrup says this Tara is both peaceful and wrathful and so has two mantras. The peaceful mantra is OM TARE TUTTARE TURE SVAHA that surrounds the syllable *tam* at the heart. The wrathful mantra is OM NAMA TARE NAMO HARE HUM HARE SVAHA that surrounds the syllable *hum* at the heart. See Lhundrup Rigsel 2014, 85.

82. Meru, Mandara, and Vindhya are mountains that are abodes of different types of malevolent gods, nagas, and so forth who are intent on harming sentient beings. Lama Lhundrup says, "I guess the reason why Tara shakes the three worlds and the different mountains is to weaken their thoughts and their power to harm others. By doing this she is able to render them powerless and harmless." See Lhundrup Rigsel 2014, 87.

83. Kinnaras, which is Pali—the Sanskrit being *kimnara* and the Tibetan *mi'amchi*—are half-bird-half-human beings that guard the well-being of humans. Thai temples abound with beautiful golden statues of kinnaras. The Jataka tales describe them as harmless and innocent beings fond of music and song.

84. There are many interpretations of these three words. A common one is that emptiness is the lack of inherent nature, signlessness is the lack of inherent cause, and wishlessness is the lack of inherent production. See Lopez 1990, 89–91.

85. This description is adapted from Bokar 1999, 41.

86. This meditation comes from one given by Lama Zopa at Kopan Monastery, Kathmandu, May 1987.

87. Sanskrit, literally "means of accomplishment"; a ritual text showing the method to accomplish a particular meditational deity. See appendix 4 for a short Tara sadhana.

88. Quoted in Rinpoche's *Teachings from the Medicine Buddha Retreat* 2009, 259–60 (abridged). The seven qualities are a good social class, a beautiful body, a long life, a life free from illness, prosperity, wealth, and great wisdom.

89. Composed by Panchen Losang Chökyi Gyältsen, the full title is *The Concise Essence Sutra Ritual of Bhagavan Medicine Buddha Called the Wish-Fulfilling Jewel*. The

short Medicine Buddha Sadhana has just seven Medicine Buddhas, whereas *The Wish-Fulfilling Jewel* also includes Shakyamuni Buddha below the main Medicine Buddha.

90. Of another deity, Rinpoche describes coral color as the color of coral that has been broken open, a sort of reddish orange.

91. Both quotes cited in Rinpoche's *Teachings from the Medicine Buddha Retreat* 2009, 183.

92. In Buddhist cosmology, it is said that humans evolved from the form realm gods, and our lifespan was originally about eighty thousand years. As we have degenerated, with our bodies becoming grosser and grosser, the lifespan has diminished and will continue to diminish until we live no longer than ten years. See Rinpoche's *Teachings from the Medicine Buddha Retreat* 2009, 110–15.

93. Here Rinpoche is referring to how pujas are calendared according to the Tibetan lunar calendar and not the Western one. So, the Guru Puja is regularly done on the tenth and twenty-fifth of the lunar month and the Tara puja on the eighth.

94. Mitrukpa's mantra is NAMO RATNA TRAYAYA OM KAMKANI KAMKANI ROCHANI ROCHANI TROTANI TROTANI TRASANI TRASANI PRATIHANA PRATIHANA SARVA KARMA PARAM PARA NI ME SARVA SATTVA NANCHA SVAHA. (See the section on Mitrukpa in chapter 8 for more information.) Milarepa's mantra is OM AH GURU HASA VAJRA SARVA SIDDHI PHALA HUM.

95. See Rinpoche's *Heart Practices for Death and Dying* (FPMT 2008), which includes advice on helping dying and dead beings, *The Wish-Fulfilling Jewel* (*Medicine Buddha Puja*), and a very short Medicine Buddha practice, along with prayers and mantras that are especially helpful at the time of death.

96. The verse for Having a Jewel Ushnisha is "*Chom dän dä de zhin sheg pa dra chom pa yang dag par dzog päi sang gyä rin chhen tsug tor chän la chhag tshäl lo,*" which means "To the bhagavan, tathagata, arhat, the perfectly completed Buddha Having a Jewel Ushnisha, I prostrate."

97. Abridged and modified from Ngawang Losang Tenpa Gyältsän's *Medicine Buddha Sadhana*, translated by Rinpoche. © FPMT Education Publications, FPMT, Inc., 2000, 2002, 2005, 2007, 2008, 2013. All rights reserved. The colophon states: "The Medicine Buddha Sadhana was translated by Lama Thubten Zopa Rinpoche and edited and prepared for publication by Ven. Thubten Gyatso (Adrian Feldmann) in 1982. It was first published in 1982 by Wisdom Publications. It was lightly edited and prepared for publication by the FPMT Education Department in 2001 by Ven. Constance Miller. Revised March 2002, January 2004, July 2005, January 2007." See also appendix 5 for another short Medicine Buddha practice.

98. See appendix 2 for some standard preliminary and dedication prayers.

99. This aspect of the deity in union with the wisdom mother (*yab-yum*) is common in highest yoga tantra. Very often you will see it written as "deity father-mother" to emphasize that these are not two separate intrinsic beings but the deity's unification of bliss and emptiness, or method and wisdom—the male aspect representing the bliss or method and the female aspect representing wisdom or emptiness.

100. The vajra and the bell are key tantric implements. The vajra, or *dorjé* in Tibetan (literally "adamantine" or "thunderbolt"), is a four- or five-spoked implement held

in the right hand, whereas the bell is held in the left hand. As these represent bliss and emptiness respectively, the practitioner should never hold one and not the other, meaning we should never be separated from the union of bliss (or method) and emptiness.

101. A skull cup (*kapala*) is a cup made from a human skull used as a tantric implement.

102. Here "mudra" does not refer to a hand gesture but ornaments, such as vajra, bell, jewels, bone ornaments, and so forth.

103. Although "vajra posture" and "lotus posture" (or "full lotus") are synonyms in yoga, in a tantric deity such as Vajrasattva, the vajra posture is with each foot on the other thigh, soles upwards, whereas the lotus posture refers to the wisdom mother's legs wrapped around the waist of the male deity.

104. Although most kriya or action tantras (the first of the four classes of tantra) are simple and the initiation associated with them is likewise simple, there are a few "great" initiations that span two or more days and have many of the features of a highest yoga tantra initiation. Perhaps the most commonly performed in the Geluk tradition is the great Chenrezig initiation.

105. His Holiness Trijang Rinpoche (1901–81) was the Junior Tutor of His Holiness the Fourteenth Dalai Lama and root guru of Lama Yeshe and Lama Zopa Rinpoche. He was also editor of *Liberation in the Palm of Your Hand*.

106. Quoted in a slightly different translation in Pabongka 1991, 184.

107. A Kadampa is a practitioner of Kadam lineage, the order of Tibetan Buddhism founded in the eleventh century by Atisha, Dromtönpa, and their followers. Kadampa geshes are renowned for their practice of thought transformation.

108. Within Tibetan Buddhism, there are three levels of vows we can take. These are the pratimoksha or individual liberation vows that serve as the foundation for keeping our morality pure, which can be the five lay vows taken for life (not killing, stealing, committing sexual misconduct, lying, or taking intoxicants) or the novice vows and full ordination that monks and nuns take. There are also the eight Mahayana precepts taken for one day. With a tantric initiation, we take the bodhisattva vows to enter the bodhisattva path, and (with a highest yoga tantra initiation) the tantric vows. Both have root and secondary vows.

109. Verse 8. Taken from FPMT's *Essential Buddhist Prayers, Volume 1*, 2011, 94.

110. This meditation is adapted from FPMT's *Essential Buddhist Prayers, Volume 2*, 2009, 201–207. © FPMT Education Services, FPMT, Inc., 2000. The colophon states: "This teaching was given by Lama Zopa Rinpoche during the Vajrasattva retreat, Land of Medicine Buddha, Soquel, California, USA, 1999, and revised in New York, November 1999. Edited by Nicholas Ribush, 2001. Lightly revised for inclusion in *Essential Buddhist Prayers, Vol. 2* by Venerable Constance Miller, FPMT Education Department, 2001."

111. The intermediate state (*bardo*) is the state between this life and the next.

112. See appendix 2.

113. This can also be referred to as the *Sutra of the Three Heaps* (*Triskhandhadharmasūtra*; *pungpo sumpé do*), the three heaps being homage, confession, and rejoicing or dedication. For the whole practice, including reciting and prostrating to the names of the Thirty-Five Buddhas and the Medicine Buddhas, the confession prayer, and the

general confession, see FPMT's *Confession of Downfall: Prostrations to the Thirty-Five Buddhas* or *Essential Buddhist Prayers and Practices, Volume 1,* 39–55.

114. Khensur Denma Locho Rinpoche (1928–2014) was an expert in Yamantaka, a wrathful form of Manjushri. Highly learned and greatly respected, he was abbot in monasteries in India and the United States.

115. Ngulchu Dharmabhadra (1772–1851) was a renowned scholar who wrote many tantric commentaries as well as important texts on Tibetan grammar. Because Rinpoche has based his teaching on Dharmabhadra's, Atisha's, and Gyaltsap Jé's commentaries, with only occasional references to the author, it's not always clear which explanation comes from which commentary.

116. The phonetic rendering of the Tibetan is slightly different here from the rest of the book as it is directly taken from FPMT's prayer book and is the one they use for prayers. The part of the verse that changes is usually just the buddha's name, although in the case of Shakyamuni it includes his epithets.

117. See Dharmabhadra 2016, 4.

118. See Dharmabhadra 2016, 5.

119. See FPMT's *Preliminary Practice of Prostrations* 2003, 65.

120. Ibid.

121. See FPMT 2003, 66.

122. See Dharmabhadra 2016, 7.

123. Ibid.

124. See Dharmabhadra 2016, 9, and FPMT 2003, 67.

125. See Dharmabhadra 2016, 9.

126. See FPMT's *The Preliminary Practice of Prostrations,* 2003, 67.

127. Ibid.

128. See Dharmabhadra 2016, 10.

129. See FPMT's *The Preliminary Practice of Prostrations* 2003, 68.

130. Ibid.

131. See Dharmabhadra 2016, 12.

132. *Tsatsas* are small images of holy objects, usually buddhas, and usually made of clay or plaster. One of the preliminary practices before a long retreat is making a large number of these, often one hundred thousand. Storage then becomes an issue, and so it is common to have a building or "*tsatsa* house" made where they can be respectfully kept.

133. This meditation is abbreviated and adapted from FPMT's *Essential Buddhist Prayers, Vol. 1,* 39–55. © 2008, FPMT Education Services, FPMT, Inc. See also FPMT's *Confession of Downfall: Prostrations to the Thirty-Five Buddhas.*

134. See appendix 6 for these.

135. This topic is covered extensively in *Liberating Animals from the Danger of Death and Other Ways to Benefit Them,* by Lama Zopa. There is also a CD of mantra recitations by Rinpoche. See also "Practices for Benefiting Animals" on the LYWA website.

136. Dorjé Naljorma: a female meditational deity from the mother class of highest yoga tantra.

137. See also the Medicine Buddha chapter, chapter 5, where Rinpoche lists the mantras

to say if you eat meat, specifically Medicine Buddha, Mitrukpa, Milarepa, and the special mantra to bless the meat: OM AH BIRA KHE CHARA HUM.

138. One of the eight great bodhisattvas, who vowed not to achieve buddhahood until all hells were emptied.

139. Lama Yeshe (1935–84) was born and educated in Tibet. He fled to India, where he met his chief disciple, Lama Zopa Rinpoche. They began teaching Westerners at Kopan Monastery in 1969 and founded the Foundation for the Preservation of the Mahayana Tradition (FPMT) in 1975.

140. Mundgod is a town in Karnatika, India, near which are many Tibetan monasteries.

141. This is an amalgamation taken from a forthcoming LYWA book by Rinpoche on refuge; McDonald 1984, 34–36; and the FPMT's *The Preliminary Practice of Altar Set-up and Water Bowl Offerings* booklet, © 2003, 2007, 2008, 2016 Foundation for the Preservation of the Mahayana Tradition, Inc. The colophon states: "Altar Set-up and Water Bowl Offerings" compiled by Ven. Gyalten Mindrol from advice given by Lama Zopa Rinpoche, and from Ven. Sarah Thresher and Kendall Magnussen in the FPMT Ritual Training. "The Practice of Making Offerings" and "Guidelines for Completing 100,000 Water Bowl Offerings" were extracted from teachings given by Lama Zopa Rinpoche in a commentary to the Ganden Lha Gyäma given during the Second Enlightenment Experience Celebration in Dharamsala, India, March 1986. Provided courtesy of the Lama Yeshe Wisdom Archive (www.lamayeshe.com)."

142. Statues are often sold empty and, as such, should not be placed on an altar because it is inauspicious. There is a procedure for filling them that should be carried out by a qualified teacher. If you have a statue, check with a Dharma center to see how you can have it filled.

143. More traditionally, there are said to be six preliminary practices: cleaning the room, setting up the altar, sitting in a meditation posture such as the seven-point Vairochana posture, visualizing the merit field, creating merit by offering mandala, prostrating and the other parts of the seven-limb practice, and making the requesting prayer to the lineage lamas to receive blessings and be granted realizations.

144. Verse 2. See FPMT's *Essential Buddhist Prayers, Volume 1*, 2011, 249.

145. Taken from FPMT's *Essential Buddhist Prayers, Volume 1*, 2011, 34–37.

146. Adapted from the meditation given by Lama Zopa during the Enlightened Experience Celebration 2 at Tushita, Dharamsala, March 1986, and the FPMT's *Lama Tsongkhapa Guru Yoga*, 13–23. © 2020, Foundation for the Preservation of the Mahayana Tradition, Inc. All rights reserved. The colophon states: "*Hundred Deities of Tushita (dga' ldan lha brgya ma)*, composed by Dulnagpa Palden Zangpo, consists of only the invocation verse followed by the seven-limb prayer. The Common Meditations for Migtsema Recitation is adapted from *A Storehouse of Precious Treasure of Instructions* (*zab lam dga' ldan lha brgya ma'i rnal 'byor nyams su len tshul snyan brgyud zhal shes lhug par bkod pa'i man ngag rin chen gter gyi bang mdzod*) composed by Pabongka Rinpoche, which is in turn based on the works of earlier Geluk authors. This whole practice was translated and compiled by Lama Zopa Rinpoche. Transcribed by Ven. Lhundup Nyingje (Paula Chichester) in Madison, Wisconsin in Summer 1998, and Aptos, California in October 1998. Lightly edited

by Ven. Constance Miller, FPMT Education Department, August 1999. Revised edition, July 2001. Updated in 2003, 2006, 2008, and 2009. Revised and edited by Ven. Tenzin Tsomo, Ven. Joan Nicell, and Joona Repo, FPMT Education Services, July 2016, based on Lama Zopa Rinpoche's commentary, Rinpoche's original translations from May and October 1998, Rinpoche's way of leading the practice, and the Tibetan texts of *Hundred Deities of Tushita* and *A Storehouse of Precious Treasure of Instructions*. Phonetics checked and amended by Ven. Tenzin Tsomo, June 2016. The sequence of prayers and translation revised by Lama Zopa Rinpoche, July 2020. Edited by Ven. Joan Nicell and Ven. Ailsa Cameron, July 2020."

147. Tsongkhapa's "two sons" are Khedrup Jé (1385–1438), who became the first Panchen Lama, and Gyaltsap Jé (1364–1432), who later became the first Ganden Tripa.

148. The original uses the Sanskrit name, Avalokiteshvara.

149. This comes from *A Short Practice of Green Tara: Including Praises to Twenty-One Taras*, by Lama Zopa Rinpoche and Lama Thubten Yeshe. © 2000, 2003, 2009, 2014 FPMT, Inc. All rights reserved. The colophon states: "This daily meditation practice of Green Tara is based on *The Essential Nectar: A Simplified Condensed Yoga Practice of Tara* by Lama Thubten Zopa Rinpoche. The *Glance Meditation on the Lamrim* was written by Sera-je lama, Purchog Jampa Rinpoche, said to be an incarnation of Maitreya Buddha. It was translated by Lama Zopa Rinpoche and edited by Ven. Thubten Dondrub, February, 2001. The practice in its entirety has been edited by Ven. Constance Miller, FPMT International Office Education Services, November 1998. Revised version, March 2001. Additional corrections, August 2002 and November 2003. This practice was revised by FPMT Education Services and enhanced with the Praises to Twenty-One Taras sections, February 2014."

150. This comes from *Healing Buddha: A Practice for the Prevention and Healing of Disease* by Padmasambhava. © FPMT, Inc, 2001, 2008. All rights reserved. The colophon states: "This healing meditation practice was translated by Lama Thubten Zopa Rinpoche at Tara Institute, Melbourne, Australia, on 1 September 1991. The motivation and dedication sections were added later to the original text. Reformatted by Murray Wright, FPMT Central Office, May 1993. Originally published by Wisdom Publications, Boston, in 1994. Additional revisions by Ven. Constance Miller, FPMT Education Services, June 2001. Mantras transliterated by Joona Repo and Ven. Tenzin Tsomo, FPMT Education Services."

151. To find out more about the mantras Rinpoche recommends, visit the mantra section of the FPMT website: fpmt.org/education/teachings/texts/mantras. For extensive advice from Rinpoche about the benefits of reading, writing, or reciting particular mantras not covered in this book, or how to engage with mantras to eliminate or reduce potential or ongoing obstacles, please consult Lama Zopa's Online Advice Book (www.lamayeshe.com/advice/lama-zopa-rinpoches-online-advice-book), and Advice from Lama Zopa Rinpoche (fpmt.org/teachers/zopa/advice/).

152. This is adapted from FPMT's *Ten Powerful Mantras to Recite at the Time of Death* (© FPMT, Inc., 2010) and other advice given by Rinpoche taken from LYWA's Advice from Rinpoche webpages.

153. Adapted from various teachings by Rinpoche, as well as from the FPMT's *The Four Dharmakaya Relic Mantras and Their Benefits*. © 2013, 2020 Foundation for the

Preservation of the Mahayana Tradition, Inc. All rights reserved. The colophon states: "This section is adapted from a compilation of advice from different occasions: one was dictated by Lama Zopa Rinpoche to Ven. Holly Ansett, Kachoe Dechen Ling, Aptos, November 2002. Section of the benefits is from the Kangyur, which is the essence of all the Buddha's teachings. Additional benefits for the Stainless Beam mantra have been extracted from 'Zung of the Completely Pure Exalted Beam Stainless Light,' translated by Lama Zopa Rinpoche and dictated to Ven. Matthew Tenzin, Kachoe Dechen Ling, February, 2005. Lightly edited by Holly Ansett and Kendall Magnussen, May, 2005. Additional teachings on the benefits of these mantras are from a teaching given by Lama Zopa Rinpoche at Kachoe Dechen Ling on November 26, 2006. Transcribed by Ven. Lobsang Yangchen, checked and arranged by Ven. Holly Ansett, and edited by Ven. Gyalten Mindrol, FPMT Education Department, May 2007."

154. Rinpoche is referring to the Descent from Tushita stupa at Kópavogur, south of Reykjavik.

155. Rinpoche has not explained this term, but it probably refers to the hell realm, where the beings are tortured by fierce yamas, guardians of that realm, or the hungry ghost realm, where the yamas stop the hungry ghosts from attaining even a morsel of food or drop of drink.

156. For another explanation about the mantra, the correct pronunciation, and further discussion on the benefits see appendix 7, Daily Mantras.

157. Source not found.

158. This is adapted from *The Method to Transform a Suffering Life into Happiness (including Enlightenment)*. © 2018 Foundation for the Preservation of the Mahayana Tradition, Inc. The commentary comes from various teachings. The indented text is the root text by Great Yogi Khyungpo; the other text is commentary on the root text by Lama Zopa Rinpoche. Note that where diacritics have not been used in the rest of this book for simplicity, they are included here as Rinpoche explains pronunciation in some detail.

159. Great Yogi Khyungpo, or Drubchen Khyungpo, also known as Khyungpo Neljor, a Tibetan scholar of the eleventh century, was the founder of the Shangpa Kagyu tradition of Tibetan Buddhism. He received mahamudra teachings in India from Niguma, the wisdom mother or sister of Naropa, and established the monastery of Zhangzhong Dorjeden in the Shang valley of Tsang, in central Tibet.

160. The seven precious objects of a king's reign are the precious wheel (mindfulness), the precious elephant (wisdom), the precious horse (energy), the precious jewel (joy), the precious queen (tranquility), the precious minister (concentration), and the precious general (equanimity). The eight auspicious signs are the right-turning conch, the glorious endless knot, the golden fishes, the lotus, the parasol, the treasure vase, the wheel, and the victory banner. The eight auspicious substances are the mirror, the precious medicine, yogurt, long-life (durva) grass, bilva fruit, the right-turning conch, cinnabar (vermilion powder), and mustard seeds.

161. Lama Zopa Rinpoche is referring to how these syllables are written according to the International Alphabet of Sanskrit Transliteration.

162. A ritual knife.

163. This entire section is a translation, combined with some commentary, of a section of *Ritual for Blessing Stupas: Exalted Stainless Beam Totally Pure Light Mantra* (Tib. *chod rten byin gyis brlab pa'i cho ga rig pa chen mo bi ma la uṣhṇīṣha'i gzungs*), found in the Kangyur.

164. Tib. *rig pa chen mo bi ma la uṣhṇīṣha'i gzungs.*

165. You can also recite OM PADMO UṢHṆĪṢHA VIMALE HŪM PHAṬ and blow on an animal skin, such as a fur coat. This purifies the negative karmas of the animal even though it has been born in another realm. It is also very good to recite this mantra and blow on meat, whether you are actually eating the meat or not. Like the story of the fully ordained monk who broke all four root vows and was born in hell but was then liberated by someone reciting this mantra.

166. In the *Lamai Naljor* published by Sherig Pharkhang, it says to recite this mantra three times.

167. The Heaven of the Thirty-Three (Trayastrimsha) is the highest of the god realm abodes in Buddhist cosmology. It is atop Mount Meru and ruled by Indra.

BIBLIOGRAPHY

Sutras

Flower Garland Sutra. Avatamsakasutra. 1993. Published as *Flower Ornament Sutra: A Translation of the Avatamsaka Sutra.* Translated by Thomas Cleary. Boston: Shambala Publications.

Lakkana Sutta: The Marks of a Great Man. 1897, 1995. Published in *The Long Discourses of the Buddha: A Translation of the Dīgha Nikāya.* Translated by Michael Walshe. Boston: Wisdom Publications.

Mahaparinibbana Sutta, The Buddha's Last Days. 1897, 1995. Published in *The Long Discourses of the Buddha: A Translation of the Dīgha Nikāya.* Translated by Michael Walshe. Boston: Wisdom Publications.

Indian and Tibetan Works

Nagarjuna. 1998, 2007. *Precious Garland* (*Ratnavali*). Published as *Nāgārjuna's Precious Garland: Buddhist Advice for Living and Liberation.* Translated and edited by Jeffrey Hopkins. Ithaca, NY: Snow Lion Publications.

Pabongka Rinpoche. 1991. *Liberation in the Palm of Your Hand* (*Rnam grol lag bcangs*). Translated by Michael Richards. Boston: Wisdom Publications. Also published as *Liberation in Our Hands: Part One—The Preliminaries,* 1990; *Liberation in Our Hands: Part Two—The Fundamentals,* 1994; *Liberation in Our Hands: Part Three—The Ultimate Goals,* 2001. Translated by Geshe Lobsang Tharchin and Artemus B. Engle. Howell, NJ: Mahayana Sutra and Tantra Press.

Ribush, Nicholas (editor). 2005. *Teachings from Tibet: Guidance from Great Lamas.* Boston: Lama Yeshe Wisdom Archive.

Shantideva. Forthcoming. *A Guide to the Bodhisattva's Way of Life*

(Bodhisattvacaryavatara, Jang chub sem pa chö pa la jug pa). Translated by L. O. Gómez. Boston: Wisdom Publications.

————. 1987. *A Guide to the Bodhisattva's Way of Life (Bodhisattvacaryavatara, Jang chub sem pa chö pa la jug pa).* Translated by Stephen Batchelor. Dharamsala, India: Library of Tibetan Works and Archive.

Further Suggested Reading

Practices Available on the FPMT Website

These practices, which are available on the FPMT website (shop.fpmt. org), are commonly used within the FPMT. Some are only for people who have taken a tantric initiation in that deity (these are indicated), some are intended for initiates but can be done without an initiation if you don't visualize yourself as the deity, and some are practices without any restrictions. Most are available as pdf downloads (many free).

General Practice

FPMT. 2008, 2011. *Essential Buddhist Prayers, Volume 1.*

————. 2002, 2004, 2006, 2009. *Essential Buddhist Prayers, Volume 2.*

————. 2020. *Lama Tsongkhapa Guru Yoga.*

————. 2018. *The Method to Transform a Suffering life into Happiness (including Enlightenment). A Commentary by Lama Zopa Rinpoche.*

————. 2003, 2007, 2008, 2016. *The Preliminary Practice of Altar Set-up and Water Bowl Offerings.*

Shakyamuni

Gönpo, Jigten. 2003. *Shakyamuni Buddha: Praises by Way of the Twelve Deeds.*

Paldan, Ngawang. 2013. *Shakyamuni Buddha Long Puja.*

Zopa, Lama Thubten. 2018. *A Daily Meditation on Shakyamuni Buddha.*

Chenrezig

FPMT. 2007. *Chenrezig Singhanada: Exalted Lion's Roar Chenrezig Who Dispels All Disease.*

———. 2008. *Chenrezig, The Light of the Moon that Clears the Pains and Sufferings of Heat.*

———. 2020. *The Welfare of Living Beings That Pervades Space: The Meditation-Recitation of the Great Compassionate One.*

Gampo, Songtsen. 2018. *Prayer to Chenrezig; Compassionate-Eye-Looking One.*

Gyalpo, Thangtong. 2020. *The Welfare of Living Beings That Pervades Space: The Meditation-Recitation of the Great Compassionate One.*

Gyatso, Tenzin, the Fourteenth Dalai Lama. 2003. *The Inseparability of the Spiritual Master and Avalokiteshvara.*

Zong Rinpoche. 2017. *Chenrezig Who Liberates from the Lower Realms.*

Zopa, Lama Thubten. 2003. *Meditation on Thousand-Arm Chenrezig.*

———. 2007. *Praise to the Six-Syllable Great Compassionate One.*

———. 2011. *Short Practice of Four-Arm Chenrezig.*

Manjushri

FPMT. 2010. *Manjushri Arapatsana: Orange Manjushri According to the Sakya/Gelug Traditions.*

Gyatso, Ngawang Losang, the Fifth Dalai Lama. 2014. *A Meditation on Orange Manjushri.*

Tara

FPMT. (date unknown). *108 Names of Tara.*

———. 2017. *Illustrated Praise to the Twenty-One Taras.*

———. 2005. *Meditations on White Tara.*

———. 2007. *The Method of Performing Tara Purification Night.*

———. 2020. *The Twenty-One Forms of Tara According to the Tradition of Lord Atisha.*

Pabongka Dechen Nyingpo. 2001. *Tara Chittamani Uncommon Guru Yoga.* (initiates only)

Trijang Rinpoche of Gaden. 2009. *Four-Mandala Ritual to Chittamani Tara*. (initiates only)

Yeshe, Thubten. (date unknown). *Chittamani Tara Retreat Sadhana*. (initiates only)

Zopa, Lama Thubten, and Lama Thubten Yeshe. 2014. *A Short Practice of Green Tara*.

Medicine Buddha

Dagri Tulku. 2014. *Medicine Buddha Jangwa: Freeing the Wretched from the Chasm*. (initiates only)

FPMT. 2011. *Medicine Buddha: Long Retreat Sadhana*. (initiates only)

Gyältsen, Panchen Losang Chökyi. 2009. *The Concise Essence Sutra Ritual of Bhagavan Medicine Buddha Called the Wish-Fulfilling Jewel*.

———. 2013. *A Short Medicine Buddha Sadhana*.

Gyatso, Ngawang Losang, the Fifth Dalai Lama. 2012. *Medicine Buddha: The Wish-Granting Sovereign*.

Wangchug, Thubten, the Shakya Gelong Kelsang. 2011. *Source of Goodness: Medicine Buddha*.

Zopa, Lama Thubten. 2018. *A Brief Meditation-Recitation of Guru Medicine Buddha*.

———. 2008. *Healing Buddha: A Practice for the Prevention and Healing of Disease*.

———. 2008. *Heart Practices for Death and Dying: As Recommended by Lama Zopa Rinpoche*.

———. 2013. *Medicine Buddha: The Benefits of the Medicine Buddha Mantras and Practice*. (initiates only)

Vajrasattva

FPMT. 2009. *Liberating Animals*.

———. 2003, 2004, 2005, 2011. *The Preliminary Practice of Prostrations*.

———. 2010. *The Preliminary Practices of Vajrasattva*.

———. 2010. *Vajrasattva Retreat Sadhanas*. (initiates only)

Zopa, Lama Thubten. 2010. *Short Vajrasattva Meditation*.

Thirty-Five Confession Buddhas

Dharmabhadra, Ngulchu. 2016, 2018. *The Flowing Water of the Ganga: A Thorough Praise of the Thirty-Five Sugatas.*

FPMT. 2011, 2020. *Confession of Downfall: Prostrations to the Thirty-Five Confession Buddhas.*

The Great Mantras

FPMT. (date unknown). *Four Dharmakaya Relic Mantras.* (Tibetan script for filling stupas etc.)

———. 2010. *Ten Powerful Mantras at the Time of Death.*

Zopa, Lama Thubten. 2010. *Liberating Animals from the Danger of Death and Other Ways to Benefit Them.*

Other Suggested Reading

Blofeld, John. 1978. *The Bodhisattva of Compassion: The Mystical Tradition of Kuan Yin.* Boston: Shambala Publications.

Bokar Rinpoche. 1993. *Chenrezik Lord of Love: Principles and Methods of Deity Practice.* Translated by Christiane Buchet. San Francisco: ClearPoint Press.

———. 1999. *Tara: The Feminine Divine.* Translated by Christiane Buchet. San Francisco: ClearPoint Press.

Chodron, Thubten. 2006. *Cultivating a Compassionate Heart: The Yoga Method of Chenrezig.* Boston: Snow Lion Publications.

———. 2013. *How to Free Your Mind: The Practice of Tara the Liberator.* Boston: Snow Lion Publications.

Ladner, Lorne (compiled and edited). 2000. *Wheel of Great Compassion: The Practice of the Prayer Wheel in Tibetan Buddhism.* Boston: Wisdom Publications.

Lhundrup Rigsel, Khensur Rinpoche Lama. 2014. *A Commentary on the Praises to Twenty-One Taras.* Boston: Lama Yeshe Wisdom Archive.

Lopez Jr., Donald S. 1990. *The Heart Sutra Explained: Indian and Tibetan Commentaries.* New Delhi: South Asia Books.

Mackenzie, Vicki. 1999. *Cave in the Snow.* London: Bloomsbury Publishing.

McDonald, Kathleen. 2010. *Awakening the Kind Heart: How to Meditate on Compassion*. Boston: Wisdom Publications.

———. 1984, 2005. *How to Meditate: A Practical Guide*. Boston: Wisdom Publications.

Phunsok, Khenpo Yeshe. 2015. *Vajrasattva Meditation: An Illustrated Guide*. Boston: Wisdom Publications

Sherab, Palden, and Sewang Dongyal. 2007. *Tara's Enlightened Activity: An Oral Commentary on the Twenty-One Praises to Tara*. Ithaca, NY: Snow Lion Publications.

Urgyen, Tulku. 2011. *Skillful Grace: Tara Practice for Our Times*. Berkeley, CA: North Atlantic Publishing.

Ringu Tulku. 2011. *Chenrezig: The Practice of Compassion*. Newton Abbot: RingulTrust Publications.

Wangchen Rinpoche. 2009. *Buddhist Fasting Practice*. Boston: Snow Lion Publications.

Willson, Martin. 1996. *In Praise of Tara: Songs to the Saviouress*. Boston: Wisdom Publications.

Wooten, Rachael. 2020. *Tara: The Liberating Power of the Female Buddha*. Louisville, CO: Sounds True.

Yeshe, Lama Thubten. 2003. *Becoming the Compassion Buddha: Tantric Mahamudra for Everyday Life*. Boston: Wisdom Publications.

———. 2012. *Becoming Vajrasattva: The Tantric Path to Purification*. Boston: Wisdom Publications.

———. 1987, 2005, 2007. *Introduction to Tantra: The Transformation of Desire*. Boston: Wisdom Publications.

Zopa, Lama Thubten. 2017. *Abiding in the Retreat: A Nyung Nä Commentary*. Boston: Lama Yeshe Wisdom Archive.

———. 2013. *The Perfect Human Rebirth: Freedom and Richness on the Path to Enlightenment*. Boston: Lama Yeshe Wisdom Archive.

———. 2001. *Teachings from the Mani Retreat*. Boston: Lama Yeshe Wisdom Archive.

———. 2009. *Teachings from the Medicine Retreat*. Boston: Lama Yeshe Wisdom Archive.

Zopa, Lama Thubten, and Kathleen McDonald. 2010. *Wholesome Fear: Transforming Your Anxiety about Impermanence and Death.* Boston: Wisdom Publications.

Zopa, Lama Thubten, and Lama Thubten Yeshe. 1979. *Wisdom Energy 2.* Ulverston, UK: Wisdom Culture.

ABOUT THE AUTHOR

L AMA ZOPA RINPOCHE is one of the most internationally renowned masters of Tibetan Buddhism, working and teaching ceaselessly on almost every continent.

He is the spiritual director and cofounder of the Foundation for the Preservation of the Mahayana Tradition (FPMT), an international network of Buddhist projects, including monasteries in six countries and meditation centers in over thirty; health and nutrition clinics, and clinics specializing in the treatment of leprosy and polio; as well as hospices, schools, publishing activities, and prison outreach projects worldwide.

Lama Zopa Rinpoche is the author of numerous books, including *Patience, The Six Perfections, Bodhichitta, The Four Noble Truths, Transforming Problems into Happiness, How to Enjoy Death, Ultimate Healing, The Door to Satisfaction, How to Be Happy, Wholesome Fear, Wisdom Energy,* and *Dear Lama Zopa,* all from Wisdom Publications.

ABOUT THE EDITOR

Gordon McDougall was director of Cham Tse Ling, the FPMT's Hong Kong center, for two years in the 1980s and worked for Jamyang Buddhist Centre in London from 2000 to 2007. He helped develop the Foundation of Buddhist Thought study program and administered it for seven years. Since 2008 he has been editing Lama Zopa Rinpoche's teachings for Lama Yeshe Wisdom Archive and Wisdom Publications.

ABOUT THE PAINTER

Peter Iseli, born in 1947, studied thangka painting with Chating Jamyang la and his master student Sherab la; with Jampa la, the Tibetan state artist; and at the Library of Tibetan Works & Archives. Iseli lives in Bern, Switzerland.

WHAT TO READ NEXT FROM WISDOM PUBLICATIONS

Patience
A Guide to Shantideva's Sixth Chapter
Lama Zopa Rinpoche

"Often in the West we think that patience is passive aggression: waiting for that horrible thing to go away. Lama Zopa Rinpoche shows us in great detail how to cultivate actual patience, the practice of the bodhisattva: wholeheartedly welcoming the problems. Rinpoche's powerfully experiential teachings give us the confidence to know that we can do it, too."
—Ven. Robina Courtin

Six Perfections
The Practice of the Bodhisattvas
Lama Zopa Rinpoche

"A jewel of a book, containing much practical advice on how we can start working on these six precious practices, even if we are not yet bodhisattvas."
—Sangye Khadro (Kathleen McDonald), author of *How to Meditate*

Bodhichitta
Practice for a Meaningful Life
Lama Zopa Rinpoche

An accessible, inspiring book on one of the most important topics in Tibetan Buddhism, written by one of its renowned masters who has an international following of thousands.

The Four Noble Truths
A Guide to Everyday Life
Lama Zopa Rinpoche

The Buddha's profound teachings on the four noble truths are illuminated by a Tibetan master simply and directly, so that readers gain an immediate and personal understanding of the causes and conditions that give rise to suffering as well as the spiritual life as the path to liberation.

How to Be Happy
Lama Zopa Rinpoche

"Rinpoche works with determination and great sincerity in the service of Buddha's teachings and sentient beings."
—His Holiness the Dalai Lama

Transforming Problems into Happiness
Foreword by His Holiness the Dalai Lama
Lama Zopa Rinpoche

"A masterfully brief statement of Buddhist teachings on the nature of humanity and human suffering. . . . This book should be read as the words of a wise, loving parent."
—*Utne Reader*

How to Face Death without Fear
A Handbook by Lama Zopa Rinpoche

"The reality of death is an important opportunity for spiritual transformation. Kyabje Lama Zopa Rinpoche's combined teachings and practices lead the reader to an understanding of this reality and help the person who is dying to achieve a better future life. Rinpoche's clarity and blessings will be tremendously beneficial."
—Yangsi Rinpoche, president, Maitripa College

Bliss of Inner Fire
Heart Practice of the Six Yogas of Naropa
Lama Thubten Yeshe
Foreword by Lama Zopa Rinpoche

"An impressive contribution to the growing body of Buddhist literature for an English-reading audience."
—*The Midwest Book Review*

Introduction to Tantra
Lama Thubten Yeshe
Edited by Jonathan Landaw
Foreword by Philip Glass

"The best introductory work on Tibetan Buddhist tantra available today."
—Janet Gyatso, Harvard University

Becoming Vajrasattva
The Tantric Path of Purification
Lama Thubten Yeshe
Foreword by Lama Zopa Rinpoche

"Lama Yeshe was capable of translating Tibetan Buddhist thought not only through language, but by his presence, gestures, and way of life."
—Gelek Rimpoche, author of *Good Life, Good Death*

Ultimate Healing
The Power of Compassion
Lama Zopa Rinpoche

"This truly is an awesome book."
—Lillian Too

About Wisdom Publications

Wisdom Publications is the leading publisher of classic and contemporary Buddhist books and practical works on mindfulness. To learn more about us or to explore our other books, please visit our website at wisdomexperience.org or contact us at the address below.

Wisdom Publications
199 Elm Street
Somerville, MA 02144 USA

We are a 501(c)(3) organization, and donations in support of our mission are tax deductible.

Wisdom Publications is affiliated with the Foundation for the Preservation of the Mahayana Tradition (FPMT).